Sociology AS

The Complete Companion

OCR

Patrick McNeill

•

Jonathan Blundell

•

Janis Griffiths

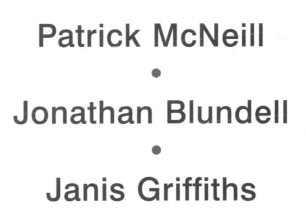

Published in 2003 by:

Nelson Thornes Ltd
Delta Place
27 Bath Road
CHELTENHAM
GL53 7TH
United Kingdom

03 04 05 06 07 / 10 9 8 7 6 5 4 3 2 1

A catalogue record for this book is available from the British Library

ISBN 0–7487–7544–7

Commissioning Editor: Rick Jackman

Production Editor: James Rabson

Project Manager: Fiona Elliott

Cover Designer: Nigel Harriss

Designer and typesetter: Patricia Briggs

Picture Researcher: Sue Sharp

Production Controller: Amanda Meaden

Illustations by Harry Venning and Oxford Designers and Illustrators

Printed and bound in Italy by Canale

Acknowledgements

The authors and publisher would like to thank Steve Chapman
for his invaluable advice and assistance in the development of
this resource.

The authors and publisher would like to thank the following for
permission to reproduce material in this book:

The Child Support Agency for the table on page 69; The Daily Mirror
for the text extract on page 28; Dorling Kindersley for the text extract
on page 18; *The Guardian* for text extracts on pages 35, 61, 73, 79,
81, 91 and 93; © Her Majesty's Stationery Office for material on
pages 23, 29, 30, 47, 54, 56, 60, 61, 64, 67–9, 71, 75, 134 and 135;
The Independent for the text extract on page 77; *The Observer* for
text extracts on pages 21, 25, 59, 71 and 148; and *Sociology Review*
for tables on pages 60 and 69.

The authors and publisher would like to thank the following
organizations for permission to reproduce illustrations as follows:

Advertising Archive for the image of a Surf advert on page 58; Jane
Alexander/Photofusion for the image of texting on page 90; © Andes
Press Agency/Carlos Reyes-Manzo for the image on page 15 and
the image of a woman in a sari on page 22; Apple for the image of
a computer on page 9; Associated Press for the image on page 49;
Associated Press, HO for the image on page 57; Associated Press,
POOL for the image on page 79; BBC Photo Library for the image
on page 112; BBC Picture Library for the image of Amanda Burton
on page 102; Patricia Briggs for the image on page 27; © Bubbles/
Loisjoy Thurston for the image on page 10 and the image of a father
and child on page 58; Bubbles Photo Library/Katie Van Dyck for the
image on page 75; Mark Campbell/Photofusion for the image on
page 4, the image of teenagers on page 32 and the image of a
shopping crowd on page 124; Channel 4 for the logo on page 100;
Corbis for the image of a family watching tv on page 90; © Paul
Doyle/Photofusion for the image on page 46; Education Photos/John
Walmsley for the image of sociology students on page 6; Colin
Edwards/Photofusion for the image on page 76; Mary Evans Picture
Library for the image on page 62; Judy Harrison/Photofusion for the
image of a father at parenting class on page 4; Hulton Archive for
the image of Ziggy Stardust on page 66; © Pam Isherwood/
Photofusion for the image on page 63; ITV for the logo on page 100;
Pete Jones/Photofusion for the image of hijjab on page 22; The
Kobal Collection for the image of Dirty Harry on page 104 and the
image on page 110; Vehbi Koca/Photofusion for the image of a man
in a kilt on page 22; Off-side Sports Photography/Mark Leech for the
image on page 29; Rex Features Ltd for the images of an American
wrestler and Pamela Anderson on page 18, the image on page 24,
the image of Oxford students on page 32, the images on pages 36
and 94, the image of Arnold Schwarzeneger on page 104 and the
images on page 106; © Rex Features Ltd for the image on page 98;
Carlos Reyes-Manzo/Andes Press Agency for the image on page 69,
the image of school children on page 124 and the image on page 125;
PA Photos for the image on page 92; Karen Robinson/Photofusion
for the image on page 91; Sky television for the logo on page 100;
Martin Sookias for the images of Barbie and Action Man on page 18;
Topham Picturepoint for the image of an atomic bomb on page 9,
the images on pages 12 and 20 and the 'Bebe' advert on page 102;
Topham Picturepoint/Universal Pictorial Press for the image of Vinnie
Jones on page 66; © Trip/H Rogers for the image of a French village
on page 6 and the images on page 16; © Trip/M Jelliffe for the
image of an African village on page 6; and © Harry Venning for the
cartoons on pages 51, 52, 56, 64, 73, 126, 128, 131, 132 and 134.

Contents

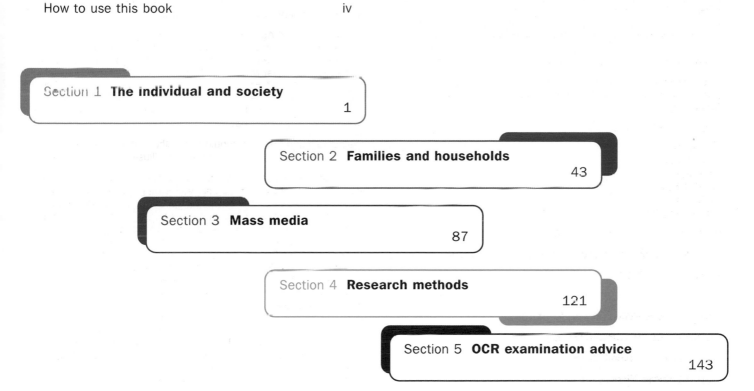

How to use this book

This book is designed to encourage active learning, i.e. to help you to think about and respond to what you are reading. The material is presented in double-page spreads that include a range of special features.

 This sign in the margin introduces a short note, comment or question relating to the main text.

Important studies

These are short summaries of key pieces of sociological research.

Research issue

These describe issues that sociological researchers who study the topic must think about.

Coursework advice

This is advice for students who have the opportunity to do some sociological research as part of their course.

Watch out

These are warnings about things to avoid when you are taking your sociology exam.

Glossary terms: Some words are printed in **bold**. These are particularly important sociological terms and are defined for you on the page and in the Glossary at the end of the book.

Think it through

These are activities and exercises designed to help you think about what you have been reading. They help you develop some of the skills that you will need in the exam but they are not set out in the same way as exam questions.

Round-up

These are short summaries of the material on the double-page spread.

At the beginning of each section, you will find a **mindmap**. This is a way of presenting an overview of the section in a visually appealing way. We suggest that you produce your own mindmaps as you work through the sections.

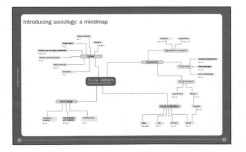

At the end of each section, you will find:

- a **summative review** – this summarises the section.
- **self-assessment questions** – these are designed to help you test how much you have learned. It would be a good idea to get together with some fellow-students to write more of these questions and to test each other on them.
- a **timeline** – this is designed to give you a picture of key developments in the history of sociology.

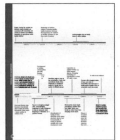

The final section in the book includes an explanation of the OCR examination papers, plus examples of exam answers, with advice and comments written by senior examiners. These answers have been written specially for this book and are not 'real' examples.

Section 1 The individual and society

The individual and society: a mindmap

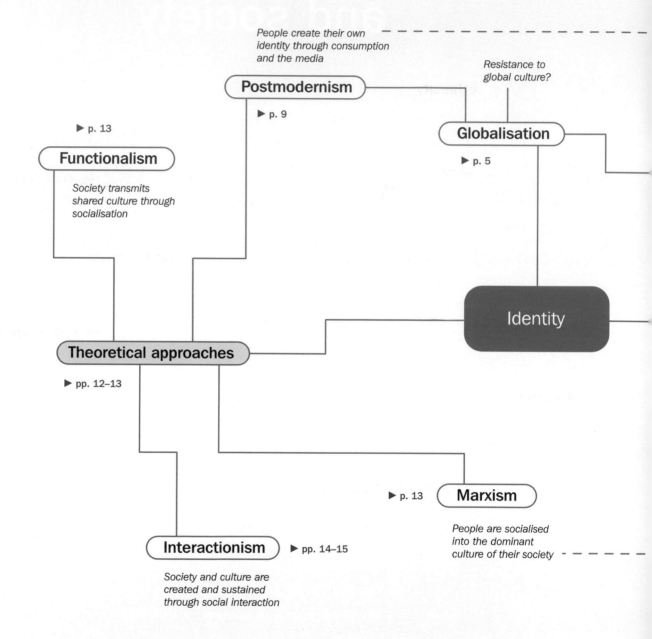

People create their own identity through consumption and the media

Postmodernism
▶ p. 9

Resistance to global culture?

Globalisation
▶ p. 5

▶ p. 13
Functionalism

Society transmits shared culture through socialisation

Identity

Theoretical approaches
▶ pp. 12–13

▶ p. 13   **Marxism**

People are socialised into the dominant culture of their society

Interactionism   ▶ pp. 14–15

Society and culture are created and sustained through social interaction

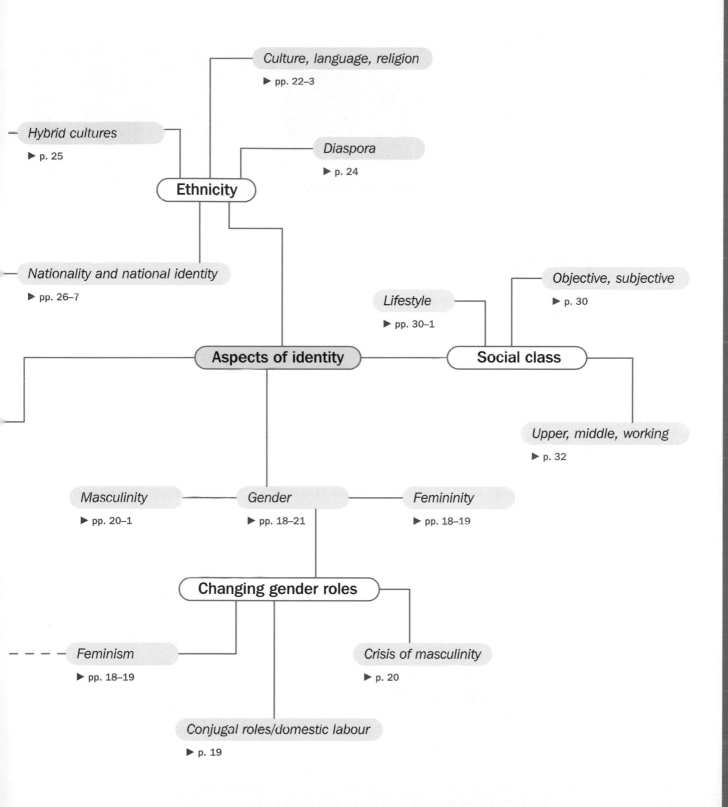

Culture, language, religion
▶ pp. 22–3

Hybrid cultures
▶ p. 25

Diaspora
▶ p. 24

Ethnicity

Nationality and national identity
▶ pp. 26–7

Objective, subjective
▶ p. 30

Lifestyle
▶ pp. 30–1

Aspects of identity

Social class

Upper, middle, working
▶ p. 32

Masculinity
▶ pp. 20–1

Gender
▶ pp. 18–21

Femininity
▶ pp. 18–19

Changing gender roles

Feminism
▶ pp. 18–19

Crisis of masculinity
▶ p. 20

Conjugal roles/domestic labour
▶ p. 19

What is sociology?

Sociology is the study of people in society

The simplest answer to the question posed above is that sociology is 'the study of people in society'. But what do we mean by 'society' and what is distinctive about sociology as a way of studying people in society?

We can start by making two statements about sociology.

1 *Sociology is an academic subject that is taught in schools, colleges and universities.* Most British universities have a sociology department. The first professor of sociology was Emile Durkheim at the Sorbonne in Paris in 1902. Usually, however, sociology is said to have begun about seventy years before this, with the writings of Auguste Comte – a Frenchman who developed some of the key ideas of what later became sociology.

The period from 1750 to 1850 is often called the 'Age of Revolutions' because there was so much social and political upheaval in Europe and America.

2 *Sociology is a way of trying to understand society, and is linked to changes in society.* Comte lived in the century following the French and American revolutions, when ideas about liberty, equality and democracy led to the overthrow of the old political order and the creation of new societies. Since then sociology has been divided between those who see its purpose as being simply to describe society, without offering judgments, and those who want to understand society in order to change it.

The early sociologists often tried to understand the new modern society that was emerging around them by comparing it with society in the past.

What do sociologists study?

You can get some idea of the wide range of topics that are studied by sociologists by looking at the specifications from the awarding bodies (AQA and OCR). Topics include:

HEALTH   SOCIAL STRATIFICATION   WORLD SOCIOLOGY   SOCIAL POLICY

FAMILIES AND HOUSEHOLDS   MASS MEDIA   WEALTH, WELFARE AND POVERTY   RELIGION

POPULAR CULTURE   POWER AND POLITICS   EDUCATION   PROTEST AND SOCIAL MOVEMENTS

YOUTH AND CULTURE   CRIME AND DEVIANCE

What do sociologists do?

Like all scientists, sociologists carry out research. The aim of the research may be simply to describe a social context, or it may be to explain it. Description may be the first step towards explanation. Either before they start their research, or while they are doing it, a sociologist will work out a possible explanation of some aspect of social life, and then do **empirical** research to test their idea (known as a 'hypothesis'). The evidence from the research may lead to the hypothesis being accepted, modified, or rejected. Theory and research go together; they are both essential.

Empirical: Based on observation or experiment rather than on theory.

Structure and action

Some students find it hard to accept that sociology seldom offers clear answers. There is disagreement in all of the natural and social sciences, but it is particularly difficult to reach firm conclusions in sociology because of the complexity of the subject matter – people. Research findings can be interpreted in different ways and sociologists often do not agree amongst themselves. However, the nature of these disagreements often makes it possible to group sociologists together using labels that indicate the approach they favour. For example, one major division is between those who focus on social structure and those who focus on social action. This has resulted in two main approaches to sociology, which are explained in greater detail on pp. 12–15.

Macro and micro approaches

In brief, the 'social structure approach' tends to focus on the large (macro) scale of social life; for example, on the education or legal systems, or on how these systems are connected. By contrast, the 'social action approach' focuses on the small (micro) scale. Taking this approach, a sociologist interested in education might study and analyse social interaction in a single classroom.

Watch out

Remember that any way of dividing sociology into two or more 'perspectives' is a simplification. Sociologists occupy a whole range of positions on a continuum, from those who are concerned with macro structural questions to those who study the smallest micro details of social interaction, and individual sociologists may change their views during their careers. Be careful not to oversimplify these divisions.

For an explanation of research methods, and of the concepts of validity and reliability, see p. 128.

Globalisation: The processes by which societies and cultures around the world become increasingly interdependent economically, culturally and politically.

There are literally hundreds of websites about sociology. A good site to start from is: www.atss.org.uk

Research methods

Sociologists use a wide range of research methods. Almost any source of information about people in society can be helpful, provided that its reliability and validity can be assessed.

The main methods used by sociologists are social surveys (including question-naires), interviews, ethnographic methods (including participant observation), and analysis of secondary data.

Social surveys can be used to study large numbers of people, by asking questions either of all of them or of a representative sample. Ethnographic methods are more appropriate when studying a small number of people, usually in a group. Secondary data are data already available from other sources such as government surveys.

Explaining social change

One of the biggest problems sociologists face is in explaining how societies, and people's lives within societies, change over time. Sociology began as a way of trying to make sense of the dramatic upheavals in politics, work and social life in the late eighteenth century and early nineteenth century. Some sociologists were opposed to what they saw happening, and hoped that societies could remain stable despite the changes. Other commentators hoped for that stability to be overturned, because stability meant that wealth and power would continue to be held by a small minority. They wanted revolutionary change rather than gradual, evolutionary progress. Their concern with inequalities of wealth and power remains at the heart of much sociology today.

In these two different attitudes to change, you can see how difficult (and perhaps undesirable) it is for sociology to be just about describing society. Almost inevitably, sociologists have opinions about what they study.

The pace of social change has quickened and sociology is as relevant as ever. Some of the changes in British society are the result of changes that are happening on a global scale. **Globalisation**, which describes the many ways in which people now find their lives connected to others around the world, has become a central concern of sociologists over the past ten years.

Value freedom

Can sociologists be completely objective, not allowing their opinions and feelings to influence their work? How far should sociology be concerned with changing the social world, and how far with just understanding it? Here again, there is a division of opinion. Some sociologists argue that it is their duty to be as objective as possible; sociology should be like natural science, where the scientific researcher is not influenced by their values (in theory, at least). This is much harder in sociology, because it is about people. An alternative view is that sociologists should accept that they are bound to be influenced by their values, so they should be open about these, leaving the reader to judge how far their work has been influenced by their values.

Social policy

Some sociology has the aim of improving society and social welfare in the belief that through greater understanding we can develop more enlightened policies on health, education, crime, etc. Sociology that has this practical aim is called 'applied sociology'. For example, a sociologist might try to find out which methods of responding to juvenile crime are more likely to reduce it. The findings might lead to a change in government policy.

Jargon

The language of sociology can be off-putting. Sociologists sometimes use unnecessary jargon (words that would not be understood by non-sociologists – a sort of private language), and seem to be stating the obvious in a complicated way. This is a common failing of academics in every subject! However, some of the jargon is useful, because – once you have learned it – it helps you express complex ideas with fewer words.

Round-up

Sociology is an academic subject, in which sociologists study many aspects of social life using a wide variety of theories and research methods. Because of its subject matter, sociology is often linked to attempts to improve aspects of social life. Sociologists face particular issues relating to value freedom.

What do all societies have in common?

Social life can only be maintained if there is a certain degree of social order, based on acceptance by the majority of at least some basic rules for behaviour. If this order did not exist, there would be no society. This basic agreement forms a large part of a society's culture. Sociologists have analysed these aspects of social life using a set of related concepts: norms, mores, rules, values, attitudes, statuses and roles.

THE INDIVIDUAL AND SOCIETY

Norms

Norms are the unwritten and usually unspoken rules of everyday life, referring to specific situations. Young children are taught some norms during socialisation, but we all learn new norms constantly throughout our lives as we encounter new situations. Norms are usually learned through observing the behaviour of others and how others react to what we do. Sanctions against people who break norms vary from silent disapproval through verbal rebuke to physical punishment.

Mores

Mores (pronounced 'more-rays', coming from the Latin for 'manners' or 'customs') are a stronger form of norms. They have a moral aspect and are about upholding standards of behaviour that are widely felt to be the 'right thing to do'. Because of this moral aspect, the sanctions against people who break mores are often stronger than against those who deviate from norms.

Rules

Rules – and laws – are stronger than norms and mores and there are specified sanctions for breaking them. Schools and other institutions have rules and have the power to punish those who break them. Laws apply to the whole of society, and many people (judges, the police, lawyers, etc.) are employed to identify and deal with those who break the law. Rules and laws are formal, usually written down, and those who break them are normally aware of the consequences of being caught doing so. Sanctions can range from a warning to fines, imprisonment or even execution.

Values

Values are the beliefs and moral views that are deeply held by most of the people in a society, and so can be taken as typical of that culture. Values lie behind norms. If you know the values of a society, you may be able to work out what the norms are likely to be in a particular situation.

Attitudes

Attitudes are not as deeply held as values. A society can tolerate a wide variety of attitudes, but not of values. For example, people in Britain have a wide variety of attitudes towards political parties and their policies, but there is the underlying value, shared by the majority, that a democratic political system (one in which there are parties with different policies) is the best system.

Status

Status means a position in society. Everyone has several statuses, and together these are referred to as a 'status set'.

Some statuses are based on characteristics that the person is born with, for example, position within a family, age, sex and ethnicity. These are 'ascribed statuses'. They cannot be changed by an individual, although collectively people may be able to challenge disadvantages arising from that status. For example, women have challenged the lower status of females.

Other statuses are 'achieved' by individuals, sometimes by competing against others – for example, by passing an examination, or getting a job.

Norm: A rule of behaviour in everyday life.

Values: The beliefs and morals that underlie norms.

Status: A position in society.

Think it through

1 What are the roles in this situation?

2 What norms, mores, and rules apply to the students?

3 Are the norms or mores different for different groups (e.g. for males and females)?

4 What values underlie these norms and rules?

5 What sanctions might be applied to someone who breaks the norms, or the rules?

There are almost always some common elements to be found between different societies

Roles

With each status there is a set of expectations – norms that the person with that status is expected to follow. This is a **role**. Just as everyone has a status set, so everyone also has a role set. Roles can sometimes clash; for example, students who have part-time jobs are sometimes asked to work extra hours when they should be studying. This is 'role conflict', between the roles of student and employee.

Cultural diversity

Cultures vary from one society to another. The differences cover every aspect of social life: language, religious beliefs and practices, food and drink, clothing and decoration, cultural practices such as art, music and dance, uses of technology, and so on.

In many parts of the world, and especially in cities, there are societies made up of people from diverse cultural backgrounds. In London, for example, there are people from many different ethnic groups, speaking different languages and following different beliefs. This is the result of global migration, fuelled in the past by slavery and colonialism and today by globalisation, war, disasters and political repression. London can therefore be described as 'multicultural'. Some societies have a single dominant culture, and are 'monocultural'. Japan is an example of a modern industrial society that is still fairly monocultural.

Cultures borrow freely from each other and even cultures thought of as 'traditional' are continually evolving.

Research issues

Researchers studying other cultures and subcultures often aim to gain an insider's view by joining a social group and observing the participants 'from the inside' and on their own terms (see pp. 132–3 on 'participant observation').

The processes of globalisation are spreading Western (and particularly American) culture around the world. Some sociologists have seen this as 'cultural imperialism', in which local cultures are swamped by Western culture with its values of **individualism** and consumerism. However, the transfer of culture is a two-way process and Western culture has itself absorbed and been changed by aspects of many different cultures. Many people in Britain, for example, eat food prepared in the style of a wide range of different cultures.

Subculture

In modern societies, different social groups may have different cultures and ways of life. For example, people living in rural areas may have a different way of life from those in urban areas. A social group with its own particular values and way of life is a subculture.

Deviance

Deviance refers to actions that break the norms and values of a society. 'Crime' refers to actions that break laws. Some deviant acts are criminal. However, some criminal acts are so common (e.g. speeding on the motorway) that it could be argued that they are not deviant. There is a continuum from eccentricity through mildly anti-social behaviour and deviance to seriously anti-social behaviour and crime.

Norms, values and laws vary between societies, so what is counted as crime and deviance may also vary.

Important studies

The Channel 4 film *Baka* (1988) showed the way of life of the Baka people who live in the rainforest of southern Cameroon. Aspects of Baka culture include the following.

• Everyone belongs to a clan, and members of a clan cannot marry each other.
• There is no marriage ceremony, but the man must give gifts to his wife's parents.
• Parents share equal responsibility for looking after children.
• Status depends on age – old people, both men and women, are very highly regarded.
• Children sometimes play all day but, even from about four years of age, are also expected to help with preparing food and looking after babies and infants.
• The Baka do not read or write but have many stories, songs and rituals.

Role: The set of norms and expectations that go with a status.

Deviance: The breaking of norms, mores, values or rules.

Individualism: An emphasis on individual people – e.g. in terms of happiness and success – rather than on groups, communities or societies.

Watch out

We are all members of a culture. It therefore follows that in studying other cultures or subcultures, we look at them from our own cultural point of view. There is a danger here of ethnocentrism, of assuming that our own culture is 'normal' and that it provides a sort of benchmark against which other cultures can be judged.

Round-up

Social order, based on sharing of aspects of culture, is essential for the smooth running of society. There are wide differences between cultures. Within modern societies there are often distinct subcultures as well as the majority culture. The breaking of cultural expectations and rules is called 'deviance'.

How have societies changed?

Sociology and the modern world

As you have seen, sociology had its origins in the attempts by people in the early nineteenth century to make sense of the massive social changes that were taking place in Western Europe and elsewhere. However, although sociology emerged in a particular kind of society, it can still be applied to the study of other types of society.

The myth of 'traditional society'

One way in which early sociologists tried to make sense of their own societies was by contrasting the emerging modern way of life with how life was assumed to have been in the past. 'Modern' societies were contrasted with 'traditional' societies. The differences between these two concepts, modern and traditional, formed the basis of much early sociology.

It was suggested that there had been changes in:

• scale – from small to large
• the basis of economies – from being based on agriculture to being based on industry
• where people lived – from most of the people living in the countryside to most living in towns and cities
• people's relationships with others – in the modern world, more relationships are impersonal and fleeting; this was sometimes seen as a change from 'community' to 'society'.

The picture of a 'traditional society' that is implicit in this list of comparisons is not a flattering one. Traditional societies tend to come across as being rather primitive and stagnant – although some writers also see that they had important values (such as in family and community life) that are in danger of being lost in the modern world.

In fact, the idea of 'traditional societies' is misleading. It lumps together the vast range of societies that existed before about 1750 – from hunter-gatherer societies to the complex and urban-based empires of pre-modern Europe, Asia, Africa and the Americas. Supposedly 'traditional' societies usually turn out to have been dynamic (constantly changing), while apparently ancient customs are found to be of more recent origin. Well-known examples in our own society include many of our Christmas traditions, such as Christmas trees and cards, which date back only to the Victorian period. All societies are always in a process of change.

Industrialisation

The Industrial Revolution refers to the transformation of Britain from a predominantly rural and agricultural society to a predominantly urban and industrial one. This transformation is usually dated from about 1750 (though its origins were much earlier) to 1850. Subsequently, other nations – Germany and the USA first, then others – went through a similar transformation. This change is referred to as '**industrialisation**'.

During the Industrial Revolution changes took place in each of the following areas.

• *Population* – the population grew rapidly; the death rate fell; people migrated from rural to urban areas where they became the new industrial working class. '**Urbanisation**' occurred (i.e. there was an increase in the proportion of a country's population living in cities).
• *Technology* – this was an astonishingly inventive period in which new methods such as the use of steam power greatly increased production.
• *Transport* – this included the canal system, much improved roads and the railways. Together these made it much easier both to take raw materials to industrial areas and to distribute manufactured goods.
• *Agriculture* – improved techniques led to rising yields. The resulting greater prosperity of farmers, who became a rural middle-class, made them an important market for new industries.
• *Industry* – this was transformed by new technology and large investments of capital.
• *Empire* – Britain expanded its trade and then its empire, in search of sources of raw materials and new markets. Potential competition to British industry – such as the thriving Indian textiles industry – was destroyed.

This enormous and rapid transformation provided the early sociologists such as Comte and Durkhein with much to try to understand and analyse. This was a period of great optimism and faith in progress. It created what we can call the 'modern world', or '**modernity**'. The idea that societies could be improved, even perfected, led to political ideologies such as communism – which was not just aimed at understanding the world, but also at changing it. This optimism survived the two world wars. After World War II, in Britain and other western countries, a Welfare State, protecting the most vulnerable, was created and there was state intervention in the running of industries. There was general acceptance of this arrangement by both right-wing and left-wing politicians, which is referred to as the 'post-war consensus'. It began to break down in the 1970s as the role of governments in providing welfare and in running industries was increasingly questioned.

Industrialisation: The set of changes by which a society moves from being predominantly rural and agricultural to being predominantly urban and industrial.

Urbanisation: The increase in the proportion of a country's population living in towns and cities.

Modernity: The period of history from the late eighteenth to late twentieth centuries, marked by a belief in progress through science and rationality.

What do we mean by progress?

Into postmodernity?

The mood of certainty and optimism associated with modernity was called more and more into question by events in the twentieth century. Advances in science and technology improved health and living standards, but also led to modern warfare, killings on an unprecedented scale and degradation of the environment. Moreover, the rising living standards of developed countries were achieved only through the exploitation of their colonies in what later became the 'Third World'. The pace of social change is continually accelerating, but we have no clear idea in what direction we are heading.

Some sociologists and others have suggested that the pace and scale of change means that the world is now very different even from only a few decades ago. They describe this as the change from living in modernity to living in **postmodernity**. Much of what we took for certain – gradual progress, better lives for our children, experts who could tell us what to do – has been lost. Some of the features of postmodernity have been said to be as follows.

- The mass media dominate our lives to the extent that we confuse media images with reality.
- Economies are now based on information and knowledge rather than manufacture of goods.
- Sources of identity such as class have become less important; people increasingly have multiple and cross-cutting identities. Identities are also increasingly based on lifestyle and consumption (which can be more easily changed).

Other writers, however, have argued that these changes have not been so sweeping, and that the period we are now living in is better described as 'late' or 'high' modernity.

Postmodernity: The period of history after the modern period.

Think it through

Look at the images above. Draw a table with two columns and list in one column ways in which life today has improved compared with the life lived by our ancestors; in the other column list ways in which life is not as good. Which of the ideas that you have listed can be attributed to advances in science and technology?

Important studies

■ Lyotard (1984) argued that we live in a postmodern world because the two major myths or 'meta-narratives' (big stories) of the modern world can no longer be believed. These are:

• the myth of liberation – that science and progress can make us more free. This myth has been destroyed by the way scientific knowledge has been used in great crimes such as the Holocaust and weapons of mass destruction
• the myth of truth – the status of knowledge and the idea that we can find out the 'truth' about things are now in question. This myth has been destroyed by theories that say that we can never know what is true and that all truths are relative.

Research issue Many descriptions of 'primitive' societies were written by military invaders, colonists and missionaries, and can be seen as helping to justify the so-called 'civilising' of the societies in question.

Round-up

Sociology has always been interested in the changes that have led to the creation of the modern world. The most significant historical changes that students of sociology need to have some understanding of are industrialisation and its role in creating the modern world, and the emergence of the post-war consensus and its replacement by a diverse and uncertain postmodern world.

How do we learn to be social?

The biological and the social

What are the main influences on how people behave in society? For some writers, our behaviour can be explained by referring to biological factors (our 'nature'). For example, in recent years there have been claims that criminal behaviour, health, intelligence and sexual preference are linked to, even determined by, our genes and their DNA. This theory is known as **determinism**. Most sociologists, however, take the view that human behaviour can be explained by referring to social factors (our 'nurture' or upbringing).

Ways in which sociology is affected by the nature–nurture debate		
Area of study	*Possible biological factors*	*Possible social factors*
Educational achievement	Inherited intelligence	Class, ethnicity
Criminal activity	Inherited criminal personality	Class, family, culture and subculture
Gendered behaviour	Genetic differences between men and women	Patriarchal authority

Determinism: The view that all events are fully determined (caused) by previous events. In the context of human social behaviour, it is contrasted with 'voluntarism'.

 The long-running 'nature vs. nurture' debate is about the importance of these different factors in relation to each other. It is undeniable that there are biological differences between men and women; the question is how far these influence the social behaviour of men and women.

Primary socialisation

Socialisation: The processes by which people learn the norms and values of a society.

'**Socialisation**' is the process by which people learn to become members of a society. This involves:

- internalising the norms and values of the society (internalising means that although initially these norms and values exist outside the individual, he or she will eventually be able to accept them as being their own)
- learning how to perform social roles.

 Older textbooks often imply that primary socialisation takes place only within families. However, in Britain and other developed countries today, many pre-school-age children spend more of their time away from their families (for example, at playgroups and nurseries) than used to be the case.

 Theories suggesting that behaviour can be explained by inherited, biological factors are sometimes referred to as 'genetic determinism'.

'Primary socialisation' refers to the first and most important phase of socialisation in infancy and early childhood, which takes place mostly within the family. During this period, the child learns basic norms and values – for example, norms about eating behaviour, and the value placed on being 'good'. Adults reinforce their children's learning through positive and negative sanctions – smiles and words of approval for success and conformity, disapproval and possibly punishment for failing to behave as required.

Some socialisation takes place through the child observing and imitating. Some involves parents explicitly instructing their children. Children constantly try out different behaviour, to see what the response of their parents and others will be. Socialisation is not a one-way process in which children are slowly filled up with norms, values and roles; rather, children can and do reject and modify them. Both 'structure' and 'agency' (see pp. 14–15) are at work.

 Sociologists sometimes refer to cases of supposedly 'feral' children as evidence of the crucial role of primary socialisation in enabling people to fulfil their human social potential. Visit www.feralchildren.com

Important studies

Buss (1998) studied differences between how men and women choose their partners. Questionnaires were sent to over 10 000 people in 37 countries. The results showed that men chose women who were young and good looking, because these factors indicated fertility, while women chose men who had money or income and could therefore look after their wife and children. The genetic-determinist interpretation of this would be as follows.

- Men and women are programmed differently by their genes.
- In both sexes, the aim is for the genes to be passed on to the next generation.
- Men have evolved to be competitive and to seek as many mates as possible in order to have as many children as possible.
- Women have evolved to seek protection from a man while they raise children.

This interpretation can, however, be challenged by a social explanation. This might argue that women need a man with money because the opportunities for women to be financially independent are limited.

Secondary and adult socialisation

After primary socialisation, the child begins to experience a wider range and variety of social situations and influences. The child is still learning norms, values and roles. This phase is called 'secondary socialisation'.

Socialisation continues throughout life as people encounter new situations and have to learn new norms, values and roles. The term 'adult socialisation' is used for the learning by adults of new roles for which earlier socialisation may not have fully prepared them, such as becoming a parent or starting a new job.

Agents of socialisation

While the family is the main agent of primary socialisation, there is a range of agents of secondary socialisation.

- *Schools* – in schools we learn how to get on with other adults and children, how to conform to rules and how to become independent of parents; we also acquire knowledge and skills for later life.
- *Peer groups* – children are aware from an early age that there is a 'child' role, and they observe other children to try to learn what is expected of them.
- *Mass media* – these are of growing importance in modern times. Some media products have an explicit educational or socialising purpose, but all media contain messages of some kind that children will take in.
- *Religion* – this provides strong guidelines for behaviour and for many people remains a powerful source of values and mores.

Socialisation and social control

All sociologists accept the need for socialisation. It is the mechanism by which societies ensure that there is continuity (but also some change) from one generation to the next. However, functionalists and Marxists differ in how they see socialisation.

- For functionalists, it is vital that all members of a society learn the same core values; this creates a 'value consensus', which acts to hold a society together and prevent discord and breakdown. All societies must have ways of socialising the next generation, although these may differ between societies. Everyone benefits from this.

- Marxists, on the other hand, see socialisation as involving the instilling into the population of the values of the ruling class. Only the ruling class benefits from this.

Socialisation requires individuals to accept a set of norms, values and roles. Failing to meet society's requirements can be defined as 'deviance' or crime and may lead to punishment. With socialisation goes social control.

Functionalists see social control as necessary and working to the benefit of all. For Marxists, however, social control is used by the powerful in society to force or persuade the less powerful to behave as they want them to. Marxists argue that what we have called the agencies of socialisation are used by the ruling class to propagate its ideology, a world-view that justifies existing inequalities. The power of these agencies – schools, the media, and religion – is such that the ruling class ideology achieves **hegemony** and becomes widely accepted. It thus becomes difficult for other world-views (such as Marxism) to be heard or gain currency.

The French Marxist Louis Althusser (1971) argued that the ruling class in capitalist societies secured its power through the ideological state apparatuses (ISAs). These are the institutions that were not directly controlled by the state but which served the interests of the state – and thus the ruling class. In the past, religion was the main ISA, but Althusser maintained that schools had taken over this role. When the ISA fails to ensure that the working class accepts their position, the ruling class can turn to the repressive state apparatuses (RSAs) – police, armed forces – to deal with 'troublemakers'.

Social control: The ways in which societies control the behaviour of their members.

Different sociologists adopt different perspectives on society. Two of the most influential perspectives within sociology have been functionalism and Marxism (both described in more detail on pp. 12–13).

Agencies of socialisation can also be described as 'agencies of social control'.

The socialisation function of families and the mass media is explained in greater detail in later sections of this book.

Hegemony: The dominance of an ideology in a society.

Think it through

Watch some television programmes made for pre-school children, such as *Teletubbies*, *The Fimbles* and *The Tweenies*.

1 What might children learn from these programmes about the norms and values of our society? What might they learn about the roles that children are expected to take on in our society?

2 Now watch some programmes (e.g. early-evening soap operas) that, although not made for pre-school children specifically, they are likely to watch.

What might children learn from these programmes?

Round-up

There is a continuing debate about the relative importance of social and cultural, as opposed to biological, factors in influencing human behaviour. Sociologists emphasise how, in order to be fully human, people have to learn to become members of a society through the process of socialisation. Socialisation is seen by functionalists as essential for the stability and continuity of societies, but for Marxists it involves the imposition of an ideology and the enforcement of conformity.

How does society shape our lives?

A s you learned earlier, there are two main approaches to sociology. One focuses on 'social structures' (the macro approach) and one on 'social actions' (the micro approach). These two approaches reflect different views about the nature of society and of social life, and can be summed up as follows.

- *The social structure approach* – by social structure, we mean all the institutions of society and the ways in which they shape our lives. We are born into families and communities, educated in schools, employed in business organisations, ruled by governments, and so on. These institutions existed before we were born and will survive long after we have died. Some sociologists are interested primarily in the way these institutions work, and the effects they have on us. This is the social structure approach. It focuses on how our lives are shaped by the social forces around us and puts less emphasis on how we can influence or change those forces. Emile Durkheim was one of the early sociologists to take this approach.

- *The social action approach* – other sociologists however, stress that social institutions are created and maintained by people. For example, a school is a social institution because of the actions and behaviour of the pupils, teachers and others who are involved in the life of the school. This means that, while social institutions may seem to control our lives, we can change them (together or perhaps alone). The institutions may seem to set rules or guidelines about how we live, but rules can be broken. Sociologists who take the 'social action approach' are interested primarily in how people interact, and in why we act as we do. By focusing on how people interact, and the meanings they give to their actions (how they explain them and what they mean to them), this approach pays less attention to how social behaviour is shaped by structural forces. Max Weber was one of the early sociologists to take this approach (see p. 16).

 All three sociologists mentioned so far are men. Durkheim and Weber, together with Karl Marx, are often referred to as the 'founding fathers' of Sociology. In the nineteenth century, women were excluded from universities and thus from much academic life, though writers such as Mary Wollstonecraft made important contributions to social philosophy in the eighteenth and nineteenth centuries.

Max Weber (1864–1920). Durkheim and Weber, together with Karl Marx, are often referred to as the 'founding fathers' of sociology.

Think it through

For functionalists, the institutions of society work together so that society is healthy and stable, in the same way as the systems of the body work together. If something goes wrong in one part, this will have effects elsewhere.

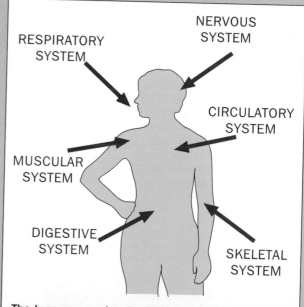

RESPIRATORY SYSTEM

NERVOUS SYSTEM

CIRCULATORY SYSTEM

MUSCULAR SYSTEM

DIGESTIVE SYSTEM

SKELETAL SYSTEM

The human organism is made up of related systems

1 In what way do the family and the education system work together?

2 In what way do the political system and the criminal justice system work together?

3 How would other social institutions, and society as a whole, be affected if the family ceased to function as it is supposed to?

The social structure approach

This approach emphasises the extent to which human behaviour is constrained by social forces beyond our control; in simple terms, the extent to which we are slaves to society. Social structures and institutions seem to take on a life of their own and dominate our lives. Society has an existence above and beyond that of the individuals who comprise it. This approach is deterministic.

Two perspectives in sociology, functionalism and Marxism, take this social structure approach but each one has reached it for very different reasons.

Functionalism

For functionalists, the institutions that make up the social structure work together, like the different parts of a body or machine, making up something that is more than the sum of its parts. Each part of the social structure fulfils a function that contributes to the overall well-being of the society, and enables it to function smoothly and survive. Society is based on a consensus, a basic agreement about the way things should be. This is known as **value consensus**.

Marxism

For Marxists, the institutions of society also work together, but against the interests of most of the people. Marxists see modern industrial societies as divided into two classes as a result of the economic system, (capitalism). The class division is between:

- the bourgeoisie (the ruling class, who own the economic capital) and

- the proletariat (the working class, who own only their ability to earn a living).

The bourgeoisie's economic power enables them to control all aspects of society, and to use this control to maintain their dominance of the proletariat. The bourgeoisie is able, most of the time, to ensure that the proletariat accepts that the rule of the bourgeoisie (and the way things are) is just and fair.

Marxists agree with functionalists that there is basic agreement on values – but argue that the majority has been persuaded to accept a set of ideas, the dominant **ideology**, which justifies the way things are and so acts against their interests. The dominant ideology is conveyed by the mass media (see pp. 92–3), religious institutions, and so on. To support its interests and protect its power, the bourgeoisie has set up the State, which, in a democracy, appears to be neutral but in fact serves the interests of the ruling class.

Marxists argue that the conflict that is implicit in the way things are will eventually lead to revolution when the proletariat will overthrow the bourgeoisie and bring about a new, fair, social order.

Marxism has been a strong influence on European sociology (it was always much weaker in the USA). This influence has been undermined, but not completely ended, by the failure of the communist states that based themselves on Marxist ideas.

Determinism assumes that all events are fully determined (caused) by previous events. In the context of social life, it argues that human freedom of choice is therefore an illusion.

Value consensus: Agreement on a set of strongly held, fairly permanent beliefs about what is right or important.

Functionalism was the dominant form of sociology for the first half of the twentieth century. Today, however, it is often spoken of as being rather out of date and unable to explain the social conflicts and accelerated social change of the late twentieth century. Nevertheless, its insights continue to underpin much sociological and 'common-sense' thinking about society.

Ideology: A set of ideas and claims that together produce a fairly coherent world-view. In Marxist usage an ideology is always false (the ideology exists to serve the interests of a class rather than to explain reality.)

Marxists see the economic system as deciding the nature of the social system; this is an 'economic determinist approach'.

Important studies

The basics of Marxism are set out in *The Communist Manifesto* by Marx and Engels, first published in 1848 (available in Penguin Classics). It is short, readable and still easily available, including on the internet.

Watch out

Both functionalism and Marxism should be thought of as broad schools of thought, able to encompass differences of opinion. In summarising complex ideas, simplification is unavoidable. However, some of the common criticisms put forward in textbooks in relation to both functionalism and Marxism are based on oversimplifying and even caricaturing them. These views are not entirely opposed; for example, Marxists would agree that social institutions have functions, but they would not describe them in the same terms as functionalists.

Research issue When studying and trying to explain social structures and social change, sociologists compare one society with another. The 'comparative method' is the basis of most scientific explanation (see Research methods pp. 136–7).

Round-up

Sociologists differ in the emphasis they place on the influence of social structures or of human agency in explaining social behaviour. The social structure approach takes two main forms – functionalism and Marxism. In their different ways, both functionalists and Marxists tend to see society as having an existence beyond the people who make up society, and as shaping our lives.

How much choice do we have?

The social action approach

In the previous section, you read about the social structure approach. As mentioned, this can be contrasted with the social action approach, which emphasises the extent to which people are conscious of their actions and how much individual social behaviour is the result of real choices (even though the range of choices may be limited by social contexts). The social action approach believes people give meaning to their actions and those of other people (they 'interpret' social actions) and make choices about how they will behave.

In this approach, people are often described as '**agents**' or actors, whereas in the structure approach they are more like puppets whose strings are being manipulated. 'Social actors' sometimes act alone (individual agency) and sometimes in groups (collective agency). The social action approach sees people not as slaves but as free – at least within certain limits. It is therefore a **voluntaristic** approach.

Agency: The ability of people, individually or collectively, to take decisions and to act.

Voluntarism: The assumption that individuals are agents, with some choice and control over their actions. Usually contrasted with determinism.

Varieties of social action theory

Within the social action approach, as within the social structure approach, there are different perspectives.

Symbolic interactionism

In your study of sociology you will come across 'symbolic interactionism'. This was developed by George Herbert Mead in the 1920s (Mead, 1934). He was interested in how people give meaning to their social actions on a one-to-one basis. He emphasised that we are constantly monitoring how we act, assessing how other people respond or will respond, and deciding on our next action. As we do this, our ideas about who we are (our self-concept and identity) are changing and developing all the time.

 The action approach is usually traced back within sociology to the German sociologist Max Weber (see p. 12). This makes it the younger of the two approaches, although its origins go back to much earlier philosophical views of the nature of social life.

 To some extent, all sociologists use the concept of social construction. It is something that distinguishes sociology from other disciplines. But the emphasis on social construction is much greater in the action approach.

Phenomenology

Phenomenology places even greater emphasis on the extent to which all social phenomena, including society itself, are created by social interaction. The core idea is the concept of social construction. This term is used to describe how aspects of society that appear to be 'real', to exist independently of people, are in fact the result of social interaction. For example, you will read in Section 2 about the social construction of childhood. Childhood might appear to be a natural stage in the development of all humans – but who is described as a child, how children are treated and what is expected of them, varies enormously between different cultures and over time. So the idea of childhood can be said to be socially constructed.

A further example of social construction, which you will come across when you study sociological methods, is official statistics such as those of crime or health. Because decisions have to be taken about what to measure and how to measure it, these statistics do not simply reflect an objective reality. For example, whether or not a crime is recorded in the official crime statistics depends on whether it is reported to the police and whether the police decide to record it as a crime. It is these decisions that make it an official statistic, not the original action (see p. 127).

Ethnomethodology

This took these ideas even further. Ethnomethodologists were especially interested in uncovering the unspoken 'rules' of everyday social interaction and observing the consequences if these rules are broken. For example, Garfinkel (1967) arranged for some of his students to behave in their own homes as if they were lodgers, and observed how this disrupted normal social interaction.

The social action approach therefore has a very different view of society from the social structure approach. In the structure approach, the institutions that make up society are powerful and real – dominating our lives. Yet those who take the action approach would say that these institutions only exist because we create and re-create them all the time. They would say that the structure approach makes the mistake of **reification** – it treats social institutions as though they exist independently of people, whereas, in fact, they are only the sum of the actions of many people. Society is made, and constantly re-made, by people interacting with each other.

Reification: When the results of human interactions seem to take on an independent reality of their own.

Important studies

■ Goffman (1969) made important contributions to the study of small-scale social interaction in everyday life. He described everyday life using the analogy of drama. People are like actors in a play. We can follow the scripts set out for us by our roles, or we can improvise. We are constantly playing to an audience, being aware of how others respond to us and modifying our behaviour accordingly; Goffman calls this 'impression management'. Our clothes, other aspects of our appearance, our houses, cars and jobs are props that we use to put on our dramatic performances. There are even backstage areas where we can relax from our otherwise continuous performances.

■ The term 'social construction' was popularised by Berger and Luckmann, in their book *The social construction of reality* (1967). They showed how society was actively created by people. We live in a world that has been made by social interaction. At the same time, this socially constructed world seems to have an existence of its own and shapes our lives.

Structuration

Of the many attempts to bring the structural and action approaches together, the most recent is that of Anthony Giddens. Giddens (1979) uses the term 'structuration' to refer to the way in which social structures not only limit how people can act but also make it possible for social action to take place at all. Social structure and social action cannot exist independently of each other. People can only make choices within social frameworks.

Think it through

In contemporary British society, older people are encouraged to conceal grey hair, wrinkles and other signs of ageing. In other cultural traditions, however, less negative interpretations are placed upon physiological aspects of old age. For the Sherbro people of Sierra Leone, incoherent and incomprehensible speech by an aged person is perceived as a positive sign. Their incoherence indicates their close communication with ancestors, who are regarded as important arbiters of destiny (McCormack 1985, cited in Hockey and James, 1993). Similarly for the Venda-speaking people of Southern Africa, old age is regarded as a 'pleasure'. Signs of old age, such as greying hair or the birth of a grandchild, are welcomed as indications of a person's approaching contact with the 'real' world of the spirits (Blacking 1990, cited in Hockey and James, 1993). In cultures where the afterlife is accorded great significance, old people's proximity to death enhances rather than reduces their status (Pilcher, 1995).

1 'Old age is socially constructed'. Explain and discuss this statement, referring to this extract and using some of the terms you have read about in this section.

Research issues

The social action approach is associated with ethnographic research methods, which produce qualitative data and which, if done well, have high validity. The main aim of these methods is to try to understand why people behave as they do by seeing things from their point of view, and understanding the meanings people give to their actions. To describe this, Weber used the term 'verstehen', normally translated as 'understanding'.

Round-up

The social action approach emphasises human agency, the extent to which we can choose how to act. It can be contrasted with the social structure approach, which emphasises how society seems to have an objective reality that dominates our lives. Several perspectives within sociology, including symbolic interactionism, adopt this view. A key concept in sociology, derived largely from the action approach, is social construction, which is used to explain how the social world is made by people rather than having a separate existence. The more recent structuration theory aims to show how structure and action are interdependent.

How equal are we?

Sources of inequality

One of the main interests of sociologists has always been social differences, for example in wealth, income, status or power. These kinds of differences are known as 'social inequalities'. When groups of people can be ranked hierarchically (that is, in order) for differences such as wealth and power this is called 'stratification'.

For most sociologists, at least until very recently, the main form of stratification in modern societies was social class. The equivalents for earlier societies were caste, **estates** and slavery.

Over the past few decades, gender, age and ethnic or racial differences (which previously had usually been taken as a part of class stratification or as being less important than class stratification) have come to be seen as being just as important as class – and perhaps even more so.

Social inequalities exist in many forms, both within and between societies and social groups

Life chances

The importance of stratification can be measured by its impact on life chances. The following measures (among many others) can show differences between classes, between the genders and between ethnic groups:

- life expectancy
- levels of health and illness
- income
- wealth
- housing
- achievement in education
- the likelihood of being convicted of a crime or being the victim of a crime.

Caste compared with social class

In understanding class it is useful to be able to compare it to other, earlier forms of stratification. The caste system in India was based on occupation, but both occupation and caste position were decided at birth. For example, the son of a priest would be destined to be a priest and to belong to the priestly caste. This means that caste is ascribed; it is not the outcome of individual effort or mobility. Occupation in the class system, by contrast, is not fixed at birth, and is an achieved position.

Both caste and class involve fairly strict hierarchies, but in the caste system it is almost impossible to move from one level to another while the class system allows some mobility – though how much is a matter of debate.

Social class

Social class is a commonly used term for a recognised form of stratification, but there are wide differences between the theories of class given by different sociologists.

- Functionalists see class as a necessary and inevitable aspect of modern societies. Social-class differences emerge out of differences in talent and ability that deserve different rewards. Differences in wealth and power are justified and act as an incentive to all.

- Marxists see social-class differences as arising out of exploitation – the ruling class (the bourgeoisie) own the means of production and exploit the working class (the proletariat) by not paying them the full value of their work and taking the surplus as profit. This basic clash of interests between the classes is 'class conflict', which will ultimately lead to revolution and the overthrow of the ruling class.

- Max Weber, whilst agreeing that social class is an important source of inequality and power, also argued that religion, ethnicity, gender, age, etc. were other sources of what he called 'status differences' (Weber, 1978). These differences may result in conflict but not in revolution. This view was very influential in sociology in the latter part of the twentieth century.

- In recent years, postmodernists have questioned the importance of social class and suggest that people no longer strongly identify with it. Instead, people are more likely to define themselves through their lifestyle – that is, through what they consume.

Estates: The system of stratification in the medieval period, with division between clergy, nobility and commoners.

 The sociology exam requires you to be familiar with four main aspects of stratification: class, gender, ethnicity and age. Stratification can also involve groups that are different in other ways, such as ability and disability, or sexual preference.

Important studies

The French sociologist Pierre Bourdieu (1984) argued that class was still of great importance in modern societies, but he offered reasons as to why this was not always recognised. His concept of 'cultural capital' explains how class differences are made invisible, because they are routinely reproduced in ways that seem natural. For example, the 'right' accent, effortlessly acquired within the family, may give a middle-class person an advantage over someone who has in the same way acquired a regional accent. Class differences are strongest when people are least aware of them.

Think it through

Like Marx, Weber recognised the existence of social class but he also highlighted status divisions within classes, based on education, skill, pay and consumption of goods as represented by lifestyle choices. Moreover he noted that membership of particular status groups which were unrelated to class sometimes conferred benefits on people and sometimes denied them access to rewards. For example, members of different ethnic minorities or religions, women and disabled people in the UK may be denied access to top jobs, whatever their social class position.

Adapted from: Woodward, K. (ed.) (2000)
Identity: Gender, class and nation, Routledge/Open University, London

1 Identify three status differences that might exist within the medical profession.

2 Identify and explain three other sources of inequality in society other than social class.

3 Assess the view that status is the key to understanding inequality in society.

Gender

Feminists argue that gender differences are an important division in society today and they draw attention to 'gender stratification'. They point out that modern societies are often **patriarchal** and that this is reflected in male domination of areas of social life such as employment and politics.

Ethnicity

The term 'ethnicity' came into use in sociology when it was recognised that the idea of race was deeply flawed. Members of an ethnic group may share some attributes that can be considered racial (for example, skin colour) but ethnicity refers to shared *cultural* rather than physical or other characteristics. These cultural characteristics may include: language, religion, family and marriage patterns, a common historical origin and a sense of shared identity.

Most modern societies are **multicultural**, with, usually, a dominant ethnic majority and one or more minority ethnic groups. The cultural characteristics of the minority groups in such situations are not survivals from the past but are shaped by their existence in a multicultural society. If that society is marked by prejudice and discrimination, the result can be a defensive strengthening of aspects of culture that mark the minority group as different.

Watch out

Everyone has an ethnic identity. It is a common mistake to think that ethnicity refers only to minorities. In Britain, the white majority is also an ethnic group (or, more accurately, several ethnic groups).

Ethnicity cuts across class stratification. For example, members of a minority ethnic group in Britain today, such as Indian people, may belong to the middle class or to the working class.

Age

Stratification by age is a characteristic of many societies. In Britain and other Western countries today, there are fairly clear differences in the situation of different age groups. Children have a different legal status from adults. They are closely protected and seen as having rights while also having their freedom severely curtailed (for example, they may be obliged to attend school). Older people, on the other hand, can suffer prejudice and discrimination and old age has a low social status. So, both the old and the young are treated as being less competent as those in between. This is 'age stratification'.

In other societies, age groups may be just as clearly marked (for example, with very clear transitions, marked by rites of passage, from childhood to adulthood and to becoming an elder). Identity based on belonging to an age **cohort**, experiencing events such as **rites of passage** together, can be very strong.

Patriarchy: A system where men have social, cultural and economic dominance over women.

Multicultural: The intermingling of a number of cultures.

Cohort: A group of people who share a significant experience at a point in time, for example, being born in the same year, or taking A levels in the same year.

Rite of passage: A ceremony to mark the transition from one stage of life to another; for example, marriage ceremonies.

Round-up

The main dimensions of stratification considered in AS and A level sociology are social class, gender, ethnicity and age. These provide a theme running through the course. In the past, social class was the dimension that attracted the most attention from sociologists. The acknowledgement of the importance of the other dimensions is relatively new. The idea that modern – or postmodern – societies are characterised by a range of cross-cutting social divisions calls into question the idea of stratification.

What is the difference between males and females?

Sex

The term 'sex' refers to a biological concept and means the physical differences between males and females that are determined before birth. Most (though not all) of us are born with a clearly identifiable sex. Many writers, such as Desmond Morris (1975) and, more recently, Robert Winston (2002), have proposed the view that these biological differences lead to social differences between males and females. This view is known as 'biological determinism' or 'evolutionary psychology'. Sociologists tend to reject this view of human behaviour because gendered behaviours (see below) vary so dramatically from culture to culture and also change over time within cultures.

Gender

The term 'gender' is a sociological concept. It refers to the **socially constructed** ideas of how the different sexes should behave in social terms. Different norms and values apply to both male and female behaviour in our culture. Women are expected to wear different kinds of clothes, drink different alcoholic drinks, and participate in different sports and hobbies from males. Even their gestures, body language and manners are expected to be different, so females tend to sit with their legs together and gesture more with their hands. There may be an emphasis on body adornment: decoration of hair and nails, for instance. Masculinity is often associated with positive attributes such as bravery, power, intelligence and dominance (see the table opposite).

Primary socialisation

Gender is taught and learned within the family through primary socialisation (see pp. 10–11). In many families, male babies are cuddled less, spoken to less and offered firmer discipline. From an early age there are expectations of male behaviour so that boys are less likely to be picked up if they fall – and if they do fall, they are discouraged from crying or expressing emotion. Male and female children are offered different toys, clothing, television programmes, video games, books, bed linen, sports and activities, shoe styles, hairstyles, videogames and comics. As the children of the family grow older, the female children may be expected to take on more domestic work and may begin to have their freedom restricted. This has a cumulative effect on the development of the adult personality; and this means that expected adult male and female social behaviours are very different.

Socially constructed: An agreed social definition of how to think or behave.

In British culture, the drag queen or pantomime dame is a traditional form of entertainment. It's worth considering the ways in which these men impersonating women present an exaggerated form of femininity in order to mock female behaviour.

These images of toys represent stereotypes of male and female qualities that are often reinforced by media imagery

Think it through

The following passage comes from a popular children's book series designed for adults to read aloud to their young children.

When they came down from the ladder Mummy bought them each a little fire-fighter's helmet.

'I'm going to be a fire-fighter when I grow up' said Kerry.

'Can girls be fire-fighters?' asked Topsy.

'I don't think so' said Tim.

'Yes they can!' said the lady who was selling the toy helmets.

'I'm a fire-fighter, just like Kerry's Dad. Women can be fire-fighters, but they have to be as strong and as brave as the men.'

To show how strong she was, she gave Tim a fireman's lift.

Adamson, Jean and Gareth (1999) *Topsy and Tim meet the Firefighters* Dorling Kindersley, London

1 Identify traditional female-gendered roles in the text.

2 Outline and identify ways in which traditional gender roles are challenged in the passage above.

3 Evaluate the suggestion that British society is patriarchal.

Secondary socialisation

Secondary socialisation can reinforce gender so that even in families where attempts are made to prevent younger children becoming gender stereotyped, exposure to social influences may well undermine those attempts. These influences include the following.

- *Books* – traditional reading materials for children offer male heroes and images of female passivity. Traditional fairy stories feature female characters cherished for their beauty. Children's storybooks often revolve around male characters such as Thomas the Tank Engine or Bob the Builder, while female characters have a secondary role.
- *Education* – this had a strongly masculine aura until feminist challenges were issued in the 1970s and 1980s. Textbooks generally used male examples and traditional uniforms required females to wear jackets, white collar and ties – a masculine form of dress.
- *Peer groups* – these may exert pressure so that people accept the dominant norms and values of those of a similar age and status to themselves. Children often use terms such as 'gay' and 'woman' as terms of abuse before they fully appreciate the significance of what they are saying.
- *Media* – the media produce gender-specific consumer products, such as films directed for women ('chick flicks') and novels specifically aimed at women ('chick lit'). Even when the product is the same (e.g. deodorants or cars) it is marketed and sold differently to men and women.
- *Religion* – many faiths offer an image of a male God and teach traditional marriage and gender roles. Religious ceremonies may show differing gender patterns for males and females with men carrying out the ceremonial roles while women support them.

Important studies

Oakley (1981) argues that gender socialisation has four central elements:
- *Manipulation* is where parents encourage gendered behaviour.
- *Canalisation* is where parents direct children towards gendered activities and games.
- *Verbal appellations* such as pet names are used to describe children's characteristics.
- *Differentiated activities* are where girls are encouraged to take on domestic roles but boys are sent out to play.

Stereotypical characteristics of a traditional man and woman

	Traditional male	Traditional female
Physical type	Hard, dominant, big, tall, muscular	Small, dainty, little, weak, fragile
Employment	Physical labour, skilled manual, managerial	Variation on female domestic roles – cooking, cleaning and caring
Domestic life	Practical – takes responsibility for technical side of domestic life, cars, and maintenance	Responsible for cooking and feeding family, takes on chores
Intellectual	Clever, intellectual, scientific, mechanical, rational	Unintelligent (or if intelligent – then unsexy), at mercy of hormones, irrational, emotional, unpredictable
Emotional life	Unemotional and controlled, except whilst watching sport	Emotional, tearful and at the mercy of hormones. Care giver and emotional control for males
Sexual	Sexual predator, experienced	Innocent, asexual, or if sexual then a slut or prostitute
Social characteristics	Active and judges himself by the standards of other men	Passive and judges herself by the standards of males
Leisure	Team games, sport, drinking alcohol	Domesticity, social activities with family
Archetype	James Bond, any action hero	Cinderella, any fairy tale princess

Status

In addition to the physical and cultural differences between men and women, there is another dimension: that of status. Men and women are not viewed as equally important in many cultures. The lives of male children are sometimes seen as more valuable than the lives of female children. In our own society, men tend to earn more, and have more social freedom than women. A dual sexual morality is applied to men and to women, whereby male promiscuity is tolerated and female promiscuity is likely to be condemned. Although females may take on male forms of dress and behaviour (such as the wearing of trousers), males can lose status if they behave in a way that is seen as being feminine. Many terms exist to condemn males who act in a female way, but probably fewer exist for those women who display masculine characteristics.

This difference in status between males and females was far more marked in the 1950s than in the present day. This led many women to question the traditional gender roles and to call themselves 'feminists'. They gave a name to male dominance of society – 'patriarchy'. It was argued that males dominated society, and women, through violence and sexual exploitation. In addition, the male view of the world has become hegemonic, so that people are unable to challenge it easily.

Round-up

Traditional gender roles in British society emphasise the dominance and power of men, with women being encouraged to be more passive and domestic. These roles, although challenged by both men and women, are still powerful because they are socialised into children in the home and in wider society. Children are taught gender patterns through both primary and secondary socialisation and this has an impact on their adult roles and personalities. More importantly, gender socialisation can also reflect how the different genders have access to power and economic wealth in our society.

Go through some of the children's products of the major catalogue companies such as Argos or Littlewoods. Identify which products are gendered. Look at toys, bed linen, clothes, books and games in particular. Which personal characteristics, styles and pastimes are associated with girls and which with boys?

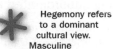
Hegemony refers to a dominant cultural view. Masculine hegemony refers to a view of the world that is masculine in terms of the dominant ideas about how the genders should behave.

How are gender roles and gender identities changing?

Gender roles

In recent years there has been considerable change in the traditional views of the roles of men and women. Evidence for this can be seen in a number of trends, including:

- in popular culture, where many celebrities have been sexually ambiguous in their behaviour – for example, the pop stars Marilyn Manson or Michael Jackson

- in daily life, where more women are employed in roles that were traditionally the preserve of men. They are now found as Members of Parliament, as company directors and as lawyers.

Feminists tend to claim that the changes have come about because women are freeing themselves from male domination, whereas postmodernists are more likely to suggest that it is because society is changing and people no longer accept many traditional social values. Men and women are beginning to learn to see each other as partners in life. Judith Butler (1999), an eminent postmodernist, asserts that whereas gender roles were once in opposition, in modern society gender roles can be viewed as a continuum. She claims that some men may display feminine characteristics and that females can be masculine without fear of social stigma.

Patterns of gendered behaviour for men and women in British culture are changing. Are these changes significant or are traditional patterns still there under the surface?

Changing gender patterns

New Men

This concept was identified in the late 1970s. It was argued that males were becoming more like females and that they were willing to take on domestic tasks and talk about their feelings. It was, however, a **contested concept**, because many feminists did not believe that New Men were numerically significant.

New Lads

'New Lads' are a more recent phenomenon. It is argued that as a reaction to increasing female claims on traditional masculinity and in response to the New Man, some young men display aggressively male attitudes masked with humour. An example of new laddishness is the content of *Viz* magazine.

Ladettes

Some young women have developed attitudes that were previously associated with masculinity. Hard drinking and aggressive sexuality are signs of the ladettes. Well-known ladettes include Radio presenter Zoë Ball in her younger days, and TV presenter Davina McCall.

Crisis in masculinity

It is claimed that males have had their traditional roles challenged by women but have not discovered a new identity that allows them to be separate from women. If to be a man means that a person is not female, is not a wimp and is not gay, this leaves few role options for young males. Based on his studies of Australian males, R M Connell (1995) claims that men have taken on a variety of new identities and are looking for a sense of who they are.

Homosexual men and subordinated masculinity

Homosexuality was **decriminalised** in Britain in 1967. Before this date, most gay men hid their true sexual orientation from others – and often from themselves. There has been an increasing acceptance of gay men in public life, with politicians publicly acknowledging gay relationships and openly gay behaviour on television and the media. Nevertheless, gays are still vulnerable to physical and verbal attack.

See pp. 66–7 for a discussion of changes in the domestic roles of men and women.

Contested concept: Debated and discussed, with disagreement.

Important studies

Brittan (1989) suggested that there is a difference between 'masculinity' and 'masculinism'. He claims that masculinity is socially constructed and changes through history. It has traditionally been associated with care for the weak and with paternalism. The New Man offered a new direction for masculinity in the 1980s. Masculinism, however, is still apparent throughout society and takes the form of a desire to dominate and control social relationships and situations.

Decriminalised: When behaviour is no longer punishable by law.

Publicly [men] subscribe to the myth of the young single life where you don't have to clean up and you can drink all day, watch porn and shag endlessly. But a lot of men are really thinking, 'I have done that for two years and actually I've been pretty low'.

There is much to be uncomfortable with in this brave new world. Traditional models of masculinity crumble and are replaced by David Beckham. Women hunt in packs in All Bar One while men skulk, fearful of rejection and humiliation. Glass ceilings are broken, playing fields are levelled out and many men find that difficult to deal with.

Cary Cooper says: 'Women have decided that there is more to life than just getting married and having children and having a job. They have decided that they want to have careers, they are entering male-dominated domains and that is causing a certain amount of tension. I think that a lot of men in the 25–30 age group feel threatened by women.'

Compton, N. (2002) 'Can't live with them, can't live without them...' *The Observer*, Sunday 28 April

1 List two stereotypical images of the male role illustrated by the passage above.

2 Suggest two reasons why males may feel threatened by the changing roles of women.

3 Evaluate the suggestion that the gender-role changes that have taken place in modern British society have been exaggerated.

But are gender patterns really changing in British society?

Despite the new phenomena listed above, there are ways in which nothing has radically changed – as described below.

Gender roles are changing ...	But ...
It is claimed that females are becoming more criminal. Elkins and Olangundoye (2000) point out that the number of women in prison is at its highest since 1901.	There are still nearly 20 times as many men in prison as women.
Women are found in increasing numbers in the workplace.	According to Department of Trade and Industry figures, women in full-time work earn 18.1% less than men. Seventy per cent of low-paid workers are female.
Girls do better in school and tend to get better examination results.	Twenty years ago, when boys achieved better results than girls in schools it was not seen as a problem. Now that boys are not keeping pace with the standards of girls, it is seen as a problem that must be tackled by government and schools.
It is acceptable for men to undertake domestic chores in the home. Males participate in domestic labour and carry out childcare duties.	Studies have consistently shown that in many households, women still undertake the vast majority of domestic labour and childcare. This pattern continues even when both partners are in full-time work.
Males have become a market for fashions, toiletries and male cosmetics. They buy creams and items that once would only have been consumed by females.	Does this reflect a real change in male roles in society or simply changing norms of masculinity?
Some female celebrities are acting in a way that was previously seen as traditionally masculine and dominant.	Many of the women who have challenged traditional male roles are also conventionally attractive. Modern celebrities of both sexes are marketed on their looks as well as their talents for singing and acting.

There are a number of American sites dedicated to 'girl power' and encouraging women to take on leadership roles. The site at **www.girlpower.gov** *is aimed at younger teenage girls, and is sponsored by the US government.*

Round-up

Gender is a significant social identifier. We are taught appropriate gender roles in the home and these are reinforced by a variety of agencies of socialisation. Whilst gender roles have undoubtedly changed in recent years, they may not have changed as much as some sociologists claim. Behaviour that challenges traditional gender roles, such as showing explicit same-sex affection, may be acceptable on television but how far is such behaviour tolerated on the streets of modern Britain?

What is race and ethnicity?

Factors that can transmit cultural or ethnic identity

✳ Early scientists were keen to categorise human 'types' by measuring distinctive features of their faces and build. This developed into the now discredited 'science' of eugenics that was used by the Nazis to identify Jews.

Race

Race: A concept that views human beings as belonging to separate biological groupings.

Ethnicity: Shared culture based on common language, religion or nationality.

Culture: The accumulated knowledge, norms and values of a particular group; their way of life.

✳ Every individual has an ethnicity, a sense of belonging to a particular group. People are more likely to be aware of their sense of ethnicity when they are in a foreign country than when they are at home.

The idea of **race** is an increasingly outdated concept. It originated with attempts made by early scientists to classify human beings into types (e.g. Negroid, Caucasoid, mongoloid) and was sometimes used to justify domination and abuse of one ethnic group by another. However, the science of genetics has subsequently shown that the genetic differences between racial groups are actually very small. The differences between individuals are far more significant than the variations between 'racial types'. The human genome project showed that humans share a very large proportion of their genetic material. Rose (1998) points out that, despite this, skin colour has been used as a basis for differentiating between one group and another in a variety of cultures. In Western culture, the reasons for this are bound up in religious symbolism. For example, in medieval wall paintings the Devil was often painted as black. The legacy of this is that the modern English language has itself become racist – 'black' is used to describe things that are unpleasant, for example, blackmail, black look, black-hearted. Racism has become part of many cultures and is often at its most obvious in jokes and humour that are based on cultural stereotyping.

Ethnicity

Ethnicity is a far more useful concept than race and means being part of a group of people who share a **culture** that consists of particular traditions and beliefs. This culture differentiates them from other groups. People who share an ethnicity feel included and part of a larger social group. Their ethnicity group often gives people a sense of pride and identity. They will emphasise their differences and signal them to others.

Ethnicity is also significant because it marks out as 'other' those who do not share that particular ethnicity, and these people are excluded. Ethnicity is a far more useful concept to sociologists than race because people who consider themselves as sharing an ethnicity may not in fact be very different from those whom they consider as 'other'. Consider the case of the Scots and English; it would be difficult for a non-European to recognise the cultural difference between these ethnicities, but to a Scottish person, these differences may be very important. Sometimes these ethnic differences may include longstanding religious and political disputes that have resulted in bloodshed. Northern Irish Catholics and Protestants recognise subtle cultural differences that would not be obvious to an outsider.

There are a variety of ethnicities present within the British population. These ethnicities have languages that pre-date modern English, e.g. Welsh and Scottish Gaelic. Minority ethnic groups found in Britain include Chinese, Pakistanis, Bangladeshis, Somalis, Jews, and various West Indian groups, as well as Poles, Greeks and Australians. The non-white British population is mostly derived from those migrating to Britain from the Caribbean, South Asia and East and West Africa since the mid-1950s. Modood (1997) points out that the majority of non-white people currently living in Britain were born in the UK and consider themselves to be British.

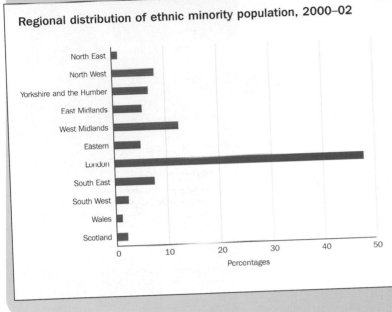

Regional distribution of ethnic minority population, 2000–02

North East
North West
Yorkshire and the Humber
East Midlands
West Midlands
Eastern
London
South East
South West
Wales
Scotland

0   10   20   30   40   50
Percentages

In 2001–02 minority ethnic groups made up 9 per cent of the total population in England compared with only 2 per cent in both Scotland and Wales. Chinese people made up around 0.3 per cent of the total population in each country. 48 per cent of the total minority ethnic population lived in the London region, where they comprised 29 per cent of all residents.

Source: Annual Local Area Labour Force Survey 2001/02, Office for National Statistics

1 Where were members of minority ethnic groups most likely to live? Summarise the patterns shown in this graph.

2 Explain why most members of minority ethnic groups live in metropolitan and urban areas.

3 Evaluate the view that Britain is a multi-ethnic and multi-cultural society.

Adapted from www.statistics.gov.uk

How is ethnic identity transmitted?

Ethnic identity is transmitted through processes of socialisation within the home through language, custom, tradition and food traditions. Goffman (1969) pointed out that minority languages are often used in the home, whereas English becomes the language of business and education. Agencies of secondary socialisation are also very significant:

- *Religion* – this is very closely allied to a sense of ethnic identity so that young Asians may consider their religion a more significant identity than their nationality.
- *Media* – the media are strongly associated with creating a sense of ethnic identity, particularly associated with sporting events.
- *Education* – it is argued that the curriculum promotes a British view of historical events so that we learn little of the history of British minority ethnic groups.

Assimilation

Some immigrant groups have become so established in Britain that it is difficult to recognise that they were ever non-British. The term to describe this process is 'cultural assimilation'. There is some debate as to whether cultural assimilation is taking place among more recent minority ethnic groups. Modood (1997) has suggested that British Asians and African Caribbeans think of themselves as mostly British but are not entirely at ease with this identity because they don't feel that the white British accept them as being fully part of British culture. However, John Rex (1996) suggests that societies that include minority ethnic groups may respond in one of three ways:

- The minorities become equal citizens but lose their separate identity.
- The minorities are treated as second-class citizens.
- Minority groups may retain their separate identity at home but may have to subscribe to the dominant culture in the workplace and in the political sphere.

British or English?

It's worth noting that within Britain there is often confusion between the notion of being British and English, so that the distinctiveness of Welsh, Irish and Scottish culture is lost. Hechter (1975) has referred to the way in which English culture has become the dominant culture of the British Isles as 'cultural imperialism'.

Round-up

The concept of race does not help us to understand the differences between different cultural groups of human beings. Differences between individuals are far greater than the differences between racial groups. Nevertheless, race has been used to justify discrimination, prejudice and cruelty. The British population is made up of individuals with a mixed heritage and the British culture has assimilated ideas from many other cultures and languages. There are a number of different ethnic and cultural traditions to be found in what we loosely call 'British' culture.

www **www.bbc.co.uk/education/20cvox/immigrate.shtml** *provides first-hand accounts of the experience of immigrants to Britain after the end of World War II. There are accounts from the Asian and West Indian communities. For the West Indian story, click on 'Windrush'. For more detailed information about the human genome project, visit their website at* **www.genome.gov**

How is ethnic identity changing?

The question posed by the heading of this section is one of the most important current debates in sociology. Postmodernists suggest that the world is no longer a place of certainties in which people 'know who they are'. People are now aware of lots of ideas about the world but do not know what to believe in. People can make choices about how to act according to their gender, their age, their class or even ethnicity. Identities are not simply given, but are socially constructed from a number of sources – media, culture, and religion. An identity becomes a 'project' that a person can act upon rather than something that is determined by birth and nationality.

Diaspora

> ✳ 'Diaspora' is a Biblical term that described the movement of the Jews away from Israel and Judea. The modern term describes the spreading out and movement by peoples from their homelands.

The debate about ethnic identity has been prompted by the concept of diaspora. History has seen great movements of peoples around the world. For example, there are probably more 'Irish' people now living in America than in Ireland as a result of migrations in the nineteenth century. The process of population movement has become simpler due to improved transport and communication so that not only do people move but also we are now more aware of other cultures and ideas. It has been argued that a process known as 'globalisation' is taking place. Cultures are beginning to lose their separate identities and becoming part of a mass Americanised culture in which certain American products are found on sale all over the world, e.g. McDonalds and Coke. Global media networks that sell American-style media products in dozens of countries are hurrying this process along.

Madonna has adopted Asian cultural tradition to fit in with fashion. Does her choice of dress reflect cultural understanding as well?

Individual identity

Nowadays, there is a more personal element about the way individual people create their own sense of self. An example of this is related to the use of the term 'Asian'. This term is commonly misused to describe people whose ethnic origins are in the Indian subcontinent. However, the term is problematic because it covers a whole range of diverse cultures, languages and religions. Not all the people whom we call Asians came to Britain from the subcontinent; many came from Africa in the 1960s. Others originated from the West Indies, where they had settled in the past. Asians are not a single ethnic group any more than people from the Caribbean form a single culture. In describing a certain range of non-white cultural groups some British people may incorrectly use the term 'Asian' in ignorance of this. However, the matter is confused by the fact that the term 'Asian' is sometimes also specifically used by British Asians to refer to themselves because they feel it acts as an emblem of a shared experience of racism in our society.

> ✳ It is by no means certain that globalisation has actually occurred. Many people resist American culture and gain identity by rejecting Western ideas and returning to their own cultural roots through religious expression.

> ✳ 'Cultural resistance' is a useful term to describe how people reject the ideas given to them by a dominant culture.

EXAMPLES OF BRITISH ASIAN OR 'BRASIAN' CULTURE

- TV programmes e.g. *Goodness Gracious Me* and *The Kumars at No 42*
- Films, e.g. *East is East*, *Bend It Like Beckham*, *Monsoon Wedding* and *Langaan*.
- Music styles that fuse Western and Asian traditions.
- Jewellery styles and Asian symbols such as Bindi and henna tattoos, popular with white women.

Hybrid culture

There has been considerable mix between various cultures so that many children do not belong exclusively to one ethnic group or another. Modood (1997) showed that:

- two out of five children born to an African-Caribbean parent also have a White parent;
- nearly 20% of British men, and 10% of women, with Indian or African Asian origins live with White partners.

Many young British people are therefore able to draw on a variety of traditions in order to create multiple identities.

The terms 'fusion' or 'hybrid culture' are used to describe the new cultural mix that occurs. The impact of West Indian and American-African culture on British and American popular music has long been documented. The use of reggae rhythms in white music is an example of that process. Certain sectors of the youth community associate being black with being 'cool'.

British Asian culture has traditionally had less of an impact on cultural forms. However, recently there has been growing awareness of Asian culture and a recognition that British Asians are a market for cultural products reflecting their heritage. Ballard (1979) found that South Asians did not feel that they had to choose between their home culture and British culture, because they had actually formed a culture of their own that was a synthesis of their two cultures.

✱ Although it is now increasingly being acknowledged that British Asians and African Caribbeans have made a major contribution to the development of British culture, racism is still part of the experience of many non-white members of the British community.

✱ A 'hybrid' in scientific terms means a mix between two different species. Here the term is used to describe new cultural identities that emerge when two very different cultures mix.

Global economy: Describes the global market in which goods and services are traded across the world, particularly by multinational corporations.

Important studies

■ Gilroy (2000) suggested that Black Americans who adopt 'gangsta' fashions and develop a cult of exaggerated muscle and masculinity as a defensive reaction to racism have in fact made themselves the tools of exploitation by a White-run **global economy**. Their styles and fashions are stolen and sold to White consumers who do not actually share their views of African-American culture. Black culture has become a commodity to be bought and sold so that the essential humanity of the people who create it has become lost.

■ In his study of the role of soap opera in creating identity among Black and Asian girls, Barker (1997) identifies Sandra – a teenage girl who accepts herself as Black, but rejects the idea that it is a negative label, who recognises herself as working class but aspires to middle-class status and uses middle-class language. She identifies herself as British but feels her Blackness is important to her. She recognises that Asian girls have similar experiences of rejection and racism to herself. She has a hybrid identity.

■ Britton et al. (2002) found that the experiences of young Asians (and the extent to which they were expected to conform to traditional cultural roles) varied between the genders. Males were tolerated when seen as breaking the cultural norms but females had experienced pressure to conform, particularly with regard to marriage.

Think it through

VOXPOP – SUBCONTINENTAL DRIFT

British Asian culture has won a place in our hearts – and about time too

IT HAS BEEN AN AMAZING 10 YEARS for British Asians. The last few years, in particular, have witnessed a drastic rise in the artistic output of second- and third-generation Asians here. From a musical perspective, there has been greater interest in British Asians expressing their identity, with artists such as Cornershop, Asian Dub Foundation, Badmarsh and Shri, Fun-da-mental, Joi, Sona Fariq, Talvin Singh, Susheela Raman and State of Bengal all having an impact on the mainstream.

For a long time, many of these artists, myself included, were placed in the patronising category of 'Asian Underground', a term designed to give an edge to an imaginary movement. The real semantic effect, however, was to reduce genuine social and cultural change to a trend that reinforced marginalisation rather than challenged stereotypes.

I remember how, when I was nominated for the Mercury Music Prize in 2000, I was referred to as 'this year's token Asian' by a newspaper. For me, there could be no tokenism in a pluralistic society. In fact, I have always viewed this country's cultural diversity as a symptom of true strength and development.

Sawhney, Nitin (2002) 'Subcontinental drift', *The Observer*, Sunday 28 July

1 Explain the meaning of 'marginalisation' with reference to British Asian culture.

2 Suggest three ways in which British culture has adapted to the presence of minority ethnic groups within the UK.

3 Evaluate the suggestion that fusion cultures and hybrid cultures are gaining acceptance among the majority of the population.

Round-up

British culture is undergoing change as it adapts to the cultural stimulus provided by its minority ethnic groups. Distinctive hybrid cultures have developed that fuse the characteristics of minority groups and mainstream British culture. However, minority groups still experience marginalisation and racism, and increasingly their customs and cultures are being adapted into fashion items and used without any understanding of their meaning or significance.

What is nationality?

We each belong to a nation. This is a legal concept and relates to the idea that our nationality gives us particular rights of residence or voting. We are entitled to a passport and are considered citizens of our country, which means that our government will protect us if we find ourselves in trouble in a foreign country. In some European countries, citizenship also carries legal obligations so that males in the population may be expected to join the army for a period of time. As a result of migration and intermarriage between people of differing nationalities, many people carry a dual nationality. For the purposes of representing a country at a sport, often it is enough to lay claim to having a grandparent born in that country. People may change nationality but this is a lengthy and difficult legal process.

The issue of '**nation**', however, is more complex than that. Sociologists are interested in the way in which people find a sense of nation for themselves. This means loyalty to a particular geographical region, which is usually (but not always) a legal entity such as a state. In some cases, nationalist loyalty may be to a state that does not formally exist as a legal entity but to one that may have existed in the past or that people would like to see exist in the future. For example, Palestinians feel a strong sense of identity to a state that has not existed since 1949 when the state of Israel was created. In such cases, a strong sense of injustice or oppression by another state may be a powerful dynamic in the creation of a sense of **nationality**. One could ask whether being Welsh or Scottish would be important to people if there were not such a powerful cultural force as England against which people could measure themselves.

This is a very significant issue because **nationalism** can be a powerful emotion – one that drives people to dangerous political action such as terrorism and warfare. At its most extreme, it can appear as xenophobia within an existing state and members of the ruling majority may turn on and kill members of minority ethnic groups. This was certainly a phenomenon in the twentieth century, when massacres of minority populations occurred in states such as Turkey and former Yugoslavia.

Nation states often have their own symbols of nationalism. These are used to represent the state and its citizens. They are often used to pass on a sense of nation to children in school, via stories, festivals and traditions, as well as:

- flags and pennants – for example, the Welsh dragon, the Union Jack
- symbols such as the crescent moon and star, Star of David
- music such as national anthems and well-loved traditional songs
- traditions and festivals, e.g. Hogmanay in Scotland
- clothing and costume such as kilts
- dance and artistic productions, e.g. traditional Irish dance
- famous historical and/or mythical people who represent national characteristics, e.g. Joan of Arc, William Wallace (Braveheart)
- saints such as St Patrick
- particular places deemed special in the eyes of people, e.g. Westminster Abbey
- documents embodying the state, e.g. the American Constitution.

Many modern states deliberately attempt to encourage a sense of **national identity** among their citizens. In the twentieth century, one of the most sustained efforts to create a national identity occurred during the Third Reich in Germany (1933–45) when German symbolism and art was used to create dramatic propaganda in order to wage war. However, not all attempts to create citizenship and national identity are necessarily malicious or dangerous. As Durkheim (1964) suggested, nationalism can be a powerful force uniting people. In the United States, flags are held in all classrooms and students are expected to pledge the Oath of Allegiance. Davidson (1997) suggests that in Australia, citizenship has become a national project because it is a **multicultural, multiethnic society** and unity is of central importance to the state.

Arguably, national identity becomes most strongly evident at times when it is felt to be under threat. However, sporting events and national teams can be a major means of transmitting national identity in times of peace between nations. It is at sporting events that many of the symbols of national identity become prominent, with people carrying flags, wearing costume or singing nationalistic music. In modern times, sporting achievement can give people a sense of pride in nation, a sense of belonging to a larger grouping, and an 'other' from whom we can differentiate ourselves. Consider nationalism during major sporting events such as the football World Cup or the Olympics. There is, however, a dark side to this sporting nationalism, which is apparent in racist incidents between clubs and nations. Racism is often expressed towards non-white football players by spectators and such players also experience insults on the pitch from other players.

SOCIALISATION INTO NATIONAL IDENTITY

National identity can be transmitted to children in many ways, such as:

- education
- family
- religion
- holidays abroad
- family history
- culture in the home
- books and toys
- visits to historical buildings
- flags and festivals
- participation in sporting events
- home language
- participation in social groups for members of minority ethnic groups.

Multicultural: The intermingling of a number of cultures.

Multiethnic society: A society in which a number of different ethnic groups live together.

Many people have died in this century for reasons of nationalism. War graves often carry the Latin phrase 'Dulce et Decorum est pro Patria Mori' which means 'it is good and correct to die for one's country'.

Think it through

The following comments are adapted from a discussion board on Welsh identity run by BBC Wales North-East:

Melanie from Talybont: "Wales is my home, and definitely where my heart is. I have never considered myself to be British, and I always say my nationality is Welsh. I was born in Wales, brought up in Wales and I will never consider leaving this beautiful country… Wales should leave the British Empire… "

Ffion from Ruthin : "I am a Welsh speaker and have lived in Wales all my life. I find the topic of Welsh Identity a divisive and shameful subject that blights this country. No person, be they Welsh or English speaking, has superiority over another. Each individual living within the boundaries of Wales is a member of the Welsh nation. Arguably, those that seek to define 'Welshness' in ethnic terms, by the speaking of Welsh for example, echo the fundamental ideals of Fascism."

Mark, originally from Wales but now living in Australia, writes: "I'm from Wales and feel Wales, Ireland, England and Scotland will always be separate as in New Zealand. One man said to me 'You're English/British'. I said 'Do you call a German an Italian or a Spanish a Greek?' Another man said he walked into a pub in Wales and they started speaking Welsh. I said if you go into a French pub they speak French. We have our own language… Wales will always be Wales and Welsh part of the British Isles… "

Adapted from: www.bbc.co.uk/wales/
northeast/yoursay/topics/nationalism.shtml

1 Outline two ways in which a person can claim a Welsh identity.

2 Outline the differences between 'nationality' and 'ethnicity'.

3 Evaluate the suggestion that ethnicity is more important than nationality in giving a person an identity.

Coursework suggestion
You could carry out a survey asking a number of people what nationality they feel they have and when they feel that sense of nationality most strongly. You might compare people of different ages or ethnic origins.

Nation: This can mean 'a country' but is used in sociology to define a group of people with a shared common culture and history.

Nationality: This is a legal concept. A person's nationality refers to the country of which they are a legal citizen with rights of residence and voting.

Nationalism: This is a social and political concept that describes how people feel loyalty to a geographical region or culture.

National identity: This is a sense of belonging to a particular nation state or cultural group.

Round-up

Nationality and nation are legal concepts and identities, with a passport being one symbol of that identity. They are also strong emotional and political concepts relating to a sense of loyalty to a region, or the idea of separate statehood. In the case of nationalism, this is often prompted when people feel a sense of oppression or enmity to a neighbouring and dominant culture. This feeling can, and does, erupt into terrible violence – and outbreaks of this have marred the history of the twentieth century. People gain a sense of national identity through social institutions. In the home this sense is passed on through cultural traditions. Many nation states deliberately encourage nationalism as a positive and unifying force. Sporting events in particular may unite people with a sense of national pride, but can also erupt into violence or displays of racist behaviour.

How are national identities changing?

What does it mean to be British?

Sociological debate about changing national identities concerns the extent to which they are changing because of globalisation. As a result of globalisation, events that take place in other nations have a huge impact on our own society and nowadays we are often aware of significant world events almost as soon as they happen – for example, the impact of September 11, 2001. Lash and Urry (1994) point out that now we are all linked and interdependent through communications, mass media, economics, politics and commerce. Obviously, such a major change in the nature of world culture will have an impact on people's sense of nation. There are two main views on this.

- Marxism suggests that globalisation is basically a bad thing because it leads to domination by world capitalism. It also means that our distinctive national cultures are disappearing in the face of American cultural values and American products.

- Postmodernism claims that globalisation offers people the opportunity to make choices in terms of their identity. The media offer us new ideas and new values from which we may take our pick.

Within the political boundaries of the UK, there has been another change that affects the way in which people view nationality. There has been a rise in regionalism, with Scotland and Wales devolving (breaking away) from the UK and having regional governments of their own. Areas within England have also made claims to the same rights as the Scots and Welsh and there are demands for assemblies in other parts of the UK such as Cornwall. Clearly, global forces from above and local forces from below are challenging the idea of a nation state as a source of identity for many people within countries. At the same time, research exists suggesting that people are experiencing a sense of identity loss that is causing them to turn to nationalism in order to reclaim their cultural identity. These positions are clearly contradictory and show that there is considerable room for debate and discussion in this area.

> *Racism, violence, xenophobia, lager, vomit and fat men with tattooed beer bellies displayed like prize marrows at a church fete are not the curse of English football. They are the curse of England… the Scots and Irish do not have the profound identity crisis that plagues the English. When the broken glass has been swept away and the pools of dried blood washed from the pavement, it comes down to this – the English have absolutely no idea who they are.*

Tony Parsons (2000) *Daily Mirror*, 26 June

THE IMPACT OF GLOBALISATION ON THE NATION STATE

- The state is weaker than it once was. Consider the relationship of individual countries to the European Union or the relationship of the UK to the USA. In Britain, much opposition to the EU has been related to the loss of symbols such as the pound in favour of the Euro.

- There has been massive population movement so that nations now contain large minority ethnic groupings. People may view themselves as global citizens rather than as belonging to national groups.

- People may not identify themselves with a nationality but with a political or religious position such as Islam, feminism or anti-capitalism. They feel that they have more in common with people who share their views internationally than with their nation state. Studies have indicated that Pakistani youths see themselves first as Muslim, then Pakistani and finally, British.

- There is a blurring of tastes, attitudes and culture because we are aware of other cultures via the media, travel and communication so that there is little that now specifically belongs to only one culture and can therefore typify that culture.

THE LITTLE ENGLANDERS

Curtice and Heath (2000) surveyed more than 3000 people in England, Scotland and Wales. Many of these felt themselves to be British rather than English. These researchers claimed that people living in England generally have a weak sense of identity because they lack symbols that are exclusively English (in contrast to the strong sense of national identity among those who live in Scotland and Wales). There was a degree of ignorance of British culture and political institutions among English respondents. Among the sample of English people was a small but significant rise, compared with previous similar studies, in the percentage of those who claimed to feel English rather than British. They called this group the 'Little Englanders'.

- For many of these people, Englishness appeared to consist of a rejection of foreign culture and an appeal to nostalgia for empire and military glory.
- A significant number of those who claimed to be English also expressed racial prejudice and claimed that immigrants took people's jobs. They disagreed with equal opportunities for non-whites.
- The Little Englanders felt that being white and being born in Britain with English parents was a significant element in Englishness.
- The majority rejected the Euro as currency and 22% wanted to leave the EU.

The British fear of losing national identity by closer union with the other countries of Europe should be contrasted with its embrace of American culture through TV, film, music, food, (McDonalds), clothing (Levi jeans and sportswear) and many attitudes..

Dr Romuald E J Rudzki, (1999) *British Social Culture*, The Poland Library

Important studies

Anthony King (2000) has argued that a new way of developing a consciousness of identity is emerging which is located not in nationality but in football support networks. His study group of Manchester United fans shows that they do not see Europe in terms of nations, but rather as a base in which their team must compete in order to succeed against other European teams and cities. Fans regularly travel to away games in European cities and are fully at ease with the culture in each area they visit, whilst taking their own cultural norms and values with them. He echoes Delanty's (1995) suggestion that there can never be a European identity because there is no 'other' for all Europeans to fight against.

NATIONALITY TESTS AND POLITICS

There has been a tradition for some while among British politicians of all political viewpoints to suggest that members of minority ethnic groupings within Britain should subscribe to some form of loyalty or knowledge testing. One of the most famous examples of this was Norman Tebbit's 'cricket test', which suggested that minority ethnic people should identify which cricket team they would support when England was playing the West Indies, India or Pakistan. More recently David Blunkett has suggested that immigrants settled in Britain who apply for British nationality should undertake a test of culture and language. He is quoted as saying 'It is a two-way street. If we are going to have social cohesion we have got to develop a sense of identity and a sense of belonging.'

Think it through

NATIONAL IDENTITY – WOULD YOU DESCRIBE YOURSELF AS BRITISH?

People living in England are more likely to describe themselves as British (48 per cent) than those in Scotland (27 per cent) or Wales (35 per cent), according to *Living in Britain*, the report of the 2001 General Household Survey. Respondents were asked to select their national identity from a list comprising: English, Scottish, Welsh, Irish, British and Other. This is the first time a question on national identity has been included in the survey.

Fifty per cent of people described themselves as either English, Scottish, Welsh or Irish. Thirty-one per cent described themselves as British only, with 13 per cent choosing British and either English, Scottish, Welsh or Irish. Four per cent gave an 'other' identity; one per cent gave other combinations.

Older people were less likely to describe themselves as British; 36 per cent of those aged 65 and over described themselves as British, compared with 47–52 per cent of people aged less than 55.

People in London were the most likely to describe themselves as having an 'other' national identity; 19 per cent compared with 2–5 per cent in other areas of England, Scotland or Wales.

Source: www.statistics.gov.uk

1 Which nation group is most likely to describe itself as British?

2 Suggest reasons for the generational difference in people's sense of national identity.

3 Evaluate the suggestion that nationality is no longer significant in determining identity.

Round-up

Sociological debates on national identity centre on the extent to which people are either losing an identity because of globalisation or picking their own personal identity because they are more aware of alternatives than they were in the past. Individual countries seem to be losing importance; the EU and other groupings such as the United Nations or NATO have power to make policies that affect more than one nation state. Within countries there are large populations of people who identify with more than one nation state because they belong to a minority ethnic group. However, there are others who wish to protect and preserve national identities. Within the UK, more importance is being attached to the politics of regionalism so that the Celtic nations are reasserting their sense of nationality, distinct from the English.

36011

What is social class?

In our society, inequalities between people's life experiences can be seen in a number of ways:

- *Life chances* – some people have more opportunities for good education, health, career, etc.
- *Life expectancy* – some people are more likely to live a long time.
- *Life-style* – some people have a better standard of living.
- *Status* – some people are treated with more respect than others.

Some of these inequalities arise out of personal differences; we are not all equally clever or good-looking. More importantly for sociology, however, are those inequalities that arise out of social differentiation, where whole groups of people are unequal because of their social characteristics. We have already considered ethnicity and gender; now we look at social class.

Social class is a form of stratification (or layering) of groups in society. Those at the highest levels in the stratification system will have lives of comfort and privilege. Those in the lowest levels will have a very different life experience, possibly encompassing poverty and deprivation.

While many of us are aware of class differences and can easily recognise that there are groups of people who are above or below us in the system, class is a very difficult term to define and **operationalise**. This is because there are a number of elements that go to make up someone's class status. One important distinction is between:

- *objective class*, which refers to our class position as classified by government or by social research, whether we agree with it or not – it may be related to our income, wealth, or occupation
- *subjective class*, which refers to our personal perception of our class position, i.e. which class we think we are in. Subjective class is the basis of our class identity and the norms, morals, values and political opinions associated with this identity.

Sociological theories and class

Sociologists have different views of class depending on their theoretical perspective.

- *Functionalists* view class as a ladder or staircase. Only the most talented or hardworking in society will make it to the top; the others will slide down the scale or stay in the same position they were born in. For example, Davis and Moore (1945) believed that social inequality is necessary for the effective functioning of society.
- *Marxists* see class as the most important of social dynamics. They argue that there are essentially two classes – the proletariat or working class who sell their labour for a living, and the bourgeoisie or upper class who own the means of production and who exploit the working classes.
- *Weberians* see class as a complex interplay of status, power and wealth. They suggest that class structures are becoming fragmented as new classes develop and evolve.
- *Postmodernists* such as Pahl and Wallace (1988) reject the notion of class and prefer to see inequality in terms of patterns of consumption, i.e. the ability to purchase commodities. They do not see inequality as an issue of identity or social status.

In everyday language, people tend to talk about upper, middle, and working or lower classes. There are other terms, too, such as 'aristocracy' or 'professional classes'. However, these terms are of limited use to a sociologist because it is difficult to agree on which groups of people belong in each category.

Operationalise: To define something so that it can be measured or counted.

Functionalists: Sociologists who explain social institutions in terms of the functions they perform for the society.

Weberians: Sociologists who draw on the ideas of Max Weber (1864–1920).

One of the problems in researching social class is that sociologists often use terms to measure class that are different from those in everyday use.

Think it through

Weekly pay of employees by sex and type of work, April 2002

		Average gross weekly earnings (£)
Male		
	Manual	366.6
	Non-manual	608.7
Female		
	Manual	250.3
	Non-manual	404.0
All employees		462.6

Adapted from: *Social Trends 33*, p. 99

1 Identify two patterns in the distribution of weekly pay.

2 Suggest reasons why manual workers often have a lower standard of living and poorer life chances than non-manual workers.

3 Evaluate the suggestion that class can be identified by occupational status alone.

How does the government define class?

The government in Britain defines class by using occupation as the main indicator. This may not be sociologically valid, but government data is not gathered for sociological purposes. The two main systems you will come across are:

- the Registrar General's Scale of Social Class (the RG's scale), which was used between 1911 and 2000 for Census and other data, and
- the new National Statistics Socio-Economic Classification (the NS-SEC).

The Registrar General's Scale

Class	Occupational group	Typical jobs
I	Professional, etc.	senior management, surgeons, doctors, university lecturers, chemists
II	Managerial and technical	teachers, executives, journalists
III N	Skilled non-manual	secretaries, sales executives, officials
III M	Skilled manual	skilled crafts people; plumbers, carpenters
IV	Partly skilled	bus drivers, machine operators
V	Unskilled	labourers, cleaners

The National Statistics Socio-economic Classification

Social class		Typical employment	Percentage of working age population in 2002
Higher Managerial and professional	1.1	Company directors, Police Inspectors, Bank Managers, Senior Civil Servants, Military Officers	10.2
	1.2	Doctor, Barrister, Solicitor, Clergy, Librarian, Teacher	
Lower Managerial and professional	2	Nurses and midwives, Journalists, Actors, Prison Officers, Police and Soldiers (below NCO)	21.9
Intermediate	3	Clerks, Secretaries, Driving Instructors, Computer Operator	10.4
Small employers and own account workers	4	Publicans, Farmers, Playgroup leader, Window cleaner, Painter and Decorator	7.3
Lower supervisory and technical	5	Printers, Plumbers, Butchers, Bus Inspectors, TV engineers, Train drivers	9.6
Semi-routine	6	Shop assistant, Traffic Warden, Cook, Bus drivers, Hairdressers, Postal workers	13.0
Routine	7	Waiters, Road sweepers, Cleaners, Couriers, Building labourers, Refuse collectors	10.2
Never worked	8	Long-term unemployed and non-workers	17.5

Since the late 1990s, a new classification has been adopted and was used in the Census of 2001. The reasons for redesigning the system included:

1 the reduction in the number of manufacturing jobs
2 under the old system, over half the population was in Class III
3 the growth in the employment of women
4 the growth in service-sector jobs (leisure, food entertainment, insurance, and business)
5 the distinction between manual and non-manual occupations was no longer clear cut.

The new system is based on employment relations and conditions:

1 Job security
2 Opportunities for promotion
3 Ability and opportunity to work on your own and make your own decisions about tasks.

Income and wealth

The term 'classless society' hides the reality of the vast inequalities of wealth, income and power in our society. For example, Gordon (2000), quoting statistics gathered by the Department of Social Security, notes that the richest 10% of the population increased their share of income from 20% to 28% between 1979 and 1996. This share has increased again since 1997. Roy Hattersley (2001) pointed out that the poorest 10% of the population received 2.9% of the total share of national income while the richest 10% get 27%. When property and investment is taken into account, the differences between the rich and poor are even more dramatic.

The differences between the better-off and the poorest have led some sociologists to claim that there is a new social class developing in British society – the underclass. These are people who are below the existing class structure and who live lives of poverty and welfare dependency.

Important studies

Pantazis and Gordon (2000) found that differences in income are growing between various sectors of society. People are not becoming more equal, but less so.

Turak (2000) suggested that certain sectors of the workforce are more vulnerable to unemployment and poverty than others and that unemployment is a major cause of poverty.

The Low Pay Commission (2000) suggested that many of those in employment experience poverty through poor rates of pay.

Round-up

Social class is an important differentiator in our society, though class is a very difficult term to define. Occupation can be used as an indicator of class but this does not take into account the different elements that go to make up class, including the subjective perception of class that gives a person their class identity. Government measures of class show that Britain is an unequal society. Class is a central concept in sociology because it affects people's life chances and life-styles and is central to the organisation of our society.

Is social class a significant identity?

How do these people view themselves in relation to society around them?

 Meritocracy is the idea that people can progress upwards through society on the basis of ability rather than background. Functionalists argue that Britain is a meritocratic society because there is movement between social classes. Marxists suggest that the amount of meritocracy has been exaggerated and that, in reality, very few people are able to change their class position.

Agencies of socialisation: Groups of people or institutions in society (e.g. media, family, education) that are influential in socialising others.

Social class has a substantial influence on people's lives. Middle-class and upper-class status confers considerable social advantage on those who are born into the higher social groups. Furthermore, people in the different social classes experience different life-styles, have differing access to power and status and may have different values. Although there has been an increase in the number of middle-class jobs since the 1960s and more people now have access to luxuries such as foreign holidays, most of these improvements are due to an overall increase in national wealth. There has been limited change in the overall class structure of Britain and social class is still an important source of identity for many people.

Class identity can be passed on through a number of **agencies of socialisation**, so, for instance, working-class pupils may not understand the values, norms and culture of their more middle-class teachers. A number of writers have suggested that they are then disadvantaged through a whole series of processes that can result in them ultimately rejecting education altogether.

Occupation is another significant form of class identity. When we first meet someone, we often ask what they do for a living because work is an indicator of social class and education. These two factors may also have influenced our tastes. 'High culture' or a knowledge of arts and literature carry status, whereas a taste for 'popular' or 'mass' culture is often seen as being working class and carrying lower social prestige.

How many of the norms and values of the students in the picture at the top do these people share?

Traditional stereotypes of class

The following table is intended to show some of the stereotypical differences that exist between people of different social groupings. You could develop this by thinking of other differences that exist between the different social classes: tastes, leisure activities, attitudes, work, pets, etc.

Traditional stereotypes of class			
	Upper class	*Middle class*	*Working class*
Education	Eton or Harrow public school followed by Oxford, Cambridge 'old' universities	Private schools or 'good' comprehensives followed by 'red brick' or modern universities such as Birmingham or Sussex	Limited education; qualifications earned through apprenticeships
Speech	Recognisably 'posh'	Neutral, sounds like BBC newsreader or weather reporter	Strong regional accent
Leisure	Hunting, shooting, fishing, polo, horse racing (as owners) rowing.	Golf, tennis, hill-walking, squash	Dog racing, watching football, pubs

IMPORTANT CONCEPTS

- *Cultural capital* is an idea associated with Pierre Bourdieu (1973). He suggested that wealthy people can pass on knowledge and a particular world-view to their children as well as wealth and money. This knowledge and world-view constitutes cultural capital that gives the children an added advantage in life, contributing to social success.

- *Elite self-recruitment* is associated with the work of sociologists such as David Glass (1954) and A H Halsey *et al.* (1980), who said that wealthier groups in society were able to recruit their own children for the best jobs.

- *Class consciousness* is a Marxist term used to describe the way that the working classes would come to recognise their powerlessness in the face of class inequality. Marx predicted that they would then unite in order to overthrow capitalism. Many working-class people are able to take a sense of pride from their working-class status.

- *Old-boy network* is a commonly used term to describe the way in which people who attended the famous public schools will automatically favour other ex-pupils of similar schools. This concept has now been developed by sociologists into what is known as social capital, in the sense of 'who one knows'. Implicit in this is that people have power to help others in their careers or professional life. Scott (1982, 1986), points out that the upper classes do not willingly allow others to penetrate their social circles.

- *Hegemony* is a term associated with Antonio Gramsci (1971). Gramsci claimed that the ruling classes exercise power because it is their norms and values that dominate society. People agree to being controlled simply because they accept the ideas that they are given through social agencies (such as the media and education), which reinforce upper- and middle-class values.

- *Subcultural values* is a concept used by sociologists who believe that the working class have a different culture from the middle class. They claim that the working-class male, for instance, values masculinity and toughness. As a result of this, he is more likely to engage in risky behaviour such as drinking or criminality.

- *Instrumentalism* means that something is done for a specific purpose, e.g. instrumental workers work for a wage. This contrasts with the term 'vocationalism', which is the idea that people work to give their lives meaning. Goldthorpe and Lockwood (1969) suggested that working-class people work solely in order to earn money to buy consumer goods whereas middle-class people are more likely to work for status or pleasure.

Think it through

Higher Education was talked about as a middle-class system in which working-class students were disadvantaged and 'different', and 45% of the MORI sample agreed that 'the student image is not for me'. Some focus group respondents anticipated, or recounted, being intimidated by middle-class students.

Mature students were particularly likely to voice fears of being 'out of place'. Some mature female students also felt they did not understand the culture and language of the middle-class staff. A number of non-participant women talked about universities as 'big and scary' and 'snobby'... 'Students' were widely represented as middle class (and largely white) and therefore 'different' to oneself. Images of (middle class) students were largely negative, with students positioned as 'lacking common sense', 'immature' and as socially inadequate. This latter view was particularly prevalent amongst white respondents.'

From: Archer, L. (2002) *Social class and access to Higher Education*, A report of findings from the social class and widening participation to HE project, University of North London (www.unl.ac.uk)

1 Summarise the different ways in which working-class students felt out of place within higher education.

2 In what ways was the image of the middle-class student negative?

3 Evaluate the suggestion that class identity is significant in modern Britain.

Important studies

Marshall *et al.* (1988) found that most people could identify themselves in terms of a social class and that class is still a significant factor in people's life chances and life-style. However, this is in contrast to Savage *et al.* (1992), who suggest that classes have become fragmented and that it is no longer possible to identify a middle-class social group because people now make life-style choices. They identified three different middle-class life-style choices that people could make. (For further details on this see p. 34).

Charlesworth (2000) in his study of the Rotherham area suggests that working-class people are unable to express their experience because a feature of working-class culture is an inability to put feelings into words. Poor economic and social conditions have an effect on physical and psychological health. Males have low self-esteem and little hope for the future.

Southerton (2002) found that there were distinct social attitudes between people of different social classes within a new town in the south of England. In terms of people's understanding of their social status and position, property and consumption were seen as being more significant than class. The poorest people considered the wealthiest to be snobbish, whereas the middle-class groupings viewed the poorer people as lacking in cultural understanding. The different social groups employed different ways of understanding class as a concept.

Round-up

Traditional views of class show deep divisions between the groupings. Whilst these stereotypical or common sense views of class are often unreliable (forming caricatures of what people's lives are truly like), they contain an element of truth that many people will recognise. Behind the stereotypes of class lie a reality of inequality and deprivation for the poorer, working-class sectors of society, while the wealthier middle and upper classes often enjoy lives of considerable wealth and status.

How are class structures and identities changing?

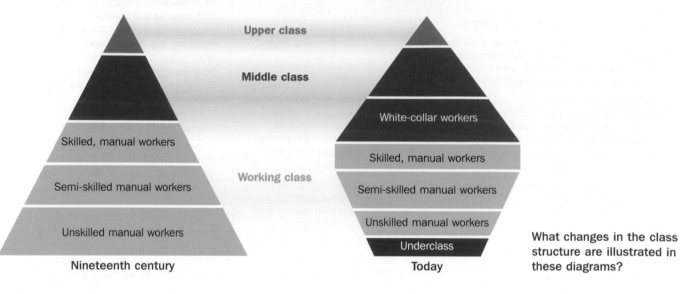

Upper class

Middle class

Working class

Nineteenth century
- Skilled, manual workers
- Semi-skilled manual workers
- Unskilled manual workers

Today
- White-collar workers
- Skilled, manual workers
- Semi-skilled manual workers
- Unskilled manual workers
- Underclass

What changes in the class structure are illustrated in these diagrams?

How are class structures changing?

Significant changes have taken place in the class structure of modern Britain, as shown in the diagrams above. Before World War II, people could identify each other's place in the social hierarchy by indicators such as education, accent and type of work. In modern Britain, there has been a blurring of the old class distinctions and new categories of social class appear to be developing. There are a number of reasons for this. Many are related to changes in the structure and organisation of industry and the nature of the work that we do.

- There are fewer work opportunities for unskilled labourers. Machines today do much of the work and there is less need for the uneducated in the workplace.
- Many items that once would have been made by skilled manual workers are now manufactured. For example, carpenters once built windows to fit holes in buildings; now, buildings are designed to fit around standardised prefabricated window frames. Wedderburn and Crompton (1972) claimed that this process of mechanisation has blurred the old class distinctions.
- Middle-class jobs increased after World War II with the expansion of the welfare state and public services. Many graduates from the new universities became teachers, social workers and civil servants.
- Traditional industries have declined, with a resulting decrease in skilled and semi-skilled manual occupations – mainly for men, such as coal-miners and dockers.
- Today, many jobs are found in the service sector, including 'McJobs' (a term used to describe the casual labour found in fast-food chains). Many of these are semi-skilled and do not contribute to a person's identity. People do not feel long-term loyalty to the company or the work. They can take no personal pride in their employment, as it is generally short-term and low status.
- Goldthorpe (1987) found that there has been a certain amount of movement between social classes so that some working-class people have been absorbed into the new expanding middle classes. The term used to describe this is 'social mobility'.
- Writers such as Buckingham (1999) and Murray (1984) have argued there has been a growth in the underclass of people who rely on benefits to survive. It is claimed that these people have become dependent on welfare handouts and are distinct and separated from the traditional working classes.
- There is increasing affluence, so even the poorest people can have a quality of life that is far better than they could have expected thirty years ago.

Proletarianisation: A process whereby middle-class people become more working class.

Fragmentation: The breaking up of class structures and loyalties.

Important studies

Savage *et al.* (1992) identified three life-style groupings within the British middle class. There were those who adopted what was described as an 'ascetic' lifestyle. These were professional people who were concerned with healthy life-styles and worked in the public services on relatively low incomes. 'Postmoderns' tended to have a life-style that comprised an interest in high and pop culture, so bingeing on food or drink would be followed by sessions at a gym. The commercial and civil-service middle classes, however, have a more conventional and 'undistinctive' life-style that involves golf, and visiting cultural sites. This suggests there is no one particular life-style associated with middle-class income but that people choose differing ideologies and ways of living.

Theories to explain changes in class structure

- *Class convergence* – A number of writers have suggested that non-manual workers have become more like workers (i.e. the working class) in terms of their status as employees. Braverman (1974) claimed that office workers were losing their lower middle-class status in the class structure as a result of automation and the loss of skills. He termed this process 'proletarianisation'.
- *Embourgeoisement* – This theory was briefly popular in the 1960s and suggested that, as the working class earned ever-higher wages, they were becoming more like the middle class in their attitudes. Goldthorpe and Lockwood's 'affluent worker' studies, published in the late 1960s, effectively dismissed this view.
- *Fragmentation* – Dahrendorf (1992) suggests that the classes are fragmenting, so that we no longer have single monolithic groups such as industrial workers. Multinational companies now own the real wealth and power. This results in individualism. People are more concerned with personal issues so class is no longer so significant. This idea is related to postmodernist theory.

How important is class in Britain?

Class is still important

- Chapman (2001) has made a strong case for the existence of an upper-class identity that is reinforced by a closed system of socialisation. The upper classes educate their children differently, marry within their own circle and use the 'old boy network' to support their efforts in business.
- Adonis and Pollard (1998) identified a new 'super class' of élite professionals and managers working in financial services. High salaries are normal and the super class own shares in the businesses that employ them.
- MacIntosh and Mooney (2000) claim that social class is our prime source of identity: it provides us with a sense of 'other'. Because we are able to measure ourselves against other people, we gain an identity.

Class is not so important

- Debate has raged around the extent to which traditional class patterns of voting behaviour have broken down due to changing class allegiances. Sarlvik and Crewe (1983) claimed that voting no longer takes place along lines of traditional class loyalties to political parties. This suggests to them that class is no longer significant.
- Both Conservative and Labour politicians have claimed that Britain is now a meritocracy where people all have equal chances of success or failure. In September 1999, at the Labour party conference, Tony Blair stated: 'The class war is over, but the struggle for true equality has begun'.
- Postmodernists have argued that consumption of goods is a more significant source of personal identity than class. They argue that social groups are divided by how much money people have and how they spend it. Slater (1997) argues that sociologists should study individual needs and wants, taking account of people's resources and the meanings they attach to what they own and what they spend their money on. Through purchase of goods, we create meaning in our lives.

Think it through

Tony Blair says we're increasingly middle class; the 68 per cent of Britons who call themselves working class would beg to differ. So what are the definitions we use to classify ourselves? *Whatever Happened to the Working Class?* (BBC4) got stuck in to a perennially fascinating subject and the result was an excellent film.

The makers mixed academic analysis with an impressive array of archive clips. We saw images of the Jarrow March, and footage of far less renown: in *Late Night Line-Up* from 1972, women factory workers in Hull sat around a table, drinking stout and discussing politics and their working lives. A film from the early 80s investigated the effect of a colliery closure upon a community in the Valleys, which demonstrated that not much had changed for the working class of South Wales since the 1950s.

In the end, the film offered no firm answer to the question the title posed. The narrator suggested that, due to the decline of manufacturing in Britain and hence manual labour, social class is nowadays denoted by things such as job security and control over one's terms of employment.

Adapted from: Redmond, C. (2003) 'And then there were none', *The Guardian TV Review*, Friday 17 January

1 Outline and identify three examples of working-class culture described by the television programme.

2 Suggest reasons why class identities have changed in modern Britain.

3 Evaluate the suggestion that the study of social class in Britain is a pointless exercise.

Round-up

The study of class has prompted a wide range of political and social debates. There are a variety of theories to account for changing class loyalties. Some writers suggest that class allegiances are breaking down and are therefore no longer significant to people's identity and sense of who they are. Others suggest that, despite superficial differences, class inequalities are as significant as ever.

Where are we going?

Global identity – a new possibility for identity?

Nowadays, new media and many cultural products are produced for sale in more than one country. Multinational chains of shops and fast-food outlets are often opened in countries all over the world. It is argued that as a result of these phenomena many traditional identities are being eroded. There are two possible perspectives on this issue:

- We are all gaining a single, new, consumer-based identity drawn from the mass media and popular culture.
- We are able to choose from a variety of identities, both traditional and new, in order to achieve personal, self-created individualities.

Postmodernism and identity

Postmodernism: The theory that suggests industrial society has been superseded by a media-saturated society in which the old indicators of identity – e.g. social class – have been replaced by new forms of identity based on consumption of style, fashion, etc.

Meta-narratives: A postmodern term to describe 'grand' theories such as Marxism.

Consumption: The process of buying and using goods and services.

It is claimed by postmodernists that religion, class, culture and ethnicity were once part of a set of ways of thinking that made people secure in an identity. People lived their lives framed by sets of knowledge about the world that postmodernists defined as '**meta-narratives**'. It was argued that these meta-narratives gave people a sense of how things should be, and that if this process was disrupted, people became disturbed and confused.

The development of the media and the process of globalisation in modern culture have meant that we are now all open to more possibilities in our lives. We are open to new choices – for example, birth in one gender no longer forces a person into a particular set of behaviours and activities; people can exercise choice in their behaviour and may be as masculine or as feminine as they choose. It is increasingly possible for people to make lifestyle choices, as traditional cultural values are affected by social change.

It is argued that we can now create a whole new set of identities based on what we can buy and use. This is known as the 'culture of **consumption**'. Baudrillard (1985), for instance, suggests that the things we buy have a meaning. Advertising works for us because we do not necessarily buy just an item, but we also buy into an image that the product reflects. We wear labelled clothing, buy named food and drink products, and drive certain makes of car in order to create an identity for ourselves that others can read. This process is known as 'commodification'. The term 'pick and mix' is often used in association with this aspect of postmodern society – people pick up cultural ideas and adopt them in a piecemeal fashion to tailor an identity or moral system that suits their own needs and desires. People are able to choose a way of living and create a 'lifestyle' through the objects they buy or ideas they subscribe to. Identity is therefore something that we can buy.

A HISTORICAL EXAMPLE OF AN ADOPTED IDENTITY

There is considerable historical documentation surrounding women who have lived as males, and even gone to war under assumed male identities. One of the best known was Dr 'James' Barry, whose real name was possibly Miranda Stuart, and who served in the British Army as a doctor for 40 years from 1813. Dr Barry gained high status and a good reputation in a number of posts. His physical existence as a biological woman was only discovered on his death. For further information see: http://www.vanhunks.com/cape1/barry1.html

The debate about how much freedom we do in fact have to change our identities continues. The main arguments are summarised in the table opposite.

SEMIOLOGY

Ferdinand de Saussure (1857–1913), a Swiss linguist and philosopher, was interested in language as a code for transmitting ideas (Koerner, 1972). He pointed out that words are symbols for things and that we transmit our messages through the use of symbols. This idea has been developed into a branch of study known as 'semiology' in which we look at the codes that people use to transmit messages about themselves and the way they view the world. If you look at individuals, their bodies, clothing and their hairstyles, for instance, you can see that they have created an intentional message about their sense of personal identity through the codes of clothing and fashion.

Can we now choose identities for ourselves? Michael Jackson has undergone radical physical change and his appearance has been transformed. To what extent is such a change possible for those of us who are not so wealthy and who live more ordinary lives?

The debate about how much freedom we do, in fact, have to change our identities continues. The main arguments are summarised below.

Are identities subject to change?	
Identities have changed ...	*But ...*
There are individuals who have been able to experiment with different identities.	This is difficult to do, and in the case of gender transformation, both expensive and painful. It is not a recent phenomenon either (consider the case of Dr James Barry opposite).
New forms of identity have emerged such as the 'new man' who is aware of the needs of women.	Feminists argue that the case for the 'new man' has been exaggerated and that women still earn less and do more domestic labour than males.
There is increased tolerance of sexual difference, particularly in the media and politics where homosexuality among males and females is often explicitly admitted.	Homophobia and intolerance are typical of many city areas. There is still a high incidence of violent crime targeted at homosexuals. 'Gay' is a term of abuse in some quarters.
Many people are able to work on a 'body project' and transform their physical shape and appearance through drugs, surgery and gymnasium work. Anorexia is an extreme expression of this trend.	Many cultures have imposed strict notions of body image on people: notable examples are Chinese foot-binding or Maori tattoos, where people have consented to dramatic body transformation.
People aim to alter their appearance and behaviour to become part of a target group, moderating regional accents, for instance, in order to pass as middle class.	Whilst people can transform themselves, will they necessarily be accepted among the social group to whom they wish to belong? Scott (1986) for instance has suggested that it is difficult to penetrate upper-class social groups.
New identities are emerging as people become more familiar with the ideas and thinking of other cultures. There is an increase in New Age spirituality and interest in alternative lifestyles and health-care.	Are people who adopt these different styles of living and thinking taken seriously?

Think it through

Changing Identities: Barry Cox becomes Gok Pak-wing

An American journalist, Gregg Zachary (1999) describes how Barry Cox, a 21 year old man from Liverpool, has pushed at the limits of how far he can change his own social identity. Cox has an English working-class background, eats meat pies and likes cricket. At high school he became fascinated by Chinese popular culture. He experimented with martial arts and enjoyed the soundtracks to the Jackie Chan movies. Hanging around his local fish and chip shops he met many of Liverpool's Chinese community, some of whom run the local 'chippies'.

Frustrated that he could not understand those Chinese who did not speak English, he studied Cantonese and found that he could understand and learn it. He worked as a waiter in a Chinese restaurant so that he could practise his language skills and now works in a Chinese grocery store. He has a Chinese name, Gok Pak-wing (meaning 'long life') and dates a British born Chinese woman. Gok Pak-wing and his partner's Shanghai-born parents are concerned that she can't speak Chinese.

Although working in a grocery store, Gok's ambition is to be a Chinese pop star. He has already won some local contests, singing such 'Canto-pop' songs in Cantonese as 'Kiss under the moon', 'Kiss once more' and 'Ten words of an angel'. The title of his original song, which his fans love, translates as 'I think I am Chinese, I want to be Chinese'. Despite his obviously English appearance, he seems to have convinced some of his fans. One asked him, 'Are you English or Chinese?' Another insisted that his intonation was so good 'his father must be Chinese'.

Cox/Gok's English mother, Valerie, says, 'He lives, breathes and sleeps Chinese. I think he'd actually be Chinese if he could.' Cox/Gok concurs: 'If I didn't mix with Chinese, what would I be doing now? I'd just be a normal person, nothing special about me. Although I know I'm not Chinese, I'm trying to put myself in a Chinese body.'

1 Outline and identify three ways in which Cox/Gok has assumed a Chinese identity.

2 Suggest reasons why we need to adopt different identities in our social lives.

3 Evaluate the suggestion that many modern identities have involved a shift away from traditional identities and towards life-style choices.

Zachary, G P (1999) in Cohen, R, and Kennedy, P (2000) *Global sociology*, Macmillan, Basingstoke, p. 346

The individual and society: summative review

Who are we?

Our social world defines our sense of who we are – our identity. From birth to death, we experience the expectations of others as to how we should act and what we should be. Even before we are fully aware of our surroundings, our society gives us an identity linked to the following social characteristics:

- gender
- age
- family and status
- social class
- ethnicity
- nationality.

These are all 'ascribed statuses' and difficult, though not impossible, to change. As we grow older, we gain 'achieved statuses' and their associated identities. These are often positive and may be marked by ceremonies or certificates of some kind – for example, becoming a:

- wife, husband or partner
- graduate
- professional.

However identities are not always positive, for example:

- having a prison record
- suffering mental ill-health or instability.

To cope with the complexity of statuses in the modern world, we often create stereotypes, or simplified images of how people should be, based on a social or physical characteristic. These stereotypes can be dangerously negative – for instance, Nazi stereotypes of Jewish people during World War II – or they can be more positive – for instance, the stereotype of nurses as selfless and caring.

What is sociology?

The discipline of sociology can be traced back to the work of the French writer Auguste Comte in the first half of the nineteenth century. European societies at the time were going through a period of dramatic social and political change, including industrialisation and urbanisation. Revolutionary political ideas were developing and people's knowledge and understanding of the world was changing as the natural sciences generated theories that challenged traditional and religious beliefs. The origins of sociology can be viewed as an attempt to understand these changes.

Sociology today includes a wide range of approaches and views about the nature of society and the most appropriate ways to carry out empirical research. However, and overarching all these differences, a shared concern of sociologists is still to understand society, social processes, and the relationship between individuals and society.

Societies and culture

All societies have a culture that provides the basis of social order and makes social life possible. It includes the set of rules and the way of life shared by a group of people. These include:

- *norms* – the unspoken and unwritten guidelines for behaviour in everyday life
- *mores* – stronger than norms; the guidelines for behaviour that people believe are essential to maintain standards of decency
- *values* – the beliefs that underlie norms and mores.

All societies also share the following common features, which are known as 'cultural universals':

- some form of religious or spiritual belief
- differences of status and power
- families and a sense of kinship.

However, there are significant differences in the forms these take in different societies and sociologists use the term 'cultural relativity' to describe how what is right or normal in one society might be considered unusual or odd in another.

How do we learn the codes of behaviour appropriate for our culture?

From birth, we learn how to behave in a way that is appropriate to our culture and our social roles. This process is described as 'socialisation'. The basic norms and values are learned within the home and family and are part of the process of primary socialisation that gives us our initial sense of who we are – our identity. As a child becomes more independent of its family, it is exposed to the rules of wider society through the agencies of secondary socialisation such as:

- the mass media
- education
- peer groups
- religious groups.

We develop our sense of identity through these wider groups. They may offer us differing values from those we learned in the home and so we become actively involved in the process of our own socialisation because we can make choices about how to behave and what sort of person we want to be.

Culture is passed from one generation to the next and transmitted through the aspects of behaviour that make up an individual's cultural identity. These include:

- language
- food and the way that we eat it
- musical traditions
- religion
- clothing and clothing rules
- festivals and celebrations.

The process of developing a personal identity is complex and involves learning that others in a culture are different from us. For example, to understand what it is to be female requires interaction with males. People from visible minority ethnic groups often learn of their differences from their first experiences of racism.

Status and identity

Not all identities carry equal status or prestige. In the past, to see oneself as female meant to accept a lesser status than that of males; laws and social codes operated unequally and often in favour of men. Similarly, poorer people of lower classes and people of certain minority ethnic groups did not expect the same treatment as those they regarded as being their 'betters'. Hegemony (the control of society through ideas) is very powerful and it takes strong individuals to challenge established norms and values, and to reject the identities they are given.

Key identities

Identities vary widely over time and between different cultures, so it is clear that they are socially constructed, rather than part of 'human nature'. There are many aspects of identity but the most important in our society include:

- gender
- ethnicity
- class.

Gender

Gender is an important aspect of identity but its meaning has been changing in recent years. Up until the third quarter of the twentieth century, the female identity was associated with domestic and caring roles, with particular attention being paid to personal appearance and to pleasing men; the male identity involved more active, dominant and aggressive activities, being the 'breadwinner' and having greater social freedom. Women were subject to negative stereotyping, often reinforced by the media. However, in recent years, these traditional social expectations have been challenged, both for men and for women.

Many women are experiencing opportunities that were previously only available to men; they are doing better in school and at university and more are employed in responsible jobs, including traditionally 'male' jobs. However, these new opportunities should not be overstated; many women are still in low-paid occupations, particularly the 'caring' professions, and many are experiencing the dual burden of being in paid employment whilst still being expected to have responsibility for domestic arrangements in the home. Nevertheless, the experience of being female is changing, especially for younger women. At the same time, men can no longer expect to play the dominant part in social relationships and in society, and the value of traditional masculinity has been called into question.

These changes have resulted in male and female identities becoming less fixed and more uncertain, with greater opportunities for individuals to make choices. It has been suggested that some men are experiencing a crisis of masculinity, as they no longer feel sure what it means to be a man.

Ethnicity and nationality

Our ethnic and national identities give us a sense of which ethnic groups and nationalities we 'belong' to, but the experience of ethnicity is changing and becoming uncertain as a result of:

- the movement and intermingling of populations
- the globalisation of culture
- multi-national marketing of media and consumer products
- rapid global communications.

Some people absorb the global culture, whereas others resist it and insist on maintaining their own ethnic and national identities.

A variety of more-or-less visible minority ethnic groups have entered Britain and become part of British society, but many have experienced racism and rejection that has challenged their sense of identity. Their children, however, have developed thriving and exciting cultures based on a combination of Western and their own cultural ideas; these are known as 'hybrid cultures'. These, in turn, have attracted other young people so that there has been movement and sharing of cultural ideas. Minority ethnic traditions are becoming absorbed into mainstream popular culture and are changing what it means to be 'British' or 'English' or 'Welsh'.

Class

There is some argument as to whether class is still a significant social identity in Britain. An individual's social class position is the outcome of a combination of achieved and ascribed statuses and has a huge impact on life-chances and life-styles, but how far people still recognise it as a significant social differentiater is arguable. There is fluidity and movement between classes and, more importantly, people are able to purchase consumer products and associated life-styles, regardless of their class origins. This has led postmodern sociologists to suggest that we are now able to 'buy into' an identity through the purchase of commodities. The case for this may be overstated, however, because social change comes about slowly, and although some people may indeed challenge tradition, most of us tend to follow the traditional culture of our society with little thought or concern.

The individual and society: self-assessment questions

1 **Link the terms to their meanings in sociology.**

a Gender
b Ethnicity
c Social class

i Shared identity based on language, culture or religion.
ii Social characteristics associated with biological sex.
iii Position in a social hierarchy, often based on occupation and income.

2 **Identify three ways in which we gain gender identity, according to Oakley.**

3 **Explain the meaning of the term 'proletariat'.**

4 **Link the terms to their meaning in sociology.**

a Reflexivity
b Determinism

i The idea that people are shaped by events and experience beyond their control.
ii The capacity to interpret and make sense of social action and behaviour.

5 **Which of the following terms refers to the unwritten and usually unspoken rules of everyday life?**

a Norms
b Culture
c Values

6 **What do the following terms mean?**

a New Lad
b Ladette
c Expressive roles within the family
d New Man

7 **Match the terms to the meanings.**

a Consensus view of society
b Conflict view of society

i Societies are held together through a set of shared beliefs, norms and values.
ii Societies have social groups with differing interests who are in opposition to each other.

8 **What is 'patriarchy'?**

9 **Which sociologist took a micro approach to the study of society? Explain your answer.**

a Marx
b Mead
c Durkheim

10 **Match the writer to the theory.**

a Talcott Parsons
b Erving Goffman

i People are self-consciously aware of the impression they make in social situations and act accordingly.
ii Religions present us with a set of moral values and an ideal of good behaviour.

11 **Name three major ethnic groups that have migrated to Britain since World War II.**

12 **Suggest one difficulty in deciding a person's ethnic identity.**

13 **What does 'peer group' mean?**

14 **Explain the meaning of the following terms in sociology.**

a Secondary socialisation
b Social interaction
c Primary socialisation

15 **Link up the words and their meanings in sociology.**

a Gendered behaviour
b Masculinity
c Masculinism

i A desire to dominate and control social situations.
ii Behaviour typically associated with men or with women.
iii The social characteristics normally associated with male biology.

16 **Link up the sociological word and its meaning in sociology.**

a Postmodernism
b Cultural relativism
c Cultural resistance

i Refusal to accept the widely held or conventional views of society and finding ways to reject them.
ii The view that there can be no fixed standards for 'normal' and 'deviant' or 'right' and 'wrong' and that these will always vary from one society to another.
iii The idea that there can be no single all-encompassing sociological theory; the belief that we live in a media-saturated society where people are more able to make their own rules and identities.

17 Suggest two ways in which people express and reinforce their ethnic identity.

18 What is the meaning of the term 'diaspora'?

19 What terms do sociologists use for the following?

a Our class position as classified by government or by social research, whether we agree with it or not. It may be related to our income, wealth, or occupation.

b Our personal perception of our class position, i.e. which class we think we are in; the basis of our class identity and the norms, morals, values and political opinions associated with this identity.

20 Suggest two reasons why the number of middle-class people is increasing in Britain.

21 Link the terms to their meaning in sociology.

a Overt racism
b Covert racism
c Institutional racism

i Racism that is implicit and well hidden but which nonetheless exists.

ii Racism that is clearly identifiable and obvious.

ii Rules and policies in workplaces and organisations that have a racist impact that may not be intended.

22 Use these words to fill in the blanks in the sentences.

a Hegemonic culture
b Hybrid culture

i _____ refers to a culture that has absorbed elements of several other cultures.

ii _____ is a term used by Marxists to suggest that capitalists are able to dominate the ideas and values of others to promote and safeguard their own interests.

23 Link the terms to their meaning in sociology.

a Globalisation
b National identity

i The process by which cultures, products, and lifestyles are increasingly shared between societies all over the world.

ii The sense of belonging to a certain geographical area and culture.

24 Link each system for classifying social class with the correct description.

a Registrar General's Scale
b The National Statistics Socio-economic classification

i A five-point scale (with one subdivision) first used in the census of 1911.

ii An eight-point scale (with one subdivision) first used in the census of 2001.

25 Which of the following is a definition of 'ethnocentric'?

a To take the view that one's own culture is the main, only or best culture.

b To be centred on one's own culture but to accept the existence of others.

c To be interested in understanding the ethnicity and culture of other people.

The individual and society: a timeline

- Sociology developing in USA; Mead and symbolic interactionism; Chicago School
- Growth in anthropology (study of non-industrial societies) based in Britain
- European interest in Marxism

- Auguste Comte introduces modern sociology

- Industrial Revolution
- Rapid growth in scientific knowledge
- Growth of cities
- Expansion of European empires in Africa, Asia and South America

- World War I (1914–1918)
- Russian Revolution (1917) based on Marxist principles
- Women gain right to vote
- 1920s Economic depression; high unemployment; political and social unrest
- Independence movements in some colonial states, e.g. India
- Rise of Fascism in Germany, Italy and Spain
- Spanish Civil War

1800   1850   1900   1914 5 6 7 8 9 1920 1 2 3 4 5 6 7 8 9 1930 1 2 3 4 5 6 7 8 9 1940 1 2 3 4 5 6 7 8 9

- Consolidation of British Empire
- Growth in civil and legal rights of working people; development of trade unions
- New social, religious and political ideas
- Mass education begins
- Origins of women's movement; suffragettes

- Marx and Engels writing (Marx dies 1883)
- Weber (social action) and Durkheim (functionalism) writing
- Growth of sociology in France and Germany

- World War II and its aftermath
- Welfare state established
- Ending of British Empire
- 'Cold War'
- Most women return to domestic work
- Increase in birth rate
- Growth in suburbs and new towns
- McCarthyism (right wing) in USA
- Increased immigration to Britain

- Dominance of functionalism in UK and USA (Talcott Parsons)
- Increase in social surveys
- Community (ethnographic) studies
- C Wright Mills (Marxist) writing in USA

- Sociology less radical/political; more research is government-funded
- Growth of post-modernism; interest moves from social inequality to issues of identity
- Sociology established in schools, especially post-16
- Attempts to bring structural and interpretive perspectives together – Giddens' structuration

- Conservative (Thatcherite) governments; increase in social inequality
- Decline of traditional industries and growth of service sector
- Rise of New Right thinking
- Collapse of Soviet Union
- Globalisation; huge growth in mass media and digital (computer) technology; growth of transnational corporations

1950 1 2 3 4 5 6 7 8 9 1960 1 2 3 4 5 6 7 8 9 1970 1 2 3 4 5 6 7 8 9 1980 1 2 3 4 5 6 7 8 9 1990 1 2 3 4 5 6 7 8 9 2000 1 2 3

- Britain becomes more 'liberal'
- Birth-control pill frees women to work
- Rise of youth culture
- Challenges to traditional class and gender barriers
- Feminism, anti-racism and Marxism develop

- Marxism, neo-Marxism, feminism and interpretivism challenge functionalist sociology
- Sociology becomes popular in UK universities

- New Labour targets child poverty, social inequality, unemployment, crime and education
- Decline of Tory party
- Devolution; regional politics more important in Wales and Scotland

- Sociology has influence on government policy; Giddens and the Third Way

Section 2 Families and households

Families and households:
a mindmap

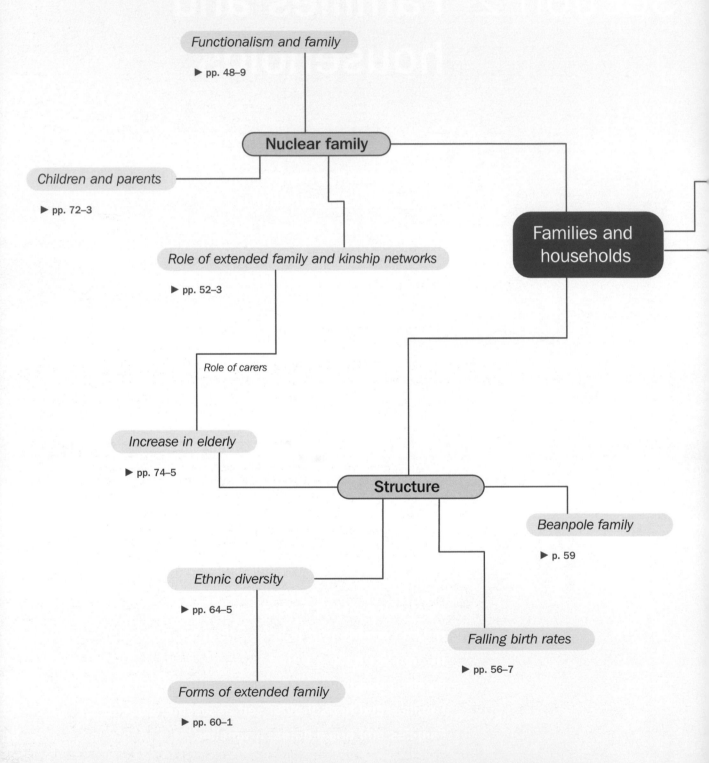

Functionalism and family

▶ pp. 48–9

Nuclear family

Children and parents

▶ pp. 72–3

Families and
households

Role of extended family and kinship networks

▶ pp. 52–3

Role of carers

Increase in elderly

▶ pp. 74–5

Structure

Beanpole family

▶ p. 59

Ethnic diversity

▶ pp. 64–5

Falling birth rates

▶ pp. 56–7

Forms of extended family

▶ pp. 60–1

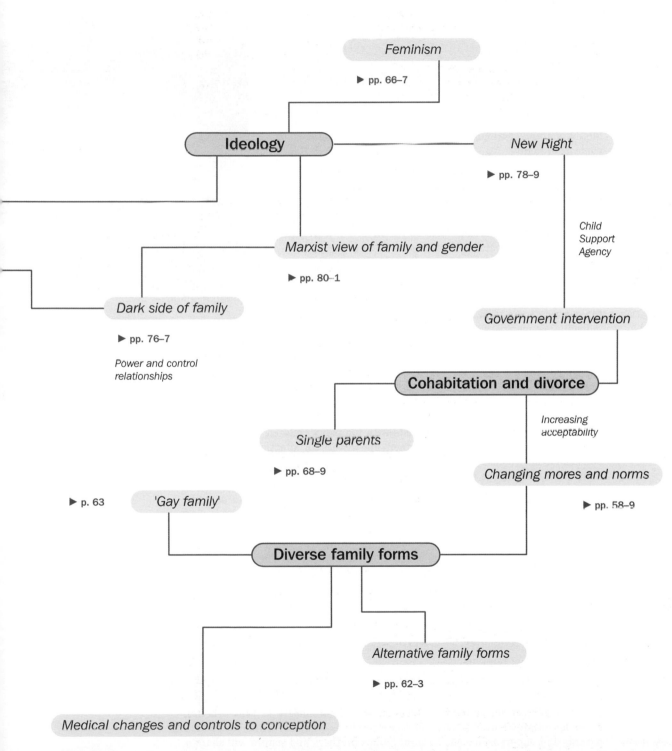

Feminism

▶ pp. 66–7

Ideology

New Right

▶ pp. 78–9

Child
Support
Agency

Marxist view of family and gender

▶ pp. 80–1

Dark side of family

▶ pp. 76–7

Power and control
relationships

Government intervention

Cohabitation and divorce

Increasing
acceptability

Single parents

▶ pp. 68–9

Changing mores and norms

▶ pp. 58–9

▶ p. 63   'Gay family'

Diverse family forms

Alternative family forms

▶ pp. 62–3

Medical changes and controls to conception

▶ pp. 56–7

What is the difference between a family and a household?

Family: A group of people to whom we may be biologically related and to whom we feel a sense of kinship.

Sociologists usually agree that there is no such thing as human nature and believe that people are the result of their culture rather than biology. However, it is worth noting that in one respect all humans do seem to be alike. They tend to form groups and choose to live with others like themselves. One of the most basic of human groups is the **family**. Very few people will have been raised without being members of some form of family unit. This means that the family is a universal cultural concept; all societies have some concept of family.

In biological terms the family is a group of individuals who share genetic material. Families often have physical characteristics in common and family members may resemble their parents or relatives very closely. We may even share habits of mood or behaviour with our relatives. However, it is at this point that sociology becomes involved in the nature–nurture argument: if we behave in a way that is similar to other family members, did we learn this behaviour or did we inherit it in our genetic material?

Household: An individual or a group of people who share a home and some meals, e.g. a family (perhaps with servants), students in a shared home or people in a community group such as a commune.

In contrast to the term family, a **household** refers to a single individual or members of a group who share a home without the special social obligations that being a family member has for the individual. A family may live as a household but a household is not necessarily a family. In Britain in the past, the household was a common social arrangement in which servants and employees would often live with a biological family unit. There would also have been considerable flexibility in social arrangements, so that parents with too many children to raise would pass on their babies to their childless brothers and sisters for adoption. Nowadays, households may consist of people who share accommodation – students, or single individuals such as the elderly, or couples and unmarried younger people.

The issue for sociologists is to define what is meant by a family and to look at ways in which people tend to organise themselves into those sets of special relationships that we know of as family

The term 'family', however, has a social meaning above and beyond a domestic arrangement. We often feel emotionally close to a set of individuals. Even if we do not actually like their company, we are obliged by a sense of duty to try to love and respect them. This special sense of obligation, or duty, is called **kinship**. We all have both an individual and a cultural concept of those whom we consider to be family. However, in modern Britain, we tend to have a fairly limited sense of family; for example, people may have biological relationships in that they are cousins, but they may never actually meet each other or make contact. Other cultures, such as Chinese or Asian people, have more complex arrangements of obligations and duties between family members and have special words to define relationships such as 'mother's brother' or 'father's brother' – words that are more specific than the English language term 'uncle'.

Kinship: The sense of duty we feel towards family members.

Nuclear family: Parents and children in a single household.

Extended family: Nuclear family plus grandparents, uncles, cousins, etc.; may share a home or keep in close contact.

The tightly formed unit of family that consists of just parents and children in a single domestic unit is known as the **nuclear family**. According to *Social Trends* in 2001 this arrangement accounted for 23% of households in modern Britain. The term **extended family** is used to describe those relations who may live close to or with parents and children. In some cultural groups brothers and sisters will share a household. This is called a horizontal extended family. In other cultural groups the elderly are very much part of family life and there will often be a number of generations living in the household. This is known as a vertical extended family.

Important studies

George Murdock (1949) wrote one of the best-known texts in the early study of the family. He concluded that all societies, no matter how variable their family structure, had at their core a nuclear family consisting of a cohabiting heterosexual couple and their own or adopted children. His definition of family structure was very rigid, and there are criticisms of his study because it was based on readings of other texts rather than on his own fieldwork.

The Census of 2001 presents a very different picture of modern British society, suggesting that a more flexible approach to understanding family and household is needed in Britain. There has been an increase in the number of single-person households but, with modern communications, this does not mean that such people are socially isolated. People are living in more varied social arrangements: they may live alone or with a partner, and then get married. If they then divorce and remarry, they are part of a sequence of nuclear families. In addition, as Britain has become more culturally varied, other patterns have emerged. Indian families tend to form households with an average of 3.6 people and Pakistani/Bangladeshi households average 4.5 people. Some of these contain members of three generations. In contrast, households headed by a Black person are substantially more likely to be lone parents with their children.

Think it through

Households

Over the past 30 years, household size has declined from an average of 2.91 persons in 1971 to 2.48 in 1991, then more slowly to 2.30 in 2000. There have also been marked changes in household consumption, with increases in the proportion of one-person households, and of households headed by a lone parent. The proportion of elderly people living alone has remained stable since the mid-1980s, but among those aged 25–44, the proportion increased from 5% in 1985 to 12% in 2000. The proportion of households containing a married or cohabiting couple with dependent children declined from 31% of all households in 1979 to 25% in 1991 and then decreased more gradually to 21% in 2000.

Families with dependent children

Changes in family composition show the same pattern as those in household composition. Thus, there has been a steady decline in the proportion of families with dependent children headed by a married or cohabiting couple and a corresponding increase in the proportion headed by a lone parent. Whereas couple families accounted for 92% of all families in 1971, they comprised 78% of families in 1993 and 74% in 2000. Most of the growth in lone-parent families has been among lone mothers, lone-father families accounting for between 1 and 3% of all families throughout the lifetime of The General Household Survey.

Source: *Living in Britain: The General Household Survey*, 2000/2001, HMSO, London, p. 5 (www.statistics.gov.uk)

1 Explain the difference between a family and a household.

2 Suggest three different forms of household structure that are commonly found in modern British society.

3 Evaluate the suggestion that both household and family structure are undergoing significant change in modern British society.

Round-up

Family members are related to each other, have a sense of kinship, and usually live in a household. Households may include only one person, or a group of people who may not be related but share domestic arrangements. In the twenty-first century, there is an increasing variety of household types.

Why do we live in families?

The functionalist view of family life

Despite continual criticisms of family life, people still carry on forming families and many appear to enjoy family life. It is this that has led some **functionalist** sociologists, such as Talcott Parsons, to look for reasons why the family is so popular as a social institution. He looked at the **functions** of the family both for the individual and for society, and viewed it as an essential institution for society as well as a cultural universal.

When Talcott Parsons studied American families in the early 1950s (Parsons and Bales, 1955), he concluded that the family had two major functions or purposes. These are:

- the stabilisation of the adult personality
- reproduction (or **procreation**) and the **socialisation** of the young.

Parsons had a very positive view of the family. However, it is clear that families have a variety of other functions besides reproduction and social stability.

The popularity of family and marriage is such that there are strong moves from many homosexuals to form couples and to create the families that heterosexual couples enjoy

---

ADDITIONAL FUNCTIONS OF THE FAMILY

- Families have more functions than Parsons claimed. For instance, families contribute to our **ascribed status** – the standing or status we have in society – over which we have no control. Obviously, membership of the Royal Family offers high status. We also have a family name, and this may indicate our ethnic or geographical origin; for instance, names beginning with O' (such as 'O'Reilly') are often Irish.

- The existence of the family is a means of regulating sexual activity because it sanctions some sexual relationships (such as those between heterosexual couples) and makes others taboo (such as those between close relatives). There can also be a negative element to this in that homosexuality for either gender is thereby not seen as fully normal in our society.

- Western society is economically and socially complex. People may be socially and economically dependent on their family until they are in their mid-twenties or beyond. Students, for instance, may need economic support for job training in professional roles such as medicine or teaching.

Critics of the functionalist view of the family

Critics of the family, such as Marxist and feminist writers, also see the family as supporting society but regard this as a bad thing because they believe society itself to be unequal and unfair.

Marxists and feminists point out that most family relationships benefit men rather than women. They argue that men have power within the family because they are likely to have higher wages than women or children. This reflects the power relationships of society, in which men dominate the political and economic world. This domination by men is known as **patriarchy**.

For a reflection of Parsons' view of the purpose of family in stabilising the adult personality and in social reproduction, you could look at any Disney cartoon from the 1950s or 1960s. These show a very traditional view of family and sexual roles. One example would be *The Aristocats*. Males are usually shown as wild until tamed by the love of a good female. The female gains satisfaction from caring for children and males. Note that while Disney-style cartoon images tend to reinforce traditional family roles and values, contemporary cartoons such as *The Simpsons* and *South Park* show a more negative and modern view of family life, while still reinforcing some traditional family values.

Important studies

In the 1950s, Talcott Parsons wrote a number of books and articles on the modern American family; he is the originator of what has come to be known as the '**fit thesis**', which suggests that family forms evolve to suit the needs of industrial society. Families have evolved into nuclear-family forms so that men have become breadwinners and women look after the emotional needs of the family. This, he argues, is because it is good for society as well as for individuals. However, this can be criticised from a number of viewpoints, particularly that of feminism – which points out that the nuclear family form is not always a good one for women because they end up socially and economically powerless in the face of male domination.

In a study of family relationships in families with teenage children, Langford, Lewis, Solomon and Warin (2001) discovered a positive picture of family life. They found that family members valued family life highly, seeing life without family as being lonely and sad. For many people, family is a 'taken for granted' assumption. It is something that they do not question. Interestingly, and in contrast with feminist writing on the family, Langford *et al.* discovered that women were more likely to be positive about family life than their husbands or children.

Melanie Phillips, a well-known journalist and commentator, is a modern writer associated with New Right thinking. In a number of articles in *The Times* and other newspapers, she has suggested that family life is in decline, partly due to what she calls a 'flight from parenting'. In other words, people are becoming less willing to accept the demands and responsibilities of being a parent. She believes that the traditional family is the building-block of our society. People who are born into traditional families have more stable personalities and a closer identification with each other. She feels that family life is in decline because people are no longer willing to participate in traditional family life.

Fit thesis: A functionalist theory suggesting that families evolve to suit the needs of industrial society.

Think it through

The passage below is adapted from the opening words of the Church of England wedding ceremony, first written in 1552.

> Dearly beloved, we are gathered together here in the sight of God, and in the face of this Congregation, to join together this man and this woman in holy Matrimony; ...is not by any to be enterprized, nor taken in hand, unadvisedly, lightly, or wantonly, to satisfy men's carnal (*sexual*) lusts and appetites, ...but reverently, discreetly, advisedly, soberly, and in the fear of God...
>
> First, It was ordained for the procreation of children, ...
>
> Secondly, It was ordained for a remedy against sin, and to avoid fornication [*sex, which was not allowed under the rules of Christianity*]; that such persons as have not the gift of continency [*being able to go without sex*] might marry...
>
> Thirdly, It was ordained for the mutual society, help, and comfort, that the one ought to have of the other, both in prosperity [*good times*] and adversity [*bad times*]...

1 What three reasons exist for families and marriage according to this version of the wedding ceremony?

2 Outline the similarities and differences between this view of marriage and that of writers in the functionalist tradition.

3 Suggest three factors that explain why many people choose to form traditional families.

4 Evaluate the suggestion that the traditional Christian view of marriage and the family is no longer relevant in modern British society.

Round-up

Despite heavy criticism from feminists and Marxists, who take a conflict view of family relationships, families seem to fulfil many social and emotional needs. Attitudes towards what makes a 'normal' family have changed significantly over the past 50 years and family forms are now more flexible so that many people retain a positive view of what families can offer to society and themselves.

What image do we have of the perfect family?

FAMILIES AND HOUSEHOLDS

Familial ideology: The view that the traditional family is 'better' than any alternatives.

Families have a social meaning that is rather more than an arrangement of people related by biological inheritance or by marriage. There is also a common view, or **familial ideology**, which suggests that certain types of family arrangements and expressions of human sexuality are 'better' than others. This type of thinking is frequently tied in with religious belief and morality, and it can be argued that this ideology of family is Christian, European and middle-class. This ideology is important because it forms government policies and politics. During the 1980s, the governments of Britain and the USA regularly called for a sense of 'traditional family **values**'.

Values: The set of beliefs and morals that people consider to be of importance.

Homosexuality is often viewed as inferior to heterosexuality. This is illustrated by government guidelines in Britain on the teaching of sex in schools, which advocate using the context of a loving family relationship and that homosexuality should be viewed as abnormal.

Stereotypes: Oversimplified images of groups of people. These images often rely on generalisations.

The common concept of the 'perfect family' in Western society is often known as the 'cereal-packet norm'. The term originates from the days when breakfast cereals were advertised with pictures of families on the front. These families were almost inevitably a nuclear family of father, mother and two children, the older of whom would usually be a boy. These **stereotypes** survive in various media representations of family, often in advertising for food products such as gravy powder or for family investment items such as housing and large saloon cars. Examples of these traditional families are much less frequently seen in the media than they were in the 1950s and 1960s, which may be a reflection of changes in family structure in modern society.

What evidence is there that some types of family are seen as better than others?

For	Against
Products are marketed to families and so food products such as pies and cakes come in packs of four.	Increasingly, advertising on television portrays non-traditional families.
Laws governing family and marriage allow only heterosexual couples the right to marry.	There has been a liberalisation of laws so that non-married partners have many of the rights of married couples.
The Child Support Agency was created to encourage fathers to contribute financially to their children's lives after family break-up.	The Child Support Agency does not restrict its activities to those who have been married, but targets unmarried fathers as well.
Media images of the family often revolve around a couple and their children. This is evident in situation comedies and in soap operas.	Television has shown some acceptance of non-traditional images such as gay sexuality and pre-marital sex.
Many politicians have made statements claiming that single mothers are a problem for society.	Some Members of Parliament have openly acknowledged their active homosexuality, which was illegal in Britain until the late 1960s.

Coursework advice
Using content analysis as a method, you could watch a number of domestic comedies or soap operas on television to study the various families shown. Trace the family trees of the characters that are represented as regulars on the programmes. How many of these programmes have a nuclear family at the centre of the action? You might like to discuss with your group the question of whether families such as *The Simpsons*, *The Royle Family*, or the families in *EastEnders*, suggest an affectionate or a critical view of family relationships.

Add your own ideas to the list in the table above. Do you find it easier to add evidence to the 'For' side of the argument or to the 'Against' side?

www.fnf.org.uk – *Families need fathers – is a compaigning website that supports the rights of fathers in the event of relationship breakdown.*

The nuclear family

Important studies

Jon Bernardes, author of *Family studies: An introduction* (1997), argues that the traditional view of the family is a 'young, similarly aged, white, married, heterosexual couple with a small number of healthy children living in an adequate home. There is a clear division of responsibilities: the male is primarily the full-time breadwinner and the female primarily the care-giver and perhaps a part-time or occasional income earner.' He argues that this model does not reflect the reality of variations of family form in either history or modern society.

Many prominent feminists such as Germaine Greer (1971) and Simone de Beauvoir (1953) have claimed that family ideology is used in a patriarchal society to tie women to men and marriage. Their view is that girls are socialised from infancy to become wives and mothers through play, story, toys and tradition. It is this that makes women tolerate the exploitation implicit in a traditional nuclear family.

Marianne Hester and Lorraine Radford (1996) suggested that The Children Act of 1989 (enforced 1991) reinforces traditional beliefs about family life and family values. When divorce had taken place because of male violence towards the women, this was not taken into account when making custody and access arrangements for children.

Watch out

Because feelings about families can be very strong, some candidates tend to express personal and political views when writing about this area in the exam. Be cautious and make sure that you back up anything you say with factual evidence or some illustrative material drawn from the studies.

Think it through

Almost every family I knew echoed, 'Father, Mother, Sister, Brother'. So, naturally, I expected to know the joys of a daughter. 'Aren't you going to try for a girl?', friends asked in disbelief. I feverishly defended my decision to stop having children. 'We only ever wanted two kids. Really. I'm thrilled with my boys.' But, in the back of my mind, I wondered who I was really trying to convince.

I was the product of a genderly balanced family. Saturdays gushed with the excitement of mother–daughter shopping trips, while my brother and father roughed it up at the hockey rink. My mother glowed as my Brownie troop leader. My father shone as my brother's soccer coach. Almost every family that I knew echoed, 'Father, Mother, Sister, Brother'. So, naturally, I expected to know the joys of a daughter. I longingly strolled through department stores, running my fingers over velvet dresses and ruffled socks.

Franco, S. *The perfect family*: www.pregnancytoday.com/reference/articles

1 Explain the meaning of the term 'traditional family'.

2 Outline one characteristic of traditional families.

3 Evaluate the suggestion that traditional families rely on the exploitation of the women in them who act as carers.

Round-up

The view that a family consists of a heterosexual couple and their children is still widely promoted and supported, even though this is a less common form of family than it once was. Those who have a strong belief in traditional family forms are often strongly religious or have conservative thinking on social issues.

How have families changed since the nineteenth century?

Debates on family change in British society are significant to sociology because there are political and ideological issues about what family changes mean for people. There are two aspects of change:

- *Structural change*: The structure of families has undergone massive change; more family structures and forms are now acceptable. Much of the evidence for such change comes from government statistics on births, marriage and divorce.

- *Qualitative change*: This debate centres on whether relationships between people within families have changed significantly. The evidence here is much less clear cut and comes from sociologists conducting small-scale research into family life.

✳ The average number of children per woman of childbearing age has been below two since 1973.

KEY STRUCTURAL CHANGES TO FAMILIES

- Fewer children are born to women so that nowadays the average completed family size is now around 1.7 children.
- Divorce rates peaked in 1993 at 180 000 but steadied to a rate around 159 000 in 1999.
- Fewer couples are marrying and those that do often cohabit before marriage. The age of first marriage is rising steadily to 29 for men and 27 for women.
- There are more single people living alone at all ages.
- People are more likely to live away from their close relatives.
- More people are likely to live as couples after their children have left home or before they have children. According to *Social Trends 32* (2002), nearly one quarter of all households consist of couples.
- There are more reconstituted or blended families. These are families that consist of children from more than one relationship living together, perhaps after divorce and remarriage. This accounts for about 6% of all families with children where the head of household is under 60 years of age.

KEY QUALITATIVE CHANGES IN FAMILIES

The key qualitative changes in families are a matter for debate. However, the main sociological points are as follows:

- Many people believe that relationships between husbands and wives are more equal. However, a number of sociologists (such as Sara Delamont, 2001) believe that the extent of change is over-rated.
- Relationships between parents and children may be less close than they once were, because there are more families where both parents go out to work. Some recent writers with a traditional view of family life, such as Peter Saunders, have suggested that this change is a cause of social problems such as youth crime.
- There is more tolerance of pre-marital sex and extra-marital affairs, which once would have been seen as a proof of low moral standards.
- People are more open about living in 'gay' relationships. This would have been well hidden before the 1960s because homosexuality was against the law.

How much have male and female roles in the family really changed?

Important studies

▨ In their book *The symmetrical family*, Young and Willmott (1973) started much of the qualitative debate when they suggested that relations between men and women in families were becoming more equal. This work is now very dated and was heavily criticised by feminists at the time.

▨ In *Women of their time* (1998) Jane Pilcher conducted qualitative research on women from the South Wales region and discovered that families at the start of the twentieth century and between the two world wars had **gendered division of labour**, but that men would and did help with housework at times of difficulty. However, she argues, there has been little change in family relationships because while contemporary men can and do help in the home, even today they still show reluctance to take on housework tasks.

Gendered division of labour: Work is allocated on the basis of gender, so women do domestic work and men work outside the home.

How does the modern family differ from the nineteenth-century family?

Although the family is in a constant state of change, there have been some significant long-term changes to family life and values in Britain since the nineteenth century.

Extended families: Nuclear family plus grandparents, uncles, cousins, etc.; may share a home or keep in close contact.

	Nineteenth-century family	Modern family
Change in status of women	Women have lower social and legal status. Fertility rates are high.	Women have greater legal and contraceptive rights and more independence.
Change in status of children	Birth rates and death rates are high, especially for working-class children. Many children go out to work before they are 10 years old.	There are fewer children and they are protected by legal rights. Children must attend school until at least the age of 16.
Changes in role of men	Men work long hours, but are dominant in the home.	Men have more leisure time and are expected to participate in family life.
Change in family form	Families are often **extended**, with relatives sharing homes or living close together.	Nuclear families are still the most common family form, but a wider variety of family types are accepted. There is greater geographical mobility.
Change in role of family	Family is significant for people's social lives; home life is valued.	Social and leisure needs are increasingly met by agencies outside the family.
Change in family morality	The moral code is rigid so that failure to comply can result in social shame. Much abuse and domestic violence is hidden and ignored.	Moral codes are flexible. Discussion of violence and sexual abuse is more open. There is some public awareness and support, so people are more able to resist poor domestic circumstances.
Change in sexual codes	Only heterosexuality is acceptable and sexual relations are expected to take place within marriage, and to result in children.	There is increasing separation of sexuality from marriage and more tolerance of alternative sexualities.

Think it through

'Cherry Norton, Social Affairs Editor of *The Independent*, argues that in the UK 'fatherhood has been transformed in the past 30 years'. Part of that transformation has been an emphasis on the importance of the father's role in children's lives. Yet the change in status of fathers... may be largely ceremonial. Certainly fewer and fewer British men are experiencing traditional fatherhood. In the 1960s, six out of ten men were living with dependent children. Today, the latest figures from the Office for National Statistics show that only 35 per cent do.

[*The passage in the book by Maushart goes on to discuss various legislative changes that are taking place in modern Britain, such as unpaid paternity leave.*]

All this is welcome, and yet the emphasis on the New Fatherhood, UK-style, has been very much on the rights of fathers rather than on the rights (let alone needs) of children. Questions of access and entitlement centre on raising Dad's claims to a level equal to Mum's claims. One survey published in 2000 by the National Childbirth Trust, for example, found that new fathers overwhelmingly wished to have more involvement in pregnancy and birth, as well as more leave to care for their babies after they were born. Prominence has also been given to research showing that 'fathers who live with young children work harder, get better jobs, are more sociable and attend church more frequently' than other men.

Maushart, S. (2002) *Wifework*: Bloomsbury, London

1 Outline the changes that have taken place in the role of fathers in modern families over the past 30 years.

2 Suggest three factors that may have contributed to changes in the role and status of fathers in the modern British family.

3 Evaluate the suggestion that the changes that have taken place in the modern British family have been exaggerated.

Can we trust official statistics?

Sociologists cannot be certain of the accuracy of the official statistics of social patterns in the past because families tended to hide problems that were considered shameful, such as divorce, or a child outside marriage. For example, mothers might have registered a grandchild as their own in order to save a daughter the shame of bringing up an illegitimate child.

Round-up

Families have been undergoing structural and qualitative changes that are closely linked to moral, social and technological change in society. While there is statistical evidence that significant change is taking place, there is a debate as to the actual extent and significance of that change when it comes to the reality of people's lives.

What has happened to the population of Britain since World War II?

Demography: The study of population.

The study of populations is known as '**demography**'. To understand something of how families have changed in British society, it is necessary to look at the population changes that have taken place in British society since the end of World War II in 1945.

The changes that have taken place in Britain are also typical of much of Western Europe and the USA. These changes could have a serious impact on the nature and structure of our society. The three main areas of change are as follows:

- the number of children being born is dropping below that which is needed to maintain a stable population
- the average life expectancy is rising and the proportion of older people in the population is growing rapidly
- people are becoming increasingly mobile, both within countries and between borders.

Social Trends is published annually and details an astonishing amount of information about changes in British society in an easy-to-read format. You can also find government statistics on the website at www.statistics.gov.uk, from where it is possible to download *Social Trends* free.

Birth rate: The number of live births per thousand of the population in one year.

Death rate: The number of deaths per year per thousand of the population.

Changes in living arrangements in later life (60+) by gender

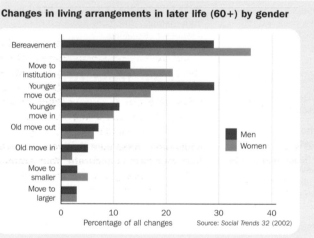

Source: *Social Trends 32* (2002)

1 What percentage of males will experience bereavement (death of a partner) in old age?

2 Which gender is more likely to experience bereavement?

3 Suggest reasons why females are more likely to move to an institution than males.

4 Discuss ways in which our society will need to adjust in order to cope with an ageing population.

Fertility rates (live births per thousand women of childbearing age) by age of mother at childbirth

	1961	1971	1981	1991	2000
Under 20	37	50	28	33	29
20–24	173	154	107	89	69
25–29	178	155	130	120	95
30–34	106	79	70	87	88
35–39	51	34	22	32	40
40 and over	16	9	5	5	8
All ages	91	84	62	64	55

Source: *Social Trends 32* (2002)

1 What trends can you identify in the rate of teenage pregnancies since 1961?

2 In which year were fertility rates for women at their highest?

3 In which year were fertility rates for women at their lowest?

4 In which age group were women most likely to give birth in all years?

5 In which age groups has the fertility rate of British women dropped least since 1961?

6 What trends can you identify in the patterns of fertility of British women?

Marriages and divorces in the UK

1 What has happened to the popularity of marriage and remarriage since 1961? Identify the main trends.

2 Which decade saw the highest rise in divorce statistics?

3 Identify trends in divorce patterns since 1961 in the UK.

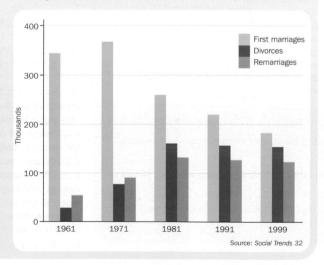

Source: *Social Trends 32*

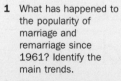 *The official government-statistics website www.statistics.gov.uk is a 'must-see' for students of sociology.*

Demographic changes in British society since 1945

	1945	Modern Britain
Birth rates	In the period immediately after World War II ended, birth rates rose very quickly in a period known as the 'Baby Boom'. This ended in 1953, but there were smaller birth-rate increases later, when the females born in the boom had children of their own.	Birth rates are dropping very significantly, with the average number of children born to each female falling. The average age of the birth of the first child has risen because women are generally starting families later than their own mothers did.
Teenage pregnancy rates	These appear to be relatively low, but statistics may not be accurate because families were ashamed of pregnancy outside marriage. Some children conceived outside marriage were hidden, abandoned or adopted in secret. Rates rose in the latter part of the twentieth century but have fallen again in recent years.	Allen et al. (1998) point out that the rates for teenage births has fallen over the past 20 years and that these are a small proportion of total births. Many of these births are to women in stable partnerships. The statistics show that the rate of teenage births is higher in Britain than most other European countries, where the fall in teen births has been more dramatic.
Changes in ethnicity	Although Britain has always been an ethnically diverse population, the majority of these people would generally have been white-skinned Europeans. Nevertheless, there were some areas, around seaports in particular, that had large and stable mixed-race communities. Immigration of non-white people from Commonwealth countries began on a larger scale in the late 1940s and early 1950s.	Britain is an ethnically diverse society, which has absorbed people from a variety of white and non-white communities. Non-white populations tend to be larger in major cities and in inner London.
Life expectancy	In 1945, life expectancy was lower than it is today. The old-age pension was set at 65 for men, on the assumption that it would only be needed for a year or so. Smoking was an extremely common social habit in all classes and many people had experienced poverty in childhood that had undermined their health. For women, regular pregnancy and childbirth brought their own risks. Many homes were poorly equipped, damp, cold and unhygienic in comparison to modern homes.	Life expectancy has increased dramatically, especially for those in the higher-income brackets who enjoy good access to health-care, quality food and leisure and who have a culture that values health and fitness. Increased longevity, however, means that many people experience a lowered quality of life in old age because, although they may survive previously fatal conditions such as strokes, they also become vulnerable to disability, Alzheimer's disease and cancers.
Child mortality rates (**death rates**)	Children were at greater risk of early death through infectious diseases such as measles, mumps, polio and TB, or through congenital deformity. According to public-health records, mortality rates for babies were high, but falling.	Children are routinely protected from childhood illness through vaccination programmes. Death rates from certain illnesses have dropped as medical technology has improved. There are higher survival rates for premature babies and those experiencing disability through birth accident. According to Social Trends 30 (2000), child death rates remain variable according to the social class, marital status and age of the mother.

Important studies

The best evidence for changes in the population of Britain can be drawn from government statistics, which are generally extremely accurate. All births and deaths must be recorded by law, and this information is supplemented by other data collection such as the National Census, which takes place every ten years. *Social Trends*, which is published annually by the government and is held in most public libraries and many resource centres, provides a brief summary of important information and changes. This material is widely used by sociologists.

As the amount of detailed data collected by the government has increased, our knowledge of the demography of Britain is fairly accurate. In addition, records have been collected for over 200 years, although the early material is generally not very detailed. We can see how patterns of population change have developed.

Watch out

Be cautious about making statements about the changing population of Britain. There are a number of popular misconceptions and misunderstandings that do not reflect the true picture of life in modern Britain. When supporting examination answers with claims about changes in population, make sure that you are certain that your data is accurate. Your examiner will spot a wild guess very quickly!

Round-up

The structure of the population of Britain is undergoing relatively rapid change. There are fewer children born, and these children are born to older mothers. Many of the mothers are not married to the fathers of their children even if the parents are in stable relationships, but this is through choice. Children are less likely to die from infectious disease than they were 50 years ago. There is an increase in the numbers of those over 65 and Britain has an ageing population. People in early retirement tend to be in better health than once would have been true for people over retirement age. The elderly old are also long-lived, but there has been an increase in the numbers of dependent old people.

Why are birth rates falling in Britain and Western Europe?

Throughout Western Europe there is a growing tendency for women to have smaller families and to delay the birth of their first child until they are over 25 years of age. This trend has been influenced by women's changing social, economic and moral circumstances, and has been aided by changes to the technology of reproduction which now enables people to make choices that were not available to their grandparents.

What woman wouldn't want to be a wife and mother?

Conceptions: by marital status and outcome (England & Wales)

	1987	1991	1995	1998	1999
Conceptions inside marriage leading to:					
	%	%	%	%	%
Maternities	56	52	49	44	44
Lebal abortions	5	4	4	4	4
Conceptions outside marriage leading to:					
	%	%	%	%	%
Maternities inside marriage	5	4	3	3	3
Maternities outside marriage	20	25	28	30	31
Legal abortions	14	15	16	18	18
All conceptions (thousands)	850	854	790	797	774

Source: *Social Trends 32* (2002)

1 What trends can you identify in the total number of women conceiving children?

2 What pattern can you identify in the number of married women conceiving children?

3 What pattern can you identify in the number of unmarried women conceiving children?

4 What are the differences between the conception and maternity choices of married and unmarried women?

SOCIAL, LEGAL AND TECHNOLOGICAL FACTORS THAT HAVE INCREASED WOMEN'S CONTROL OF THEIR OWN FERTILITY

- The contraceptive pill and other forms of contraception
- IVF treatment
- Hormone treatments
- Surrogate motherhood
- Fertility drugs
- The legalisation of abortion in 1967
- The social acceptance of birth outside marriage for some women.

One of the most notable advances in the health and life chances of women in the latter part of the twentieth century was their ability to control their own fertility. While contraceptive techniques have been used for generations, generally they were not very effective. The most effective form of contraception was the condom. However, this was invented to protect against venereal disease and was under the control of men, who could choose whether to use it or not. The advent of effective and safe contraception in the 1950s and 1960s had a dramatic effect on the lives of many women.

Women could take paid employment outside the home after marriage because they no longer faced the probability of regular pregnancy and childbirth. Note, however, that working-class women have always worked outside the home, often leaving children to be cared for by relatives.

Sexual activity for women was no longer linked almost exclusively to marriage. Women could be sexually active without the risk of childbirth and the consequent stigma of being an unmarried mother.

Changes in the social position of women and the expansion of higher education in the 1960s and 1970s meant that far more women entered higher education. Work became significant in many women's lives rather than being a time-filler before marriage. The increasing number of women in work and education led to many of them delaying the birth of their first child.

Fertility rate: The number of live births per thousand women of childbearing age (defined as 15–44 years).

Social Trends 2002 points out that, while the 25–34-year-old age group has the highest **fertility rate**, the fertility rate for women aged between 35 and 39 has doubled over the past twenty years. The average completed family size for women today is below two children, and is falling. Fertility in Britain is lower than is needed to maintain the current size of the population.

Falling birth rates

- It is often stated that some women choose not to have children so that they can focus on their career. However, the evidence is not so clear cut. It is certainly the case that combining paid work and parenthood is very difficult. Childless women do not have to make a choice between the two and so women who are promoted are often those without children, either through choice or accident. It is not so much that there is a choice between paid work and parenthood as that paid work is easier if you are not a parent.

- Parenthood has a low status in British society, despite the fact that it is a norm. For example, there is little support via the benefit or taxation systems for people with children in Britain compared with other European countries.

- A number of studies have shown that families with young children are likely to experience poverty, particularly if the mother is very young or the parents have low earnings from unskilled jobs. Gordon *et al.* (2000) suggest that 18% of families with one child and 40% of lone parents experience poverty.

- In our society, it is common for women to undertake education and establish careers beyond the years when their bodies are at their most fertile. If women choose to attend higher education courses and perhaps establish themselves in professional work, they may delay pregnancy. It can be difficult for some women to conceive without medical help when they are much beyond the age of 30. It is even possible that with the introduction of such initiatives as the student loan in 1999, graduates will feel the need to establish themselves financially before taking on the responsibility of parenting.

- Due to social and technological changes in the twentieth century, women are now able to exercise choice over fertility in a way that is quite new. Should contraception fail, there are aids such as the 'morning after pill' and abortion. Abortion was strictly illegal before 1967 and many women became infertile or died as a result of botched or unhygienic operations at the hands of illegal abortionists. There has been a steady but fluctuating rise in the number of abortions. However, abortion figures are not fully reliable because they may include pregnancy terminations of foreign nationals who are unable to obtain terminations in their home countries and will therefore travel to Britain for the operation. Abortion rates are highest for pregnant women aged between 16 and 34, but are relatively low for those under 16 or over 35.

Think it through

Certainly, the average age of mothers at first birth has increased in most Western countries. As women face increasing fertility problems after the age of 30, delaying the decision to have children may result in infecundity (*infertility*). Also, delaying a decision combined with low targets of family size may combine to result in childlessness. The classic case of 'forgetting' to have children until it is too late has been facilitated (*made easier*) by the advent (*arrival*) of effective contraception but this in itself does not create childlessness. Motivations to avoid having children may be deliberate or indirect, perhaps unwitting.

Adapted from: McAllister, F. with Clarke, L. (1998)
Choosing childlessness, Family Policy Studies Centre, London

1 Outline and identify two ways in which changes in the role of the women is changing fertility patterns in modern society.

2 Identify and explain two reasons why many couples may wish to delay parenthood until they are past their thirtieth birthday.

Important studies

In their study of both women and men who have chosen to remain childless (*Choosing Childlessness*, 1998), McAllister with Clarke, the researchers point out that many childless people feel that they have made a positive decision. They claim that parenting is a low-status occupation in our society; it is fraught with difficulty and insecurity and conflicts with other demands people have in their lives. Those who chose childlessness often set high standards for parenting and so felt it impossible to reconcile the strains that parenting brings with their other interests and concerns and their desire to live full and active lives.

Barlow, Duncan, Evans and Park (2001) pointed out that although one in five children was born to an unmarried couple, fathers had no legal rights over their children, even if they were providing financial support. An unmarried father may not take his child on a foreign holiday, cannot provide medical consent and, most importantly, has no legal right to custody if the mother were to die. Many are unaware of their lack of rights.

Watch out

Remember in any discussion of this question that although it is women who conceive and bear children, men may also be involved in the decision-making process as to whether women will bear children. Allen and Bourke Dowling with Rolfe (1998) found that fathers are often influential when teenage mothers are deciding whether to continue with a pregnancy.

Round-up

Birth rates are falling for all women. As they gain control over their bodies and their reproductive lives, many women are choosing to limit their families or to remain without children. However, the reasons for this are complex and related to the low status of parenting in our society and the high standards of care that are expected for children.

What recent social changes have affected the family?

Some fnctionalists claimed that the nuclear family, consisting of married parents with dependent children, was to be found in every society. This family form is still common in Britain, but there are also many people who do not live in a traditional nuclear family. Pressures on families to change have come from a number of sources:

- *Economic* – the movement of women into paid work is often seen as a benefit to them because as they earn money, they now have greater power to influence how it is spent. They are no longer dependent on a male breadwinner and can choose whether to marry or to remain married.

- *Moral* – Fewer people seem to subscribe to traditional religious teaching on family and marriage. This enables them to exercise sexual and moral choices that previous generations could not have accepted.

- *Pragmatic* – Many household decisions are made on practical grounds, so that as weddings become increasingly expensive, it is a rational choice to delay marriage until more significant debts such as down-payments on houses or student loans are paid off.

- *Ideological* – For many couples, particularly in the 1970s and 1980s, objections to marriage were based on political thinking about the nature of marriage as an institution that oppresses women.

- *Legal* – laws governing family and family relationships have changed and so it is easier to divorce now than ever before. In addition, as couples choose not to exercise the legal right to marry, so separating becomes simpler as well.

- *Changes in female expectations of marriage* – women may have earned the right to work, but study after study shows that working mothers carry out significantly more of the childcare and domestic labour than men. In addition, women are often expected to be emotionally supportive and nurturing of their adult male partners. They are now able to exercise a choice not to do this.

- *Social security and benefit changes* – the Welfare State will support women and their children if a relationship fails. It is sometimes claimed that young women will become pregnant in order to gain benefits, but the research evidence for this is limited. However, women who are in relationships that collapse may still retain their children and they can survive on basic levels of income, which are provided by the State.

- *Contraception and abortion* – women in Britain from the 1970s onwards were the first to be able to control their fertility with any degree of reliability. Previously contraception was in male hands or dangerous to the woman. This has freed men and women to have sex without necessarily intending marriage, or even a relationship.

- *Changes in the structure of the population* – there are proportionally larger numbers of older people and fewer younger people in the population. This means that there are more people living as couples or in single-person households. The Office of Population Censuses and Surveys suggests that there will be an increase of 50% in the number of old people over the next 30 years, reaching a total number of 14.8 million (source: www.statistics.gov.uk). The current population of Britain is 58.8 million.

What do the illustrations show us about changing family patterns?

THE POSTMODERN FAMILY?

Kidd (1999) states that, 'We cannot even say what constitutes a "family" today. The postmodern approach to the family is characterised by:

• choice • freedom • diversity • ambivalence • fluidity.

These observations mean that family relationships are "undecided" – we can only expect individualistic responses to the problems of the creation of social identity within and without the "family".'

Children of divorced couples by age of children, England and Wales 1970–91

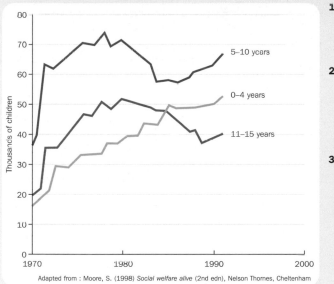

Adapted from : Moore, S. (1998) *Social welfare alive* (2nd edn), Nelson Thornes, Cheltenham

1 Approximately, what was the total number of children affected by divorce in 1991?

2 What differences do you notice between the trends for those children aged under 5 and those aged over 5 years of age?

3 Suggest reasons why the younger age of those children experiencing divorce may result in the development of reconstituted families.

Important studies

Smart, Wade and Neale (2002) interviewed 65 children who spent their time more or less equally divided between their separated parents. This arrangement where parents live separately but each retains equal share of the care of children is known as **co-parenting**. Their research is presented from the point of view of the children, but they note that co-parenting is becoming more common in Britain, particularly as a result of the 1984 Children Act, which encourages contact between children and both parents in the event of divorce or separation.

Co-parenting: Where separated or divorced parents take equal roles in caring for children, who spend some time in one household and the rest of their time in the other.

Beanpole families: Families that are very small, perhaps consisting of one or two adults and a single child, with the pattern repeated through the generations.

Think it through

NUCLEAR FAMILY GOES INTO MELTDOWN
Generations learn to link up to cope with lonely lifestyle

THE nuclear family of mum, dad and 2.4 kids is splitting up. Researchers have coined a name for the emerging British household – the Beanpoles. They 'live together' and have 1.8 children.

As Britons live longer, divorce rates rise and couples have fewer children, the traditional family – married parents with two or more children – is giving way to co-habiting couples with a single child.

A new study by the London-based research group Mintel shows family groups are getting 'longer and thinner – like a **beanpole**'. While 20 years ago the average extended family comprised three 'nuclear' generations, family groups are now made up of four generations of often co-habiting couples, each with an average 1.8 children.

'The family is undergoing radical changes under the pressure of an ageing population, longer lifespans, increased female working, the tendency to marry later in life, the falling birth rate and the rising divorce rate,' the study says.

John Arlidge (2002) *The Observer*, Sunday 5 May (www.observer.co.uk/uk_news)

1 Explain the meaning of the term 'beanpole family'.

2 Suggest three reasons for the development of the beanpole family in modern British society.

3 Evaluate the suggestion that the traditional nuclear family is no longer suited to the needs of modern society.

Round-up

The family is not a static structure but one that develops and evolves in response to changes in the social environment. It remains popular, so that even though people may divorce, they do not reject family life totally, but often go on to form further relationships. This has resulted in an elongated family structure in which many parents are older and have fewer children. They may also form a series of sexual partnerships throughout their lives.

How are traditional family structures changing?

We will now look at what is happening to families as a result of the changes discussed in earlier sections and at the various forms of family that can be found in contemporary British society.

Membership of a family is not a static situation. As we progress through life, we are members of different households and families. We may, for instance, share homes with others while we are students, or co-habit and even have children with more than one person before settling to a marriage. We may choose to live independently as adults – an increasing life-choice for many. There is a widening complexity in our kinship networks. We become parents, aunts or uncles, grandparents or step-parents. As society has become more fluid, there are more possibilities for individuals to participate in a variety of family structures.

Clearly there are more forms of family structure in modern society than would have been acceptable in the past. One of the big changes in the late twentieth century was the normalisation of family arrangements that in the past would have been a source of stigma. For example, illegitimacy and family break-up certainly did occur in the past but people would have gone to some trouble to conceal these events. Here we look at some of the ways that family forms are changing in response to the changing mores of our society.

Couple: Two adults who share a sexual relationship and a home.

Grandparenting: As life expectancy increases and more women go out to work, the role of grandparent is becoming more significant. For example, in many families, grandparents provide childcare for their grandchildren.

Modern family and household forms

Blended family	This is a family that contains children from more than one relationship or marriage within it.
Lone-parent family	This is a family that consists of one adult member and a child or children. It can be formed as a result of divorce, separation or widowhood or through choice.
Couple	Two adults who share a sexual relationship and a home. In the past, this situation occurred after children had left the home, but it is now popular with people before they settle down to children and, perhaps, a marriage. Some couples actively choose childlessness.
Empty-nest family	Parents with adult children who have left home. As life expectancy increases, a larger number of people are surviving to experience a life after their children have moved on. Sometimes this move may be permanent, but it can also be short-term, while the children are at college or experiencing work or training.
Grandparenting	Increasingly, older people may take on the care of younger family members, perhaps in the case of family break-up or to allow younger adults to work for a living.
Fostering	Children whose families are no longer capable of providing care are often placed with parent substitutes who are paid small amounts to care for these children. In the past, such children would have been placed in institutions known as orphanages.
Cross-cultural family	This is an increasingly common form, in which families are formed between people of different ethnicities and cultures.
Adoption	Parents legally accept another person's child as being their own. In the past, this was not uncommon and illegitimate children were adopted. Some adoptees, but by no means all, are from families with a history of neglect, violence or abuse and some may be older or have special needs of some kind.
Singledom	This is the state of living alone. Once this was more common among older people, but many younger people now live alone through choice. It may even be the choice of established couples who choose to have a close relationship while living in separate homes.

Household type, 16–25 year-olds (%)

	1982	1987	1992
Parental	61	58	58
Kin	2	2	2
Peer and others	5	5	7
One-person	4	6	6
Lone-parent	1	3	3
Partners	14	14	14
Parents and child(ren)	14	13	10
All (= 100%)	2925	2704	2248

Source: *Sociology Review*

1 What trend can you identify in the percentage of young people who lived in the parental home between 1982 and 1992?

2 What trend can you identify in the percentage of young people who have formed their own families?

3 What proportion of young people in 1992 were lone parents?

4 In your view, how significant are the changes that you can see in the table to the sociology of family structure?

People in employment with a second job: by gender, Spring 2000

	People with a second job (thousands)			As a percentage of all in employment		
	Males	Females	All persons	Males	Females	All persons
United Kingdom	513	696	1209	3.3	5.6	4.4
North East	13	28	41	2.1	5.8	3.8
North West	50	68	118	2.9	4.9	3.8
Yorkshire and the Humber	45	54	99	3.5	5.2	4.3
East Midlands	32	52	84	2.8	5.7	4.1
West Midlands	46	67	113	3.4	6.1	4.6
East	47	68	115	3.2	5.7	4.3
London	66	70	135	3.5	4.6	4.0
South East	76	101	178	3.4	5.5	4.3
South West	66	90	155	5.0	8.3	6.5
England	441	597	1039	3.4	5.7	4.4
Wales	17	38	55	2.5	6.8	4.4
Scotland	36	50	86	2.9	4.7	3.7
Northern Ireland	19	10	29	4.9	3.5	4.3

Source: *Labour Force Survey*, Office for National Statistics (2000)

1 Which area of Britain has the highest proportion of people with second jobs?

2 Which area of Britain has the lowest proportion of people with second jobs?

3 What gender differences do you note between the numbers of people with second jobs?

4 Which area of Britain goes against the general trend?

5 Suggest what significance the information in this table might have for family life in modern Britain.

Think it through

GRANDPARENTS 'JUGGLE CAREER AND CARING'
People in 50s and 60s feel pressure to work on

GROWING pressure on people in their 50s and 60s is set to divert grandparents from helping their working daughters and sons with childcare, according to a report today from the Joseph Rowntree Foundation.

It found a shortage of young people in the population – confirmed by the national census on Monday – would make employers do their utmost to retain older staff.

This would shrink the numbers of retired people who were able to care for their grandchildren or frail older relatives, said researchers from the Institute of Education in London.

...Almost as many men as women said they provided care, but women's caregiving was more intensive. More than a third of those providing care were doing so for fewer than five hours a week. But a quarter of women caregivers and an eighth of men were providing 20 or more hours of informal care a week.

John Carvel, Social Affairs Editor (2002), *The Guardian*, 2 October

1 Explain why employers might wish to retain older employees in the future.

2 Using the stimulus evidence, explain three family pressures that exist on people between the ages of 50 and 60.

3 What changes in family form do you consider to be most significant in British society up to now? Support your views with evidence.

Important studies

In a study for the Joseph Rowntree Foundation, Judy Dunn and Kirby Deater-Deckard (2001) discovered that children had found relationships with their grandparents to be very supportive and significant in the weeks following family break-up. Over one quarter of their sample of 460 children had not had the family break-up explained to them.

In another study for the Joseph Rowntree Foundation, Broad, Hayes and Rushforth (2001) discovered that children preferred to be cared for by extended family members in the case of family break-up or abuse. This was preferred for a variety of reasons, including the sense of being loved, safe and secure. They also valued being within their own ethnic background. They disliked the lack of freedom and the poverty associated with living with older people.

Research issues

Research into family variation might seem to you to be a sensible area for research. However, there are ethical issues related to studying family structure in cases where people may be asked to reveal information that they would rather conceal. Examples might be where an adoption has taken place or perhaps a father is in prison for a long sentence. People whose families are in the process of breaking up, or whose family break-up was recent, will feel very vulnerable to close questioning.

Round-up

Family structures are becoming more variable, although the most common family type remains the nuclear family. However, when the type is studied closely it becomes apparent that there are variant forms of nuclear family developing in our society, such as the beanpole family and the blended family. For some children, particularly in cases of family break-up, natural grandparents take the place of biological parents and create variant forms of the traditional nuclear family.

GORSEINON COLLEGE

What alternatives are there to the family?

Commune: A number of families and single adults sharing accommodation and living expenses, usually for ideological and social reasons.

Throughout history there have been attempts by various groups to set up alternatives to conventional family structures. These range from the convents and monasteries of the Middle Ages to the **communes** that became fashionable in the 1970s but which have existed at all times in history. Challenges to traditional family structures are not new, but are probably more tolerated now than they once were. However, the strain of challenging social conventions may be difficult for individuals, who are then forced to develop new forms of relationship in the absence of a traditional model.

Gay families/couples: These are same-sex individuals who choose to live in a partnership.

The communal living movement was very strong in America in the nineteenth century, where a number of such groups, including the Oneida Community, were established. Some had a religious philosophy underlying their practice, whereas others were political. Many of these groups were utopian; their members thought they were going to establish the perfect society. In the 1970s, there was a second flowering of the utopian commune movement, which was associated with 'counter-culture'. Those who rejected capitalist life-styles and adopted hippy ideals set up communes in many rural areas of the USA. Some of these communes were short-lived; others still survive to the present day. There are two basic types of communal living:

- free communes in which individuality is encouraged and rules are developed as they go along – these communes tend to have frequent changes of members and not to last for very long

- structured communes, which share a set of rules based on an underlying philosophy – there may be shared economic arrangements structure and a formal leadership system (typical of religious groupings).

Kibbutz: A form of communal living that developed among Jewish families in what is now known as Israel before World War II. It involved groups of families sharing childcare, work and domestic duties, and was often based on farming.

One of the best-known communal living experiments was the Israeli **kibbutz**. This was not designed to replace families but to help people survive in difficult conditions. It began during the early part of this century when the land that is now Israel was called Palestine and was governed first by the Turks and later by the British. Jewish people escaping ghetto life in Europe migrated to what they considered to be their Holy Land. In Palestine, the conditions were very difficult. The land was a desert and people banded together to farm. Men and women worked desperately hard and as equals. When children were born, it was simpler to ask one or two people to look after them all so that the remaining women were free to work. People shared all other jobs such as cooking and waiting on table. Some kibbutzim survive to the present day, but only a limited number of Israelis choose to live in them. Many kibbutzim have evolved over time to a more family-orientated life-style.

The ladies of Llangollen were an established, same-sex couple who lived together for 50 years at the turn of the eighteenth century and the start of the nineteenth century. They are generally described as 'close friends', despite their choice of male clothing and refusal to accept marriage to male partners

WWW http://www.thefarm.org/lifestyle/cmnl.html *This is an illustrated essay written by someone who experienced a childhood in a hippy commune. It examines the ethos and ideals of the commune as a way of life.*

Gay couples

In the current social and political structure, it is more acceptable for homosexual couples to share their lives openly, although there is still lively debate about their being able to adopt children. Many **gay** people today openly live in couples or as families. However, the extent to which this is socially tolerated remains in question. Andrew Yip (1999) points out that the stigma of being part of a same-sex couple may mean that the partners cannot expect the same degree of social support from family and friends as heterosexual couples. In addition, as Dunscombe and Marsden (1993) have pointed out, in traditional families, the female is often a subservient partner who takes primary responsibility for childcare and domestic tasks. This traditional pattern may be disrupted in same-sex relationships where such roles are negotiated.

> " *In many cases, both lesbian and gay couples have children by previous relationships or have adopted children. Thus, apart from their sexual orientation they may not wish to significantly challenge the norms of the nuclear family .* "
>
> Dallos and Sapsford, 1997

Postmodern families

More and more people delay forming their own families; some may choose to remain single or childless. This has led some sociologists (Stacey, for example) to argue that there is such a thing as a 'postmodern family'. This, she suggests, is because families and gender no longer follow strict patterns of social expectations (Stacey, 1990). People who reject traditional patterns of social life have to renegotiate family arrangements and relationships to suit their own personal needs.

EAST LONDON LADIES looking for a Dad as well as Sperm. Two happily committed girls who have been together for four years are looking to have a family. Would you like the opportunity to be part of our family? Sperm donation and co-parenting wanted.

Adapted from advertisement on www.gayfamilyoptions.org/

A Gay Pride march

Important studies

Bruno Bettelheim (1969), a psychoanalyst, studied the children of the Israeli kibbutz system in a study that became very influential in the 1970s. In it he claimed that they were particularly well adjusted socially but that their relationships were shallow because they bonded with the peer group among whom they were raised as intensely as with their parents. This work remains controversial, not the least because Bettelheim was accused of abusive behaviour, after his death, by the then grown children with whom he had worked. Nevertheless, his conclusion was that living a communal life does not emotionally damage children.

Think it through

Over the whole of Scandinavia, as in other European countries, some groups are forming residential communes based on the notion of community spirit. Such groups are normally composed of intellectuals and are often created by architects... These communes are normally composed of separate private units, with large scale communal amenities. The individual units are houses or flats of normal size composed of small private rooms with more spacious dining room and kitchen, utility room, games room and sauna... The people who live in these communes think that they can thus benefit from the combination of family and community life, which it is impossible to attain in normal residential conditions... Women feel that it is easier to organise shared household tasks within a large group than with a single man. If everyone has agreed to take part in the housework, the cooking, the washing up and child care, men cannot get out of it as easily as in a normal family.

Burguire, A., Klapisch-Zuber, C., Segalen, M. and Zonabend, F. (1996)
A history of the family (Vol. 2), Blackwell, Oxford, pp. 500–1

1 Explain the meaning of the term 'residential commune'.

2 Suggest three different reasons why people may choose a residential commune over a more traditional family arrangement.

3 Evaluate the suggestion that within a traditional household it is difficult for females to organise shared household tasks with males.

Round-up

People have made conscious attempts over the years to establish community lives that challenge traditional family structures. Those that seem to have survived best are those where there is a philosophy and shared understanding of what communal life should be like. There is increasing tolerance of family structures that are based on alternative sexuality. If a structural approach to family – such as that used by the functionalists – is adopted, then these arrangements are not family. They see family relationships in terms of organisation, blood or marriage ties. If one defines family in terms of emotion, duty and kinship, then these relationships are, in fact, family.

How culturally diverse are British families and households?

Attitudes towards families vary widely in the many cultural groups that make up modern British society. Immigrant groups that have come to live in Britain since 1945 have brought many cultural traditions with them. Minority ethnic groups have to adjust their thinking to cope with a new and sometimes threatening culture. However, terms such as 'African-Caribbean' or 'Asian' mask a huge diversity of cultural traditions, forms, religions and languages.

Indigenous British society also includes a variety of ethnicities, including the Scots, Irish and Welsh, all with their own cultural values. Researchers who assume that middle-class English culture is the same as British culture have often overlooked these groups. Similarly, the family life of the wealthier classes in Britain may not reflect family life among the poorer elements of society. For instance, there is the tradition amongst upper-class British people of sending children away to a boarding school, sometimes from as young as 5 years of age. Other classes and cultures might view this arrangement with horror, despite the fact it can confer considerable educational and social advantage on the children concerned.

'Yes, a family – heterosexual couple, monogamous shared possessions, spend social time together...'

AFRICAN-CARIBBEAN FAMILIES IN BRITAIN

In some parts of the Caribbean, society is matriarchal (based around women), a possible legacy of slavery. Other Caribbean islands have male-dominated cultures. African-Caribbean immigrants in the 1950s and later tended to carry their cultural views into Britain and reproduce their social patterns in their new country. Generally, however, Caribbean families appear to have differing approaches to family relationships depending on their attitudes, religious and political belief and their island or culture of origin. This has resulted in a very high rate of single parenthood among those of African-Caribbean ancestry. Traditionally, child-rearing is seen as a collective family responsibility, which does not necessarily end for extended relatives even after divorce ends a marriage. Berrington (1996) points out that in many African-Caribbean families males and females are in steady partnerships, care jointly for children but are in a 'visiting union', which means that they do not share a household. Mirza (1992) suggests that males are good partners, respectful of female career ambitions and supportive of their children.

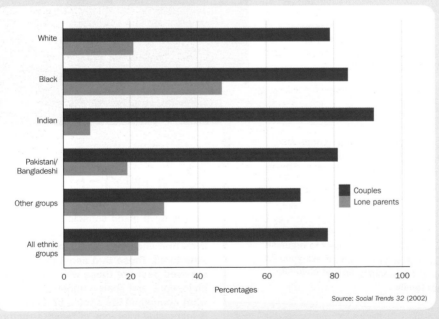

Families with dependent children: by ethnic group (Great Britain)

Legend: Couples / Lone parents

X-axis: Percentages (0, 20, 40, 60, 80, 100)

Categories: White, Black, Indian, Pakistani/Bangladeshi, Other groups, All ethnic groups

Source: *Social Trends 32* (2002)

1 Which family type is most frequent in all ethnic groups, couples or lone parents?

2 Which ethnic group had the largest percentage of lone parents?

3 Which ethnic group had the smallest percentage of lone parents?

4 What social and economic differences may exist in the category 'black', as used in the graph?

5 What social differences may exist in the category 'couple', as used in the graph?

Think it through

I'm a British born Chinese person, but my parents are from Vietnam and Hong Kong. My mother was adopted into a British family, so I've got a strong British background. My grandparents are from Yorkshire. But my dad came from Vietnam. He originally studied in France but he ended up in England, he trained to be a dentist here. My parents met over here and I was born here.

Chinese family is central to Chinese culture. It's very important to have a tight extended family. I make an effort to see my parents every week and I speak to them quite regularly. An important aspect of the Chinese community is food. We love our food. It's not only a delicious feast, it's a way of meeting up with families and friends. At Chinese New Year, in Hong Kong it's a really big celebration.

Now I am older I am really proud of my Chinese identity. I think it's important that we establish not only the Chinese part of our identity but the British Chinese identity. I have my Chinese side and my English side. I feel happy that I've got two different cultures that I can glean the best bits off really.

Sarah Yeh, 28. Adapted from text on
http://www.bbc.co.uk/radio1/onelife/personal/race/audio_chinese.shtml

1 Explain two ways in which Chinese culture is similar to traditional British culture.

2 Explain the ways in which family is central to Chinese culture.

3 Evaluate the suggestion that there is a single 'British' tradition of family life.

In *Living in rural Wales* (1993), Jones points out that for Welsh speakers, cultural notions of the family and the continued existence of the Welsh language are inextricably linked. The Welsh language includes a set of values that are based on concepts of family life, hearth and home and emphasises knowledge of the Bible and local family traditions.

Mirza (1992) studied young African-Caribbean women in two London schools in the 1980s. She found that young black women were dedicated to the idea of careers in adulthood. Their own mothers worked, often as nurses or social workers, and they expected the same from life. Many black girls rejected the concept of marriage, but still expected jobs and a family. They also expected their partners to allow them to work. Mirza portrays black males and black families as being committed to equality, with males supporting female ambition.

ETHNIC CHINESE FAMILIES IN BRITAIN

Chan and Chan (1997) suggest that the concept of family is very important in Chinese culture. Chinese couples may marry as a result of a parental arrangement, but couples also exercise personal choice of partner. It is expected that all members of the family will work to support the family economically, so males and females work together in the family business. In China, importance is placed on family honour and tradition so the family consists of parents, grandparents, uncles and aunts. Older people are perceived as having wisdom and are generally treated in a respectful manner, so Chinese children in Britain are expected to respect and obey their elders. Chinese people within Britain are often located in areas where there are few other such families. According to Smith (1991) the ethnic Chinese form nuclear families in Britain but are isolated within society. They attempt to retain social connections with family members in other areas of Britain or in the home areas, but this is difficult, especially if they are working long hours. Elderly Chinese people who have limited English and few English social connections may come to feel isolated and useless.

ANGLO-PAKISTANI AND BANGLADESHI FAMILIES

These are generally Muslim families and so there is a strong loyalty to the principles of Islam. Families are patriarchal in structure and it is expected that females will remain domestic. However, this tradition is also being challenged by a new generation of British Asian women who are less content to live within the home. Nevertheless, male children have more freedom in the home than female children (Halstead, 1994). Marriage is seen as a union between two families, and so weddings may be arranged, sometimes within the extended family.

Beishon et al. (1998) point out that females are expected to live in the family home of the husband, and to show respect to the husband's family. In Britain, fewer families are extended or share a household, though this once would have been common. Children are an important part of family life.

Coursework advice

If you are fortunate enough to embrace two cultures by being both British and a member of a minority ethnic group, this would be a very interesting area to study for coursework. You could investigate attitudes to family, to gender socialisation of children or to kinship. Someone who does not understand the cultural traditions of a different ethnic group should avoid this topic.

Round-up

People from minority ethnic cultures that have become part of British society adapt to British cultural traditions, but retain features of their own family and cultural backgrounds when they form families. These vary considerably from culture to culture and also within cultures, so it can be dangerous to generalise too strongly. Nevertheless, sociologists have identified patterns that seem typical of certain ethnic groups.

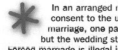
In an arranged marriage, partners consent to the union. In a forced marriage, one party does not agree but the wedding still takes place. Forced marriage is illegal in Britain.

Are conjugal roles in families changing?

Just as many women began to query their traditional female roles so, too, some men in the arts and media began to challenge traditional masculinity in the 1970s

The question for sociologists is whether the challenge to male roles in the 1970s was just fashion or whether it represented a real shift in social and domestic power

Until the 1970s there was little public querying of the roles and responsibilities of men and women within the family, except perhaps by individuals such as the French feminist, Simone de Beauvoir. In families that were studied or described by mainstream writers, the roles of men and women were seen as separate. Men lived public lives based on work and social or sporting clubs where they associated with other men. Women generally lived private lives, associated with home and children. Clearly, this is an over-simplification of reality because many working-class women did in fact have paid work outside the home, but frequently their jobs reflected their domestic roles, so most were carers, cooks and cleaners.

Academic interest was sparked by a famous, but later criticised, study in 1973 made by Young and Willmot, who produced their influential book *The symmetrical family* (Young and Willmot, 1973). Young and Willmot studied young families in a suburb in London and were among the first to notice a changing pattern in conjugal relationships. They discovered that some men were helping their wives in the home. The level and quality of the support was not high, but Young and Willmot saw it as evidence of a new equality in **conjugal roles**. They developed a theory of family that suggested men and women were becoming equal in the home.

This view was supported by a public fashion for unisex, where clothing and hairstyles were not gendered. Pop stars such as David Bowie and the rock group Queen challenged gender specific roles with glamorous feminine styles.

This gave rise to the suggestion of **new masculinities**, that was more of a journalistic fiction than a properly researched sociological phenomenon. **New men** were believed to challenge traditional male roles and take an interest in domestic life and the home. Men undoubtedly did begin to do more in the home and many took on caring roles, but whether this was a challenge to masculinity or was simply a practical response to changing female work patterns remains a matter for debate. Wilkinson used the term 'genderquake' to describe the radical changes that she perceived as occuring between the gender roles within society. Most research in this area found that men did not in fact take on much of the **domestic labour**. Employed women were doing what was known as the '**dual shift**', working by day, and doing cleaning, cooking and childcare in the evening.

Conjugal roles: The roles played by adult males and females within a family; may be 'joint' or 'segregated'.

New masculinities: This is the change in traditional male roles whereby men are enabled to get in touch with their caring and domestic side.

Domestic labour: The work of the household, usually known as housework.

Symmetrical family: A family in which men and women have some degree of equality.

New men: A man who challenges traditional male gender roles and is willing to take on domestic and other traditionally female roles.

Dual shift: The work that women do in the home after they have completed paid work outside the home.

Think it through

The author is describing a report by HMSO, the government publishers, Social focus on men (2001).

'This, the first study to focus on men's experiences of work, home, leisure and society, looks in depth at attitudes and habits. While there are encouraging signs of change – more men than ever before leave fatherhood till their mature thirties, they take better care of their health and fewer of them are the main breadwinner in their household – the report also reveals some depressingly familiar statistics. For example, despite the effects of 30 years of equality, men still outnumber women in top jobs, outstrip them in pay and fail to fully share domestic responsibilities (they play with their children for 45 minutes a night – half that of their female partners, most of whom also work).

'However, it's how men spend their leisure time that is perhaps the most interesting. They spend an average of three hours a day watching TV (favourites include football and soaps such as EastEnders) and listening to the radio and spend more than £10 a week on TV, video audio equipment and computers – double that of women. For reading material, the newspaper of choice is still The Sun (almost one-third of under 25s read it) and men are less likely than women to read a book.

Sheppard, S. (2001) 'New Man: exploding the myth', in National Statistics Horizons, Issue 19, Autumn, HMSO, London

1 Explain two ways in which male roles within the household have changed.

2 Explain two ways in which male roles within the family have seen little change.

3 Evaluate the suggestion that male and female roles within the family have undergone very little change over the past 50 years.

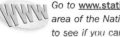

Go to www.statistics.gov.uk and have a look at the Bookshelf area of the National Statistics Website under Social and Welfare to see if you can find details of the Social focus on men report.

Important studies

Radical feminists Delphy and Leonard (1992) claimed that where a family has a male head of household, despite the relative earnings or wealth of the family, it is he who takes a dominant role. Women do not just take on domestic and childcare duties; they also fulfil a sexual and emotional role. They must support the male in his work, arrange entertainment, and flatter their husbands to keep them happy. Males, however, have more leisure, more freedom, and the best of the food and material goods. If there are two cars in the family, it is he who gets the biggest.

Beishon, Modood and Virdee (1998) discovered that amongst all minority ethnic groups, females tended to take on more responsibility for domestic labour than men. White men showed themselves to be willing to take on housework, and white households were more likely to pay for help with chores. Many men in Pakistani and Bangladeshi families felt it was a woman's duty to care for home and family, and so some were unwilling to allow their wives to work in paid employment unless it was necessary for family income.

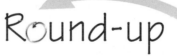 Barclays Bank conducted research in 1999 and found that 82% of their customers between the ages of 30 and 40, with incomes over £30 000 per year, employed domestic services rather than waste time on DIY or chores like washing or ironing. Mintel, the market research company, has identified a staggering growth in domestic services. Between 1988 and 1999 there was a 185% increase in domestic services.

Ward, T. (2000) 'The new reserve army of domestic labour' in Sociology Review, Vol. 10(1), September.

'In 1999 the most common reason for women to be granted divorces in England and Wales was the unreasonable behaviour of the husbands'. Social Trends 32 (2002), p. 44.

Given that most cleaners are women, perhaps there is a class dimension to the question of adult conjugal roles. Are middle-class women relying on working-class women to take on traditional female tasks such as domestic labour?

Round-up

There have been apparent changes in the roles of men and women within the family. It is not unusual to see males undertaking domestic roles. At the same time, females are more likely to participate in paid work outside the home. Whether these changes are due to fundamental shifts in male and female relationships within the family or whether they are a response to changes in the economics of family life remain a matter for discussion. Feminists feel that women still undertake more than their fair share of domestic responsibility.

Are single parents a problem for society?

> **The lone-parent family is not in itself a problem but the term has, in a similar way to step-families, become embedded in pathology. There is a sense that both mother and child are somehow losing because they can't achieve the ideals of a nuclear family.**
>
> Dallos and Sapsford (1997)

> **It is better for children to be born into a two-parent family, with both father and mother...**
>
> Warnock Report (1984)

> **As men are more likely to remarry fairly soon after divorce, and as most custodial parents are mothers, the single-parent household typically consists of a custodial mother and children. For many younger women the single-parent household phase of the process is a relatively temporary, though exceedingly stressful phase, as they are more likely to remarry or find a new partner [than older women are].**
>
> Robinson (1991)

Single parents are not a new phenomenon. There have always been single parents; it is the cause of single parenthood that has changed over the years. In the nineteenth and first half of the twentieth century, some women continued to bear children late in life and adult life expectancies were relatively short. This meant that single parents had usually experienced the death of their marriage partner.

In modern Britain, single parenthood has no single cause. People may become single parents through widowhood, separation, desertion, divorce or because they have chosen to have a child without being in a partnership. The table on the right suggests that lone mothers head 20% of all families with dependent children.

During the late 1970s, single mothers became a political debating point.

- It was widely held by politicians and some of the right-wing daily newspapers that young women were becoming single parents in order to jump housing queues for council property. In 1993, the American commentator Charles Murray actually went so far as to claim that 'the single most important social problem of our time' is illegitimacy. David Marsland has suggested that single mothers no longer need to rely on men because they survive on benefits, so they have developed a dependency culture.

- There is evidence to link single parenthood with poverty, high crime rates and delinquency. Many politicians argued that the cause of crime was the lack of male role-models in boys' lives, whereas feminists tended to argue that other causal factors, such as poverty, create both crime and single parenthood.

Families with dependent children headed by lone parents (GB) %

	1971	1981	1991	1999	2001
Lone mothers					
Single	1	2	6	8	9
Widowed	2	2	1	1	1
Divorced	2	4	6	6	6
Separated	12	2	4	4	4
All lone mothers	7	11	18	20	20
Lone fathers	1	2	1	2	2
All lone parents	8	13	19	22	22

Source: *Social Trends 32* (2002)

The New Right is a political philosophy associated with conservatism in politics and which reasserts traditional Christian family values. This view had some influence in the 1970s and 1980s but less now.

 A variety of sites offer holidays and services to one-parent families, which is an indication of the growing size of the market. Gingerbread **www.gingerbread.org.uk**, *a political pressure group, serves the interests of single-parent families and their children. Also* **www.oneparentfamilies.org.uk** *offers help and advice to single parents.*

POSSIBLE CAUSES FOR THE STATISTICAL LINK BETWEEN SINGLE PARENTHOOD AND PERCEIVED SOCIAL PROBLEMS

- Many single parents experience poverty as most of them are female, and female average earnings tend to be lower than male average earnings.

- There may have been dysfunctional adult relationships and quarrelling before the separation, which created disturbed vulnerable children.

- Family abuse and violence may have occurred before the family breakdown.

- Many families that separate come from lower social classes and there is a known link between social class, school underachievement and criminal behaviours.

- In some African-Caribbean cultures, there is a tradition of single parenthood, with mothers actively choosing to raise children without a father. There is also a known link between ethnicity, school underachievement and criminal behaviours among males. However, it is difficult to claim that anti-social behaviour is purely the result of single parenthood when African-Caribbeans may also have been adversely affeced by racism.

Are unmarried mothers a problem for society?

ECONOMIC ARGUMENTS USED IN THE LONE-PARENT DEBATE

In 2002, published government statistics showed that:

- social-security and benefit payments cost taxpayers £115 billion
- education cost £54 billion
- health and social services cost £65 billion.

Those three large government departments spend over half of the total public spending of £418 billion of this country, a fall since 1997 when they accounted for two-thirds of public spending.

A common media stereotype of the 1980s and 1990s depicted selfish young women having children and costing taxpayers money through benefit payments. However, Allen, Bourke Dowling with Rolfe (1998) found that most teenage mothers they interviewed had become pregnant by accident, but that they had been under pressure from their partners to keep the child. Many of these partners subsequently severed the relationships and had little contact with the baby they had fathered.

Who is poor in modern Britain?

	Total number (million)	Proportion poor (%)	Number in poverty (million)
Adult women	22.2	24	5.3
Children	13.0	35	4.5
Adult men	21.1	20	4.2
Elderly	9.8	31	3.0
Lone-parent family	4.3	63	2.9
Unemployed	4.6	78	2.3
All	2.9	25	14.1

Source: *Sociology Review* (Sept 2000)

This table shows that there is a very high proportion of lone-parent families who experience poverty. What other patterns relevant to the study of the family and households can you see from studying this table?

Childhood poverty

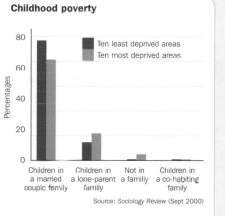

Source: *Sociology Review* (Sept 2000)

The chart shows a link between single parenthood and poverty, but does single parenthood cause poverty and a culture of welfare dependency, as the New Right suggest?

Who do children talk to?

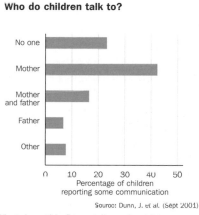

Source: Dunn, J. et al. (Sept 2001)

What does this figure tell us about how children communicate with each parent?

Think it through

Child Support Agency

Our Vision
- To deliver an excellent child support service to help reduce child poverty.

Our Mission
- Putting children first by ensuring parents meet their maintenance responsibilities.

Our Values
To continuously improve by:
- Giving an excellent service to every customer.
- Involving, investing in and dealing fairly with our people.
- Enhancing our performance by working effectively without our partners and resources.

Our Aims
Here are our main aims:
- To make accurate maintenance assessments, ensure payments are regular, and to take action to enforce paments where necessary.
- To provide a fair and efficient service that is easy for people to get access to.
- To provide clear, accurate and up-to-date information about the child maintenance system.
- To establish and maintain effective working relationships with the courts, advice agencies, customer representative groups and other organisations who are interested in our work.
- To help the Department for Work and Pensions to evaluate and develop child support policy and to make sure that we can respond effectively to change.
- To use our resources efficiently and effectively.

We also:
- trace and contact non-resident parents
- sort out paternity disputes when a man denies he is a child's father
- collect and pass on maintenance payments, taking action to make the non-resident parent pay if necessary
- deal with applications for departures from the formal assessment formula
- where appropriate, prepare and present appeals to be heard by the Independent Child Support Appeal Tribunal Service
- work with the Benefits Agency in cases where clients receive social security benefits to ensure correct payments and protect against fraud.

Child Support Agency, www.csa.gov.uk

1 What is the stated aim of the Child Support Agency?

2 How does the CSA expect to meet its aim?

3 Which government agencies work with the CSA?

4 Evaluate the suggestion that males who refuse to support their children create problems for society.

Round-up

It is difficult to prove the idea that lone parents are a problem for society as a result of their single-parent status. Much debate has been clouded by ideological views of the nuclear family as being the best form of family. In addition, there are claims that single parents are somehow inadequate because their children may experience school failure and engage in criminal activity. There are economic issues for the government as well, because providing money to support lone parents through benefits is expensive.

What are the patterns of divorce in Britain?

Marriage

A marriage is a legal contract between two people. A divorce is the legal termination of such a contract. Marriages can also be 'annulled'(cancelled), but for this to happen it has to be proved that the marriage was not actually legal when it took place and that therefore the partners are not bound by a legal contract of marriage. The traditional Christian view of marriage suggests that divorce is not morally acceptable. Many Christian churches still refuse to allow couples a religious ceremony if one or both of them has been previously divorced. Until the second part of the twentieth century, many people saw a divorce as a matter of social shame and stigma. However, there has been a massive shift in norms and values in the past 50 years so that divorce, while still seen as a personal misfortune, is no longer regarded as a source of disgrace or dishonour.

Changes in divorce legislation – a historical overview

Before 1857	Divorce was only allowed by Act of Parliament and was thereby restricted to the wealthy and powerful.
1857 Matrimonial Causes Act	Divorce was allowed in a Court of Law in England and Wales. Men had to prove adultery to obtain divorce, but women had to prove cruelty or desertion as well as adultery. Expensive legal procedures.
1923 Divorce Reform Act	This allowed wives to divorce husbands for adultery alone.
1937 Divorce Reform Act	Desertion, cruelty and insanity were added to adultery as legal grounds for divorce.
1949 Legal Aid and Advice Act	Legal aid was made available for divorce proceedings.
1969 Divorce Reform Act	'Irretrievable breakdown' of marriage became the sole grounds for divorce. Evidence can be adultery, desertion, unreasonable behaviour, or separation (two years when both want divorce, five years if one does not).
1984 Matrimonial and Family Proceedings Act	Divorce possible after one year of marriage rather than three.
1996 Family Law Act	Divorce allowed even when there is no evidence that marriage has broken down. 'Cooling off', mediation and conciliation meetings encouraged. Not fully implemented.

Divorce

Long-term trends

The overall trend in the twentieth century was for the number of divorces per thousand marriages to increase. There are several possible reasons for this.

- *Changes in divorce law* – divorce-law reform has generally made divorce more accessible to larger numbers of people.

- *Secularisation of marriage* – fewer people feel bound by traditional Christian teaching with regard to divorce.

- *Changes in the economic status of women* – women no longer require marriage as a means of economic support; other sources of income are now available to them through work or the welfare benefits system.

- *Changes in womens' expectations of marriage* – abusive relationships may have been tolerated in the past because people had fewer options; today, people know that they do not have to stay in situations that they find unbearable.

Marriages and divorces

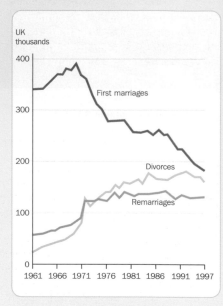

Source: *Social Trends 30*, p. 37

This graph shows that there have been significant changes in patterns of marriage, divorce and remarriage in Britain over the past 40 years. The task of the sociologist is to identify these patterns of change and to suggest reasons for them.

Watch out

It is tempting to see increasing divorce rates as evidence that marriages are not as successful as they were in the past, but this is not an acceptable argument for an examination answer. We know little about the quality of married couples' relationships in the past, because divorce was not a very easy option if a marriage failed. Your exam answers should therefore focus on the social reasons why divorce is taking place rather than the personal reasons.

 The term 'secularisation' is used to describe the gradual loss of formal religious belief from society.

Recent trends

Throughout the 1990s, the Office for National Statistics has reported a decrease both in the number of divorces and in the divorce rate. They suggest that this is because there has been a decrease in the number of first marriages, which are significantly more likely than remarriages to end in divorce.

Cohabitation

Norms and values are changing and more unmarried couples are living together (cohabiting). As a result of this, divorce statistics have become less valid as a measure of the number of relationships that break down, because cohabiting couples do not have to seek a divorce.

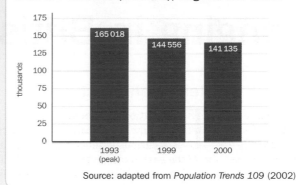

Decrees absolute (divorces), England and Wales

Source: adapted from *Population Trends 109* (2002)

Think it through

Research over 25 years suggests that the vast majority of children whose parents divorce suffer no long-term damage. E. Mavis Hetherington, professor emeritus at the University of Virginia, is touring America this weekend with this analysis from her best-selling book *For Better or Worse: Divorce Reconsidered*.

Ask an adult why they are disturbed and they often attribute their state, criminality or ill-health to divorced parents. But, by tracking 2500 people in 1400 families from childhood, Hetherington has been able to analyse not just outcomes but exact causes. Her data includes not only statistical information but tens of thousands of hours of 'secret' videotape of families at dinner, relaxing or fighting their ways through trauma and rows.

Hetherington concludes that almost four out of five children of divorce function well, with little long-term damage. Within two years, the vast majority are beginning to 'function reasonably well'. Perhaps just as important, 70 per cent of divorced parents are happier after the divorce than they were before.

Adapted from: Vulliamy, E. and Summerskill, B. (2002) 'D-I-V-O-R-C-E', *The Observer*, Sunday 27 January

1 Outline the main findings of Hetherington's research.

2 Suggest two reasons why some people regard divorce as evidence of a breakdown in society.

3 Outline and evaluate the view that divorce statistics no longer reflect the number of broken or unsatisfactory relationships in British society.

DIVORCE IN THE UK

- The average duration of a marriage is approximately 10 years.
- Just over half of all divorcing couples have dependent children under 16 years of age.
- The average age of divorce is between 25 and 29 years, but is rising. This is probably because the age of first marriage is also rising.
- Couples from the lower socio-economic groups are more likely to divorce than those in higher groups.
- Couples who marry when the bride is under 20 are more likely to divorce.
- Cohabiting couples are more likely to split up than married couples.

Grounds for divorce in 1997

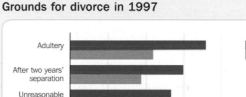

Source: *Social Trends 30*

What are the differences between male and female grounds for divorce?

http://www.fnf.org.uk/ *Families Need Fathers is a voluntary self-help society providing advice and support on children's issues from a masculine perspective.*

http://www.womensaid.org.uk/ *Women's Aid is a national charity that promotes the protection of women and children experiencing domestic violence. It takes a woman's perspective.*

http://www.adviceguide.org.uk *The Citizens Advice Bureau offer excellent fact sheets providing legal information about issues related to family, marriage and divorce, from the legal perspective.*

Round-up

Long-term trends show that there has been a steady increase in the number of divorces. There are a number of reasons for this pattern, which relate to changing norms and values in society as well as changes in the law. Recently, the number of divorces has fallen. We know relatively little about what prompts marriage breakdown. As fewer couples choose to marry, divorce statistics are becoming a less reliable measure of the quality of relationships or the number of 'broken families'.

How are parent–child relationships changing in British society?

Researching childhood

The relationship between a parent and a child is one of the most intimate areas of family life. It lies at the very core of what makes people a family, and yet it is a curiously under-researched area of social relationship. The difficulty is that the best sociological methods for understanding the meanings that people attach to family life are qualitative: observations, focus groups and unstructured interviews – and these all involve some intrusion into what is a very private area of social life. Also, the parent–child relationship involves strong emotions. Adults may not be reliable informants because they may misremember or misrepresent the events of their childhood. Children are often unable to rationalise or fully explain their emotions. Finally, it is extremely difficult to generalise from the very small samples that qualitative studies normally use.

The most frequently quoted study of childhood is the much-contested, socio-historical study by Philip Aries (1962). In his study, Aries claims that childhood as a separate status did not exist in Europe until relatively recently. This book is now over 40 years old but has not yet been replaced by a modern theory of childhood and childrearing. In Britain, the study of childhood is often related to pathological (damaged) families and those that are seen as unusual or abnormal. This means that the children studied are not typical of all children, but have experienced stress and family disruption. Other studies look at single aspects of childhood; for instance, Iona and Peter Opie investigated the playground games and culture of childhood in a series of texts and studies in the 1960s and 1970s (e.g. Opie and Opie, 1969).

Changing childhood

There are clear changes in parent–child relationships:

- The parent–child relationship is extending beyond what would have been expected 60 years ago, when working-class children began work at 14 and contributed to family income. The raising of the school-leaving age and the significance of education and training means that many people are economically dependent on their parents beyond formal adulthood at 18 years old.

- Increasingly, as life expectancies are extending, adult children may find themselves caring for their own ageing parents – a burden that typically falls on daughters, who may themselves be working or taking responsibility for their children and grandchildren.

- Where both parents are employed, they may find it difficult to spend time with their children. Where neither parent is employed, or the family income is low, parents will have little money to spend on their children.

- Parental fears over child safety mean that many children spend more time supervised and indoors than would have been the case before road traffic was heavy and the well-publicised cases of child abduction have led parents to be concerned about 'stranger danger'.

- Children are now more exposed to the media than was the case before the advent of television, video and computer technology. It is possible that, for some children, parents are a less significant agent of socialisation than once would have been the case. This is a view put forward by the feminist, Beatrix Campbell (1993), who suggests that boys in single-parent families are learning a model of aggressive masculinity drawn from action movies.

Legally, a 'child' is anyone under the age of 18. Another term for anyone under the age of 18 is 'minor'.

The term 'child' may also denote the social relationship of son or a daughter. Adults may still be children to their living parents and owe them special duties and responsibilities.

It is easy to assume that the parent–child relationship applies only to people under the age of 18. Remember that in many families, 'children' may be pensioners in their sixties or seventies who are providing care for older, living dependent parents.

Parents may be money-rich but time-poor, or time-rich and money-poor.

harry venning

www.jrf.org.uk, the website of the Joseph Rowntree Foundation, contains useful information related to a variety of social issues. Use the search engine to research parents and children.

Important studies

Philippe Aries (1962) claimed that childhood is a social construction that has developed relatively recently in Western society. Children were once perceived as being small adults; they dressed as adults did and often worked with adults on farms and in factories. Childhood as a 'special' period of life was an invention of the Victorian middle class who displayed sentimentality in their attitudes towards their own children. Nevertheless, working-class children were still employed as servants, in factories and mines. While the evidence Aries used has been criticised as being limited, the general thesis has been accepted as a sound one.

In the 1950s and 1960s, John and Elizabeth Newson (1968) interviewed large samples of parents and found evidence of differences between the social classes in child-rearing practice. Similar findings were made by Davie *et al.* in a famous longitudinal study, *From birth to seven* (1972). Both studies were concerned with social class; however, these studies found evidence that middle-class parents had different values (and used different techniques in the socialisation of their offspring) to those of working-class parents. For instance, the Newsons suggested they tended to be more verbal in their relationships with their children, talking through issues such as behaviour and attitudes.

Gillies *et al.* (2001), in their studies of teenage children, suggested that while many families experience difficulties when children go through adolescence, most of their study samples felt that family relationships underwent positive changes focused on companionship and responsibility as the children grew to adulthood and family relationships took account of the growing maturity of the children.

Think it through

CHILDREN'S SPEAKING SKILLS IN DECLINE

Some would blame the parents, others the Teletubbies. Either way, children arriving at nursery school have apparently shown a marked deterioration in their speaking and listening skills in the past five years.

Three out of four headteachers who responded to a survey, run jointly by the National Literacy Trust and the National Association of Head Teachers said they were concerned about the lack of language ability among three-year-olds. The headteachers pinned most of the blame for the decline on the time

children spent watching TV and video games. They said this detracted from the time children spent talking to their parents, interacting with them and learning to engage in imaginative play.

Neil McClelland, director of the trust, said: 'There is a concern here that children are coming into early-years classes less able to listen to each other and speak and we feel that is an issue we must tackle.'

'I don't want to give the impression that all TV and video games are bad but I do want parents to communicate

with their children more instead of just putting them in front of the TV and leaving them there.'

He urged parents to buy spin-off books from children's TV programmes and read them to their children if they had shown an interest in the show. He added: 'The right to be talked to and listened to should be the right of every toddler. Most brain development occurs between birth and the age of two so babies and toddlers need a quality linguistic environment just as much as they need nourishing food.'

Source: Garner, R., Education Editor (2002), 'Children's speaking skills in decline', *The Guardian*, 3 August

1 Explain two reasons why many headteachers feel that children's linguistic skills are in decline.

2 Explain two ways in which parents can support their children in the development of linguistic skills.

3 Describe and discuss how children's status within the family has changed over the past 50 years.

> *Parental identities based on being needed and wanted can be a source of purpose and satisfaction. So teenagers' growing independence can herald an 'identity crisis' for parents.*
>
> Langford, W., Lewis, C., Solomon, Y. and Warin, J. (2001) *Family understandings: Closeness, authority and independence in families with teenagers*, Joseph Rowntree Foundation and Family Policy Studies Institute, London, p. 26

Round-up

Parent–child relationships are under-researched in Britain, despite being at the core of family structure. There are practical and ethical reasons for this shortage of knowledge. Nevertheless, the changes that have taken place in family structure and the economic life of people in Britain have clearly had an impact on nature and quality of family life, both for children at the start of their lives and for adult children who must care for parents at the end of their lives.

What impact does an ageing population have on family relationships?

 Concepts such as 'ageing' and 'elderly' are social constructions. This means that they are not fixed by biology but are defined by social customs and practice. Just as there is no clear point at which childhood ends, so there is no defining age at which one becomes old.

An ageing population

- More people in the UK are living longer. In 1901, 1.7 million people were over the age of 65. By 2001, males over 65 and females over 60 totalled 10.8 million, from a total UK population of 58.8 million.

- The proportion of people aged over 60 is growing, from 16% in 1951 to 21% in 2001.

- Those over retirement age are sometimes divided into two groups. Those at the younger end of old age may well be fit, healthy and actively pursuing hobbies and activities. The 'elderly old' (often defined as those over 85) are more likely to be unwell or disabled. They may have become dependent on the State or on relatives to support them.

- There are more 'elderly old'. In 1984, 6.3% of the population was aged 75 and over; by 1999 this figure had risen to 7.3%. In 2001, 1.9% of the population was aged 85 and over (that's 1.1 million people), compared to 0.4% (0.2 million) in 1951.

- This increase in the proportion of older people means that in 2001, for the first time, there were more people aged over 60 in the UK (21%) than there were children under 16 (20% – a fall from 24% in 1951).

Ageing and the family

Old age need not be a social problem. Many older people continue with work, education and leisure activities and are able to support their children through services such as child-minding and baby-sitting. Many devote time to socially valued activities such as voluntary work for charities and in education. Friendship groups and reunion societies are popular with those in the 'Third Age'. They have time, money and liberty to spend on holidays and consumer goods. Many older people have realistic expectations of healthy and valuable family lives in their retirement.

 Many of the elderly come from minority ethnic backgrounds. Their expectations of old age may be different from those of the wider population. They may have specific needs that are not being met by the general provision made by social services.

 Retirement is often called the 'Third Age', as in 'the University of the Third Age'.

However, there are serious social implications arising from the increase in the number and proportion of older people in the British population. Almost every study conducted on poverty has suggested that the retired population is vulnerable to poverty. In addition, the elderly old are more liable to experience ill-health and disability than the younger old. Dementia affects approximately 20% of people over 85 years of age. (Dementias, of which Alzheimer's is probably the best known, are physical diseases that can damage a person's ability to learn and destroy short-term memory. These are very disabling conditions.)

This gives rise to concerns for families.

- Care for the elderly can be expensive, with fees for some nursing homes being well over £1000 a month. Those elderly people who have assets over £16 000 must pay for their own care. If they have property such as a house that they wish to pass on to their children, they may have to sell it in order to pay for private care.

- The elderly old may not have the same access to friendship groups and networks that younger people are able to arrange for themselves. As a result, some of the elderly may experience social exclusion and isolation. This is a particular concern for those who do not have family members living nearby.

- Many of those who care for the elderly are themselves no longer young. In 1995, 27% of carers who devoted over 20 hours a week to caring were themselves over 65 years old. Marriage partners may care for a sick husband or wife but, with increasing age, older people may be cared for by their own children who are themselves past retirement age.

- Older people are not spread evenly throughout the country and there are high concentrations in certain parts of the country. Eversley (1984) points out that the south coast of England is a 'geriatric ward' because it is attractive as a retirement area. The 2001 Census shows that Worthing is the local authority with the largest proportion of elderly old, at 4.6%. Family members may not live close enough to elderly relatives to give active support.

- The burden of caring often falls to women. In 1990, the Equal Opportunities Commission pointed out that 66% of carers are female, though men can be supportive and can also be the main carer. Coote *et al.* (1990) estimate that 25% of middle-aged women are supporting a dependent adult with no financial support from the government. Caring may reduce a person or a family to poverty, particularly if they are relying on state benefits and pensions to survive. As families are smaller and the elderly are living for longer, some children will be caring for demented or sick parents over long periods of time, when they themselves have retired from full-time work.

There is no defining the age at which one becomes old

www.ace.org.uk, the website of Age Concern, contains a remarkable amount of helpful information.

Think it through

Any changes to the supply of unpaid care could have important effects on the demand for paid care and thus the cost to individuals or the State. By unpaid care we mean care and support from family, relatives and friends, which, in terms of hours (and perhaps in terms of monetary value), far exceeds what the state and individuals provide by way of paid-for care. It is sometimes assumed that Government can influence the supply of unpaid care by taking certain measures to ensure that families and relatives care for their older people. However, in a free society a Government can do little... to influence the way in which families or relatives decide whether to care for their older members...

There are about 5.7 million people providing some hours of informal care, most of whom will be caring for older people. Most carers spend no more than about 4 hours a week providing unpaid care, but about 800 000 people provide unpaid care for 50 hours a week or more. More women than men provide informal care. People aged between 45 and 64 comprise the single largest group of unpaid carers. The largest group providing unpaid care is those providing help to their parents or their parents-in-law...

...There is genuine concern about the effects on the supply of unpaid care because of changes in family structure brought about by falls in birth rates, higher divorce rates, re-marriage, greater family mobility and less living together of families across generations.

Adapted from: Sutherland, Professor Sir Stewart, Chairman (March 1999) *With respect to old age: Long-term care – Rights and responsibilities – A Report by the Royal Commission on Long Term Care*, HMSO, London

1 Outline the typical social characteristics of a family carer of an elderly person.

2 Suggest three ways in which family members who care for the elderly are supporting the State through their actions.

3 Evaluate the suggestion that, as family structures change, the State will have to take on a greater role in the care of the elderly sick and disabled.

Watch out

When writing about older people, be careful to avoid stereotyping them all as infirm and dependent. While many elderly people are on low incomes, and a substantial minority needs to be cared for, the majority are healthier and wealthier than ever before.

Round-up

For many people in Britain, retirement can be a positive and active experience, when they can give support and help to their adult children and grandchildren. However, the very old may become vulnerable to sickness and ill health. As the population of Britain ages and the proportion of older people in the population expands, the burden of their care increasingly falls on families, often women who are themselves also working and no longer young. As families change, many of the elderly infirm may not have younger family members to care for them in their old age.

What about violent or abusive families?

Families can sometimes be difficult and dangerous places.

- People who die violently are most likely to die at the hands of someone that they know.

- Selbourne (1993) points out that the largest category of murder victims in most years is children under the age of 5 years, at the hands of a family member. The figure has remained static at about 80 children a year since 1985.

- Women's Aid groups estimate that a woman dies every three days at the hands of a partner.

In the past, much domestic violence and abuse would have been accepted or ignored, primarily because women and children had very little power, socially, legally or financially. The situation has changed radically for women, who are now in a position to make choices, although many victims still remain silent for many years. It is now more common to speak in public of domestic violence and it has become a soap-opera storyline. However, the focus on women as the victims of domestic violence masks the true picture of abuse and violence, which is more complex.

There is a variety of forms of abuse within families.

- Sexual abuse is sexual activity that occurs between close family members, particularly between adults and children.

- Neglect is when a person's physical needs for food, cleanliness or warmth are ignored.

- Physical abuse is also known as domestic violence and refers to actual physical harm, which one family member may inflict on another.

- Emotional abuse is more difficult to define, but refers to how family members may seek to dominate others through constant ridicule, shaming, rejection, or terrorising.

Feminists suggest that it is men who commit domestic violence and abuse because they are able to exert power over weaker women and children. In reality, the picture is more complex than this. There is evidence that some older people suffering from dementia are subject to violence, neglect and abuse by their relatives. Women can be violent and abusive towards men and towards their children. The sociological debates are clouded by emotionalism and fear.

Of all crimes reported to the British Crime Survey 2000, more than 1 in 20 were classified as domestic violence. (Source: Women's Aid website)

According to a WHO report, among women aged 15–44 years gender violence accounts for more death and disability than cancer, malaria, traffic injuries or war put together. (Source: website of the International Planned Parenthood Federation www.ippf.org/resource/gbv)

Families are not always a safe haven

WHAT IS ABUSE AND WHAT IS VIOLENCE?

'Abuse' is a term that is difficult to operationalise. However, a working definition is that it is behaviour that satisfies the person doing it, but upsets, hurts and offends the person to whom it is done.

'Domestic violence is physical, psychological, sexual or financial violence that takes place within an intimate or family-type relationship and forms a pattern of coercive and controlling behaviour. Crime statistics and research both show that domestic violence is gender specific – usually the perpetrator of a pattern of repeated assaults is a man.'

www.womensaid.org.uk

In everyday terms, 'violence' tends to mean physical violence. However, women's groups define violence more broadly, using it to include behaviours that others might call abuse.

This debate about the use of words reflects wider disagreements and conflicts in this area of sociology.

Coursework advice Despite the fascination that many have with questions of violence and abuse, first-hand research of those who have experienced violence and abuse is not an appropriate area for coursework. There are far too many ethical issues for a novice sociologist to handle and this is an area best left to those with experience and expertise in the study of family relationships. However, a review of secondary data, both qualitative and quantitative, might form the basis of a coursework project.

Important studies

Hester and Radford (1996), in their studies of domestic violence and the law, suggested that not only did traditional patterns of male dominance in families still exist but that The Children Act of 1989 (enforced 1991) reinforces traditional beliefs about family life and family values. When divorce had taken place because of male violence towards the woman, this was not taken into account when making custody and access arrangements for children. Males were therefore able to continue abusing and controlling their ex-wives and partners beyond the end of the marriage.

Lockhurst (1999), in his studies of male survivors of domestic violence, suggests that, because males are traditionally seen as controlling and aggressive, the problem of woman-on-man violence is underestimated, under-researched and underfunded. He claims that feminists have dominated the research so that only women are seen as victims of domestic violence.

Watch out

Like many others areas of sociology, domestic violence is a topic that can stir strong emotions. While this may make you feel particularly involved in the topic, it is important to avoid letting these emotions cloud your interpretation of the evidence.

Research issues

It is difficult to operationalise the concept of domestic violence. For example, most people in England accept the smacking of children for disciplinary reasons, but some European countries (e.g. Norway) ban this altogether and regard some English behaviour towards children as cruel and abusive. There are also qualitative differences in what may count as violent abuse. A severe beating is easy to classify as violence; however, is a slap always evidence of violence? Emotional abuse is even more difficult to define and has been claimed by men as a defence in trials when they have killed their wives.

Think it through

BRITISH ASIAN MARRIAGES SCARRED BY RISING ABUSE

The first national symposium on domestic violence in minority communities was told this week that growing numbers of third and fourth-generation British Indians and Pakistanis were sliding into depression or attempting suicide to escape their daily torment.

The suicide rate among British Asian women who suffer domestic abuse is two to three times greater than for non-Asian victims and there is growing depression and isolation. Attempts to escape the abuse, which in some cases included genital mutilation and assaults from the extended family, had seen women being traced and murdered by their families.

Research by Blackburn with Darwen Council, where about 19 per cent of the 137 000-strong population is from an ethnic minority, revealed the extent of the problem. Ghazala Sulaman-Butt, a policy officer, interviewed about 100 Asian women, many of whom were severely depressed and isolated after enduring psychological, physical and sexual violence. None was prepared to speak out for fear of bringing shame to the family izaat, or honour, which renders broken marriages taboo. Mrs Sulaman-Butt said: 'Domestic abuse is a feature of every community and is fast escalating within the Asian communities... culture and tradition plays a major part in the survivor's decision to tolerate the abuse.

'Such is the power of izaat that women have committed suicide or attempted suicide rather than leave an abusive relationship.'

1 Explain and discuss the term 'domestic violence'.

2 Suggest why some people find it difficult to believe that males can be the victims of domestic violence.

3 Evaluate the view that domestic violence is a female problem.

Source: Akbar, A. (2002) 'British Asian marriages scarred by rising abuse', *The Independent*, 12 October

www.nspcc.org.uk, the Website of the National Society for the Prevention of Cruelty to Children, has a News and Campaigns page, which comments on legislative changes that affect children. www.womensaid.org.uk, the website of the Women's Aid Federation includes a range of research findings and statistics. www.homeoffice.gov.uk/domestic violence gives details of a number of government reports on domestic violence and rape. The important criminologist and feminist, Professor Betsy Stanko, has contributed to this material.

Round-up

'Violence' and 'abuse' are difficult terms to define, but their existence within some families means that the family is not always a safe haven for its members. The privacy and intimacy of family life can be a source of danger to the vulnerable and weak, who may experience abuse, but be powerless to protect themselves. Sociological studies of domestic violence have usually been carried out by women. However, to view only women and children as the victims of abuse is to underestimate the complexity of domestic violence and abuse.

How do government policies affect families?

Britain, unlike some other European countries, has no Minister for the Family, but the law has always influenced family life, both directly and indirectly.

Direct influences

- Laws determine whom we may marry, the age we may marry, how many people we may marry, and how a marriage can be ended. A marriage certificate is evidence of a formal contract between two people, which can be ended only by law. This legislation is based on Christian morality.
- Laws affect a family's income, both through benefits such as Child Benefit and through taxation such as the allowances for married couples and for children. Laws determine the public services available for families and children, such as childcare, health and social services and community care.
- Laws influence behaviour within families, including the nature of the relationship between husband and wife (e.g. marital rape is now illegal), sexual behaviour, abortion, and the protection of children against violence and neglect.
- Recent laws have made parents responsible for the criminal actions of their children.
- **Custody** laws in the event of separation and divorce enable some parents to maintain contact, or ensure that they make financial provision for their children.
- Adoption and fostering laws and regulations govern the right of adults to take parental responsibility for a child who is not biologically their own.

Custody: Rules that govern the rights of a parent or other carer with regard to a child.

Indirect influences

Laws aimed primarily at other areas of social life may also affect families. In fact, it is hard to think of any area of policy that doesn't affect the family in some way.

- *Housing*, e.g. government policy on the balance between private- and public-sector housing will particularly affect low-income families.
- *Education*, e.g. types of school provided affect parental choice in selecting schools.
- *Health*, e.g. laws will affect the right to obtain *in-vitro* fertilisation or to use reproductive technology.
- *Transport*, e.g. the provision of public transport will affect job opportunities and, therefore, family incomes.
- *Employment*, e.g. people are affected by rules about maternity leave, or the hours that young people can work.

What is 'family policy'?

New Right: A political philosophy that emphasises traditional moral and social values, particularly with regard to the family.

While governments of all parties claim to value the family, the Conservative government policies of the 1980s and 1990s were influenced by **New Right** political beliefs, which attach great importance to the family. The resulting policies have

Alan and Judith Kilshaw paid £8 200 to adopt twin babies from the USA, via the internet. However, the children were returned to the USA as a result of legal action by another couple, who had also paid money to the birth mother. To what extent should the government intervene to control and legislate for such activity?

- Changes in the law over the past 150 years reflect changing perceptions of families and family life. Women and children are no longer seen as the property of the man, but as independent people with rights within the family. Women can control their own financial affairs.

- Non-married partners have similar but not the same rights and responsibilities as those of married partners.

- Legislation has extended into what were previously seen as areas of private life where government had no business to intervene.

Nearly 35 000 children were placed on local child protection registers in March 1995. This amounts to 0.35% of all children under 18 years of age. The Government protects these children, in theory, from abuse by neglect, violence, emotional damage and sexual exploitation via the efforts of social services departments. (Alcock, P., Erskine, A. and May, M. (1998) *The student's companion to social policy*, Blackwell, Oxford)

been continued – albeit in a much-modified form – by the post-1997 Labour governments, which continue to attach importance to the family but have taken a rather more flexible approach to policy-making.

New Right thinking affected Conservative government legislation in various ways.

- A belief in traditional family values led to legislation that emphasised parental responsibilities. For example, the Child Support Agency was set up in 1991 to encourage parents to provide financial support for children in the event of marriage break-up. This also had an impact on criminal laws, which made parents responsible if their children were implicated in delinquent behaviours.

- Government agencies were given power to intervene in situations where children are endangered or in need of protection. For instance, there are regulations governing the role of schools in the case of children who are 'cared for' by social services. Sometimes these rules are affected by ideologies of family that may be considered partiarchal or Christian in ethos.

- There was concern about the role of the biological family. The New Right had a genuine desire to see the rights of birth parents extended, so The Children Act of 1989 gives fathers the right of access in the case of relationship breakdown between parents. This has been controversial – fathers who physically and emotionally abuse mothers still have the right of access to their children. Adopted children have had the right to access archive material in order to contact birth parents since 1975. Biological parents may soon have the right to access records related to children they gave up for adoption.

- There has been a growing concern with the rights of children, which is not just an element of New Right thinking, but part of a growing global concern enshrined in the United Nations Convention on the Rights of the Child, adopted in 1989. This has meant that institutions such as schools and local authorities are encouraged to set up youth forums and student councils. Children are now consulted on their wishes by social service departments responsible for their welfare.

Think it through

ADOPTION BOOST FOR GAY COUPLES

THE GOVERNMENT TODAY promised MPs a free vote in the Commons about whether to allow unmarried and gay couples to adopt children.

Although single people and unmarried couples, including homosexuals, are now regularly approved to adopt, only one partner can be registered as the child's legal guardian, leaving the other with no legal rights as a parent.

[The Health Secretary] Alan Milburn told MPs during Commons question time: 'The government's objective is to increase the number of children who have the opportunity, through adoption, to grow up as part of a loving, stable and permanent family.'

If the measures were passed by MPs in a free vote it would be up to the courts and adoption agencies to decide who would be suitable to adopt, he explained.

Adapted from: *The Guardian*, 7 May 2002
(http://society.guardian.co.uk/adoption/story)

1 Outline the proposed changes in the law governing the adoption of children by gay and unmarried couples.

2 Suggest two reasons why some people regard these changes in the law as necessary.

3 Outline and evaluate the view that governments can have a significant impact on the family lives of people in Britain.

www.ncb.org.uk, the National Children's Bureau website, includes a list of recent legislation that impacts upon the child in British society.

THE LAW DOES NOT SUPPORT ALL KINDS OF FAMILY RELATIONSHIPS

There are areas where the law appears to fail certain kinds of families. For instance, the extended family is often disregarded by legislation. There has been some debate about the rights of grandparents to maintain contact in the event of family breakdown or adoption of their grandchildren away from the family. The issues are serious enough for interest and pressure groups to develop in this area. The Children Act allows eligible relatives to apply for access orders, but in practice, this does not always happen. Tax incentives and pension laws seem to benefit people who choose to remain single. Feminists also point out that legislation seems to assume that women are the primary carers for children by offering them maternity leave, but not encouraging fathers to spend time with young children.

Round-up

Government policies can affect families in two ways. There are direct laws (affecting family structure) and indirect legislation (relating to education, social services, benefits and the economy), which also has an impact on family life and relationships. Political and ideological beliefs about the nature of the family underlie much government legislation and there is often an assumption that men are breadwinners and women are carers, which does not reflect the reality of the lives of many people in modern Britain.

Do families have a future?

One of the oldest communes in Britain is the Findhorn community in Scotland, founded in 1962 (www.findhorn.org).

Feminism: A theoretical perspective adopted mostly by women, which sees females as being oppressed by a patriarchal society.

In the 1970s there was a serious debate both in sociology and in the media, which suggested that the family as a social institution was dying. Rising divorce rates, changing sexual morality and increasing single parenthood through choice suggested that people were looking for alternative lifestyles that did not include traditional family life. A number of young professional people in European countries set up communes of various kinds and there was a fascination with the Jewish **kibbutz** system of communal family living.

Criticisms of the traditional family came from a number of directions.

- **Feminists** saw the family as a social institution that trapped women into a culture run by and for the benefit of men. There was political pressure to recognise that women and their children experienced unacceptable violence in the home. Radical feminists advocated lesbian lifestyles as being a political choice freeing women from the oppression of men, rather than as a response to a felt sexuality. Liberal feminists pointed out that women in marriage were likely to experience depression and had higher suicide rates than unmarried women.

- Marxists saw traditional families as reflecting the capitalist structures of society. Men viewed their wives as property. Children would inherit the wealth accumulated during lifetimes of work. In addition, the family reinforced false social values that produced a conformist workforce in order to labour in factories.

- Radical psychiatrists such as Laing (1960) and Cooper (1970) argued that family life literally made people mad. They saw **schizophrenia** as a rational response to the unnatural pressures of life in a nuclear family.

Schizophrenia does not mean 'split personality'. Look this word up in a psychology textbook to find out its real meaning.

During the 1980s New Right thinkers argued that the family as we know it could die out and believed that this was a serious threat to individuals and society. Charles Murray (1993), Peter Saunders (1995) and David Marsland (1989), in common with many conservative politicians, saw the family as under threat from the same changing moral values that made single parenthood acceptable in some sectors of society. Single mothers were associated with a range of social problems, such as criminal behaviour in young men, social irresponsibility that made it acceptable to receive benefits without attempting to work, and the failure of children to thrive educationally and socially.

Many people believe in a 'golden age' when things were better in the past than they are today. There is a widely held belief that families were happier in the past because there was little or no divorce and families seemed to stay together. In reality, the picture may be more complex because people who had family problems would have hidden the evidence for fear of family shame. We have little real evidence from the past to estimate how many people lived in loveless and unhappy family homes but had to stick together because they had little or no choice in the matter.

www.princes-trust.org.uk *gives access to The Prince's Trust fact-sheets, covering a variety of issues relating to young people and social change and well supported by statistical evidence.* **www.barnardos.org.uk/future_citizens/index.html** *is a good site, with interesting questions and stimulating materials to get you thinking about families.*

No	Yes
Family structures are disappearing; many people choose not to marry.	Family structures are merely changing. People may not have legal marriages, but they still form stable and recognisable partnerships.
An increasing number of children are born outside married relationships.	The majority of children are born to married couples, but many cohabiting couples marry after their children are born.
Divorce rates are high; this suggests that people marry too quickly and then don't work at their relationship.	It is difficult to know how many marriages in the past were unhappy; divorce was not an option for those couples. In addition, many divorcees remarry – it is not marriage as such, but the partner who was unsatisfactory.
Increasing numbers of women and children report violence and abuse.	In the past, abuse within families was not taken seriously and people were unaware of the scale of the problem. People nowadays have higher expectations of family relationships. They no longer accept abuse.
The State has taken over many of the traditional family roles such as care of children's education and health.	Many people still take on the burden of care for family members; the government is effectively subsidised in the role of care by extended family members who support the sick and disabled in their own homes.
Women are finding the traditional domestic and caring role unsatisfying so they are returning to work in large numbers.	Males are adapting to the changing economics of family life. Many are taking on domestic burdens and childcare as part of their contribution to the life of the family.
More people are in non-traditional families, e.g. those headed by gay couples.	These people may have a different sexuality, but they still choose to form relationships that are recognisable as families. Some people go on to develop these relationships by having (or adopting) children.
Changes in women's working patterns have eroded their desire to have children.	Birth rates are indeed falling. However, it is not clear whether this is due to the fact of female work or to the low status of parenting and the lack of support for parents from employers.
Many children are now raised in families that do not fit a traditional pattern and experience the break-up of their families while they are still young.	There is evidence to suggest that a loving family relationship in some form is a good way to raise children; many young offenders and troubled young people come from unstable home backgrounds or have been in care.

Think it through

GOVERNMENT PROPOSES CLASSES IN NON-TRADITIONAL FAMILY LIFE

SCHOOLCHILDREN should be taught about divorce, 're-partnering' and homosexual relationships in new 'parenthood education' lessons, according to government guidelines published today.

The final draft of the new guidelines, which emphasises the importance of 'stable relationships' but acknowledges that there is 'more variety about partnerships and family form', were leaked yesterday. The guidelines encourage teachers to share with pupils their own experience of parenting and relationships to 'bring to life' their lessons.

Tory MPs today expressed concern at the changes. 'We don't want to teach children that divorce or breaking up are normal or good,' said Julian Brazier, President of the Conservative family campaign. 'Our first duty is to teach children that parenting should fall within marriage.'

The new parenting curriculum will be taught alongside sex-education classes and include a section on '21st century parenting' – such as the concept of 're-partnering', when a parent establishes a new relationship after the break-up of a marriage or former relationship.

Although the education secretary, David Blunkett, is thought to have wanted more emphasis on traditional marriage, other education experts involved in compiling the guidelines were anxious to avoid making children who come from single-parent homes or have unmarried parents feel 'second class'.

Taylor, R. (2000) 'Classes in non-traditional family life proposed by government', *The Guardian*, Friday 12 May,

1 Describe the proposed changes on parenthood education.

2 What key family values do both Tory MPs and David Blunkett feel should be taught to children in school?

3 Outline and evaluate the suggestion that changes to family structure in modern Britain imply dissatisfaction with traditional family life.

Watch out

From reading the newspapers and watching soap operas on television, you would definitely start to think that family life is on the way out. Take care to balance this view with evidence from properly conducted sociological research.

Round-up

Writers in the 1960s and 1970s tended to regard changes in family patterns as a good thing, so that predictions of the death of the nuclear family were welcomed as being liberating. Later, more right-wing writers viewed the same changes as being pathological and dangerous for society. While there are changes in family structure that are well documented and clear from official statistics, the family (in terms of emotional complexity and personal satisfaction) probably remains much as it always has been for most people.

Families and households: summative review

This image shows an idealised image of what a family should be. But what is the reality of the recent family history behind a picture showing people at a happy time in their lives? It is the job of the sociologist to recognise the difference between image and reality and to attempt to see beneath the surface in order to investigate how families really operate.

For most people, the family is their important social grouping and it is therefore not surprising that it is an area of such concern to sociologists and politicians. It is from our family that we will learn our norms, values and mores. It is with our families that we expect to experience the major rituals of our lives: births, marriages and deaths. In essence, the family is the first place where we will learn our own culture because it is within the family that we are socialised from the selfishness of childhood into the socially aware and responsive adults that we become.

Functionalists explain the role of families in our lives when they point out that families perform a number of tasks:

- the socialisation of children
- providing support and stability for adult personalities
- providing sexual control
- providing a sense of identity
- meeting the physical and emotional needs of individuals.

The debate about the nature of the family focuses on family change and family structure because there are those who insist (for ideological, legal, religious or moral reasons) that some family forms are better than others. In Britain, the mainstream ideology of the family is based on the view that a family should consist of a heterosexual couple and their children (the nuclear family). This view is based on Christian teaching, which emphasises marriage for the whole of adult life and with the purpose of procreating children. This type of family is sometimes called 'the cereal packet norm', in recognition that this form of family is the type targeted by advertisers of domestic products. Other cultures have a variety of different experiences of family organisation and structure, but in Britain these are not always accorded the same status and support as the nuclear family. Plural marriage of one partner to more than one spouse is punishable with a prison sentence in the UK, though acceptable, if not desirable to Muslims.

Is the family under threat?

Those with a strong emotional or ideological attachment to the idea of the nuclear family have argued that nuclear families were always typical of Britain, and that we should be concerned about the falling number of families that conform to the traditional pattern. There are strong arguments to counter this view – we know very little about families in the past. However, we do know that the Victorian ideology of the happy nuclear family hid the reality of a society that accepted child abuse and prostitution, wife battering, high levels of child mortality, illegitimacy, drug abuse in the home, the prevalence of mistresses and adultery, and a situation in which women and children had very little power over the activities and actions of men.

Looking at modern families, there appears to be greater tolerance of a variety of family forms. Divorce, cohabitation and single motherhood are accepted as normal life events, whereas these life situations would have been regarded as unusual fifty or sixty years ago. Those on the New Right argue that this represents a moral decline and that family life is under threat, whereas others see this as the sign of a changing society and regard it is being of no especial significance in terms of the popularity of the family.

Changes to family life since 1945

These are many and varied and can be summarised as follows.

- There are fewer children born nowadays.
- Many people are remaining voluntarily childless.
- Children are financially and emotionally dependent on their parents for longer.
- More people cohabit.
- There has been an increase in divorce, though in recent years this trend has gone into reverse.
- There has been an increase in blended families, i.e. where there are children from more than one relationship.
- There has been an increase in single parenthood so it is possible for a woman now to choose whether or not to have children alone.
- The average age of motherhood has increased.
- Marriage occurs later in life.
- Men and women tend to be more flexible in their allocation of domestic roles.
- Women are more likely to participate in the paid workforce
- There has been a highly significant fall in adult mortality so that people are now living into extreme old age.
- For those in early retirement and with sufficient income, older age can be very positive in terms of supporting their children, their own older parents and enjoying leisure.
- For those in later old age there are attendant problems, possibly with health or disability issues.

Reasons for changes to family life

There are many reasons why changes have taken place in family life, but most fall within one of the following categories.

- *Ideological and political change*
  - Many men genuinely believe in equality for women and children so they have modified their attitudes and behaviour towards their wives and daughters.
  - Many women have been affected by the ideas of gender equality promoted by feminists throughout the century.
  - The government has tried to make men more responsible for their children via the Child Support Agency.

- *Pragmatic change*
  - Men have very little choice but to help in the home if their wives and partners are working long hours.
  - House prices have risen so that two salaries are needed to pay a mortgage on a home.

- *Legislative change*
  - Divorce is easier to obtain than it once was.
  - Homosexuality has been decriminalised.

- *Moral and social change*
  - Fewer people feel the need to be bound by Christian religious teaching on family and marriage.
  - Divorce has become more widely acceptable and family forms have undergone structural change as a result.

- *Medical and technical change*
  - Contraception is more easily obtainable.
  - People live longer and in better health.
  - People can use medical technology to have children beyond the natural age of conception or as a result of donation of sperm and eggs.

Moral panics and the family

Many people consider that the family is in moral danger and this has provoked media debates on a number of issues. Over the past twenty years, there has been discussion of a variety of topics that would never previously have been mentioned in any public forum because family life was hitherto considered private and there were also taboos about discussing sexuality. A very dark side to family life has been revealed, though not all moral panics are equally grounded in factual basis. Some areas of concern have been:

- *child abuse within the family* – there is now greater awareness of very sad cases where children have experienced cruelty and murder at the hands of their carers.
- *domestic violence* – both females and males have been murdered at the hands of their partners.
- *single mothers* – young single mothers have been especially targeted by press reports as irresponsible, choosing to have children at the expense of taxpayers.

Irrespective of the validity or otherwise of the moral panic about these subjects, the public perception is such that governments have been forced into creating laws in order to show that they are acting on public concerns. Some of the panics have therefore led to major policy decisions and changes.

The future of the family

It can be dangerous to try to predict what the future will bring. However, simply from looking at current trends, one can see a number of patterns emerge that may impact on family life in the future.

- The proportion of older people in the population will grow as fewer children are born and death rates fall.
- While most older people will enjoy good health for much of their retirement, the number of dependent elderly will increase.
- The average age of first-time mothers will become steadily older; many women will remain childless either by choice or because they have no option.
- Marriage rates will continue to fall, whereas cohabitation will increase.
- People still tend to form families, but fewer of these families will conform to the traditional 'cereal packet' norm as other types of family structure become more widely acceptable.

Families and households: self-assessment questions

1   Identify the three different forms of family structure that are studied by sociologists.

2   Complete each of the following sentences using the appropriate word from the list (i–iii).
   a The term used to describe leaving paid employment as a result of age or ill-health is known as _____.
   b The term used to describe the period of retirement when people are still relatively healthy and can enjoy leisure pursuits is known as _____.
   c The term used to describe extreme old age, sometimes accompanied by ill-health or disability is known as _____.

   i   The third age
   ii   Elderly old
   iii Retirement

3   Suggest two ways in which older people can support their families.

4   Match the term with its correct meaning.
   a Marriage to multiple partners at the same time
   b Marriage to a single partner at a time
   c Marriage to more than a single partner, but only one at a time

   i   Monogamy
   ii   Serial monogamy
   iii Polygamy

5   Which of the following explanations comes closest to explaining the term 'New Right'?
   a Having new ideas about the nature of the family.
   b A political philosophy that emphasises traditional moral and social values particularly with regard to the family.
   c Voting for the Conservative party in elections.

6   What is the meaning of the word 'household'?

7   Suggest two different ways in which the concept of family can be operationalised.

8   What is the difference between a horizontal and a vertical extended family?

9   What is the average completed family size in Britain?
   a 3.5 children
   b 2.4 children
   c 1.7 children

10 Decide whether each of the following statements is true or false.
   a The average age of marriage in Britain is falling.
   b More divorce is taking place each year.
   c There are now more blended families in Britain than there were 20 years ago.

11 What proportion of British households are lone-parent families?
   a 35%
   b 15%
   c 6%

12 Suggest three factors that have contributed to family change in Britain.

13 Match each of the following terms with its meaning.
   a Parents with adult children who have left home.
   b Older people who take on the care of younger family members.
   c Children who are placed with parent substitutes who are paid small amounts to care for these children.
   d Families formed between people of different ethnicities and cultures.

   i   Grandparenting
   ii   Cross-cultural families
   iii Empty-nest families
   iv   Fostering

14 Describe two different forms of communal living.

15 The system of communal living established in Israel is known as:
 a Kaddish
 b Kosher
 c Kibbutz

16 Which of the following meanings comes closest to explaining the term 'arranged marriage'?
 a The marriage is viewed as a contract between two consenting adults, but it is negotiated between families.
 b Two adults who have never met before are married because their families insist.
 c People are forced into marriage with a stranger against their will.

17 What is the term used by feminists to describe the control of society and the family by men?

18 What sociological term would you use to describe each of the following?
 a A family where men and women have agreed some degree of equality in the home.
 b The tasks that are traditionally associated with adult male and female roles within a family.
 c Men who challenged traditional gender roles for males and who were willing to work in the house and take on domestic challenges.

19 Which of the partners in a marriage is more likely to initiate a divorce?

20 What are the causes of single parenthood?

21 Which French historian claimed that childhood is a modern social construction?
 a Philippe Pisces
 b Philippe Aries
 c Philippe Libra

22 Which of these statements about divorce are true and which are false?
 a The average duration of a marriage is approximately 5 years.
 b Just over half of all divorcing couples have dependent children under 16 years of age.
 c The average age of divorce is between 35 and 39, but is falling.
 d Couples from the wealthier socio-economic groups are more likely to divorce than those in lower groups.

23 Is cohabitation an alternative to marriage?

24 Suggest four reasons why divorce statistics tended to rise throughout the twentieth century.

Families and households: a timeline

Engels, basing his analysis on Marxism claims families are concerned with ownership and control of women and children. Capitalism is reproduced within family (1880s)

Beginnings of welfare support, improving public-health measures increase life-expectancy for children so families increase in size from start of century

Anthropologists look at family forms in other cultures

1900 1 2 3 4 5 6 7 8 9 1910 1 2 3 4 5 6 7 8 9 1920 1 2 3 4 5 6 7 8 9 1930 1 2 3 4 5 6 7 8 9 1940 1 2 3 4 5 6 7 8 9

Development of reliable contraception (the Pill). Growing acceptance of ideas of feminism

Legislation to support family, e.g. Child Support Agency. Changing technology of reproduction so that IVF child is born

Labour support for traditional view of family results in legislation that forces parents to take responsibility for children: parental imprisonment for truancy, legislation related to anti-social children

American studies into family see nuclear family as being 'normal' family. British studies look at nuclear and extended families in working-class areas. Acceptance among mainstream sociology of subordinate/domestic role of women

Feminists begin to look at the socialisation of girls into subordinate family roles; challenges to traditional notions of family from a variety of different groups

Concern with changing status of boys and crisis of masculinity. Fear that boys in single-parent families have no acceptable male role-model

1950 1 2 3 4 5 6 7 8 9 1960 1 2 3 4 5 6 7 8 9 1970 1 2 3 4 5 6 7 8 9 1980 1 2 3 4 5 6 7 8 9 1990 1 2 3 4 5 6 7 8 9 2000 1 2 3

Post-war divorce rates increase dramatically due to legal aid being introduced. Baby boom – large number of children born

Focus on changing conjugal roles, acknowledging beginnings of male willingness to take on domestic roles. Beginnings of feminism as a popular concern

Liberalisation of variety of laws affecting social rights: abortion, divorce and homosexuality. A variety of gender-equality laws make employment more attractive to women. Challenges by feminists to accepted family practice such as domestic violence

Moral panics about single parenthood, reaction from New Right, which sees family as under threat from changing moral values

Women now accepted in workplace; birth-rates fall among educated women. Increasing life-expectancy means that average age of population is growing older

Growth in policy-oriented research and research into family organisation to see what makes a 'successful' family

Section 3 Mass media

Mass media: a mindmap

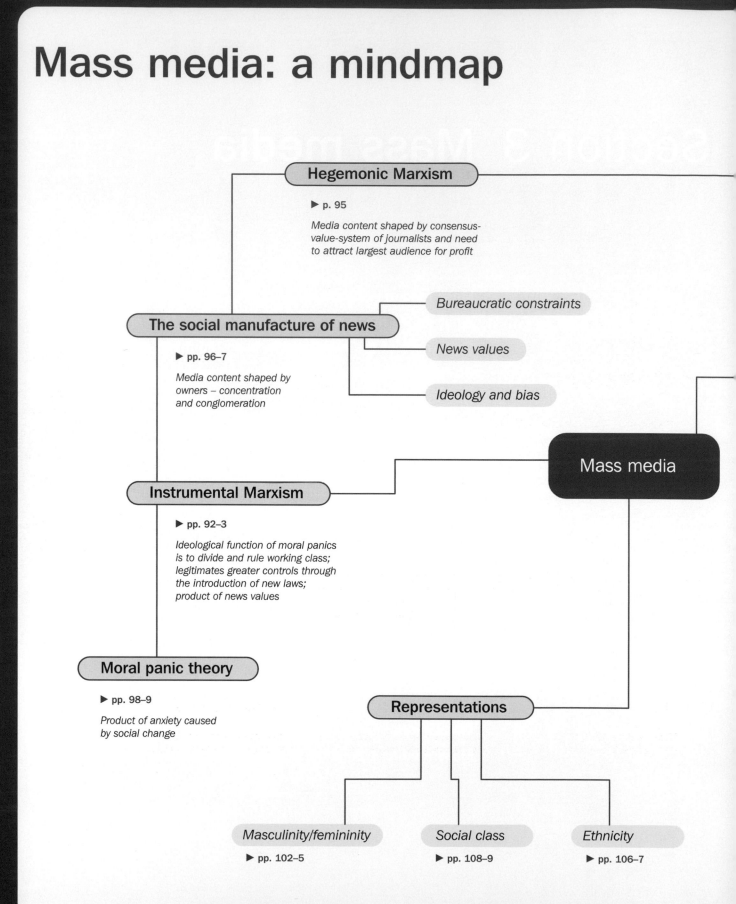

Hegemonic Marxism

▶ p. 95

Media content shaped by consensus-value-system of journalists and need to attract largest audience for profit

The social manufacture of news

▶ pp. 96–7

Media content shaped by owners – concentration and conglomeration

Bureaucratic constraints

News values

Ideology and bias

Instrumental Marxism

▶ pp. 92–3

Ideological function of moral panics is to divide and rule working class; legitimates greater controls through the introduction of new laws; product of news values

Mass media

Moral panic theory

▶ pp. 98–9

Product of anxiety caused by social change

Representations

Masculinity/femininity

▶ pp. 102–5

Social class

▶ pp. 108–9

Ethnicity

▶ pp. 106–7

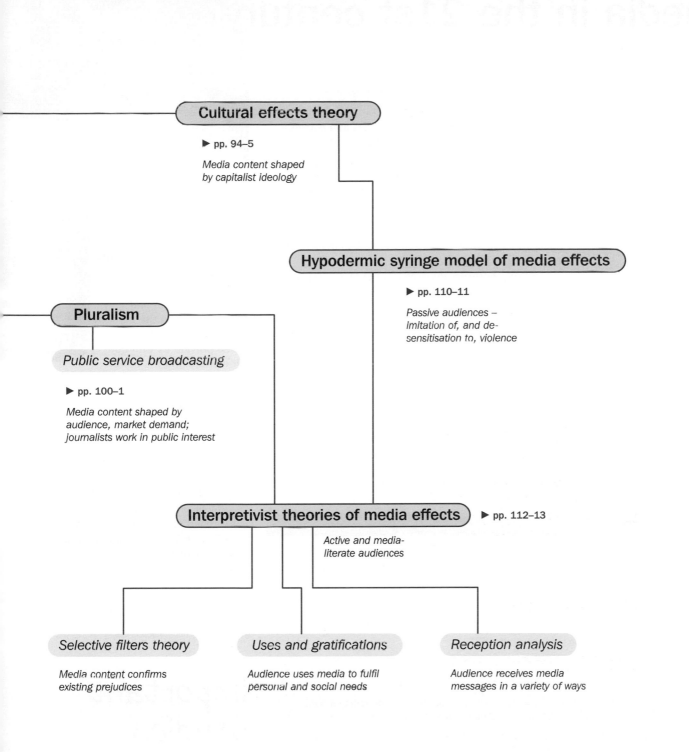

Cultural effects theory

▶ pp. 94–5

*Media content shaped
by capitalist ideology*

Hypodermic syringe model of media effects

▶ pp. 110–11

*Passive audiences –
imitation of, and de-
sensitisation to, violence*

Pluralism

Public service broadcasting

▶ pp. 100–1

*Media content shaped by
audience, market demand;
journalists work in public interest*

Interpretivist theories of media effects   ▶ pp. 112–13

*Active and media-
literate audiences*

Selective filters theory

Media content confirms
existing prejudices

Uses and gratifications

Audience uses media to fulfil
personal and social needs

Reception analysis

Audience receives media
messages in a variety of ways

What do we mean by mass media in the 21st century?

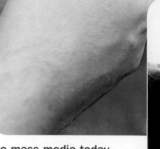

In the twentieth century, the term 'mass media' was often used to refer to two ways of communicating news, information and entertainment to mass audiences:

- the print media, i.e. newspapers, magazines and comics
- electronic audio-visual media, i.e. television, radio, cinema and music.

If we examine these forms of media closely, we can see that they have a number of things in common:

- They can reach millions of people at the same time.
- They use specialised technology, e.g. the Olympic Games and the World Cup are transmitted live to hundreds of countries using satellite technology.
- The relationship between the producers of media messages (i.e. media institutions such as the BBC, Hollywood, newspaper proprietors, etc.) and media audiences is generally a one-way relationship, i.e. they send, we receive. The relationship is not usually an **interactive** one – McQuail (1994) described it as '**asymmetrical** and unbalanced'.
- Media messages are commodities because they are generally distributed as products or services to be sold in the commercial market.

 One form of media, i.e. advertising, takes both a print and electronic audio-visual form.

 Think of the number of people you know who read newspapers or magazines; think about how few people you know who do not have televisions.

Interactive relationship: A relationship in which the parties respond to each other.

Asymmetrical: Unequal.

The mass media today are the main source of news, information and entertainment in the modern world – increasingly, the media provide us with both our identity and the means of interacting with others

A media-saturated society?

The twentieth century saw a massive growth in the range of mass-media institutions, technologies and products, to the point that we now talk of living in a media-saturated society.

The evolution of the mass media	
1910	Cinema takes off as a form of popular entertainment.
1926	The British Broadcasting Corporation (BBC) is brought under state control and BBC Radio, financed by radio licences, is set up.
1939–55	The height of popularity of BBC radio – it attracts an audience of many millions.
1953	The Queen's Coronation helps to popularise television.
1955	ITV is set up in competition with the BBC.
1957	16.7 million national newspapers are sold daily in the UK.
1962	The first live satellite pictures are broadcast from the USA.
1964	BBC2 begins. Pop music develops a major presence on **pirate radio stations**. The BBC eventually reacts by setting up Radio 1 in 1967.
1967	Colour television is broadcast for the first time. The Beatles sing 'All You Need is Love' on the first world-wide satellite link-up.
1972	Independent radio is launched.
1982	Channel 4 is set up.
1984	The first cable television channels are set up in the UK.
1989	Satellite television via Sky is broadcast for the first time in the UK.

Research issue It is not difficult to find out how many households own televisions and to collect information about the number of hours for which they are switched on. It is more difficult to collect reliable and valid data about what programmes people are actually watching.

Pirate radio stations: Radio stations that transmit illegally because they don't have government broadcasting licences.

Important studies

Lash and Urry (1994) argued that the internet was potentially a new source of inequality because information is the main means of profit and power in the post-industrial world. Wealth now depends on how well connected we are to the global information superhighway.

The developments of the 1990s

The speed of development in mass media over the past fifteen years has been phenomenal. Traditional forms of media continue to be very popular. We now have access to hundreds of television channels – terrestrial, cable and satellite – and cinema audiences have increased significantly throughout the 1990s. Videos, and more recently DVDs, sell in massive numbers. The magazine industry offers more choice than ever, whereas newspapers in the UK – especially the tabloids – continue to sell more than ten million copies a day. In the 1990s, CDs became the major music medium as vinyl records were phased out. Computer and video games, especially those linked to Play Station and the X-Box, became multi-million pound businesses in the 1990s.

Media sociologists have noted that a number of media forms are now combining to create new outputs for new markets. For examples, film companies might market a film using multiple promotion in newspapers, magazines, television documentaries, fast-food outlets, toy stores, websites, music, etc. This not only promotes the primary media product, i.e. the film, but will also promote secondary media products, i.e. the soundtrack album, the video, DVD, magazines devoted to the genre, etc. This is known in the trade as 'synergy'.

The converging mass media

There are signs that the mass media of the near future are likely to be characterised by the mass media *converging* or coming together in a technological sense. Recent developments in digital technology have led to the arrival of low-cost and accessible digital media products and increased the popularity of personal computers and the internet. These are increasingly seen as essential media in our homes, e.g. multi-media technology such as the CD-ROM with MP3 has enabled people to obtain and share music via computers and the internet in new ways. High-capacity broadband networks will probably lead to integrated digital technology replacing the separate telephones, radio, television and computers that people use today.

The internet

The internet and world-wide web only took off as forms of media in the UK in the late 1990s yet by 2002, 42% of UK households were connected (McIntosh, 2002). Women in 1999 accounted for 50% of internet users, using it to e-mail friends, to visit chatrooms and to buy books and CDs online. In contrast, men used the internet for playing games, downloading software and reading newsgroup messages.

Some sociologists are concerned about the emergence of a possible '**digital underclass**' whose existing disadvantages may be reinforced by their being unable to access the information superhighway, e.g. 80% of the richest households have internet access against only 11% of the poorest (Williams, 2000).

Research task You might decide to carry out a survey into digital inequality across social class, gender, etc. You will need to think very carefully about how you will access a representative sample. Obviously, people approached via e-mail, or outside a computer store, would not be representative.

Digital underclass: People who do not have the material means to access new media technology.

Think it through

In the latest survey of non-users of the Internet, 72% say they are very unlikely to access it in the next year. This group represents nearly one-third of all adults. 44% of them say they haven't got an interest in using the Internet. But 25% say they lack a computer, or access to one, and 20% say they lack confidence or the skills to try it out. However, those who have never used the Internet may not get the chance because other forms of media technology may supersede the personal computer, e.g. mobile phones, which enjoy near-saturation levels of ownership in the UK, will be replaced by devices with net-style information services and e-mail fitted as standard. However, despite these technological advances, it remains clear that a gulf in skills, opportunity and interest remains.

Adapted from: McIntosh, N. (2002) 'The widening digital divide', *The Guardian*, 12 October

1 Identify three reasons why one-third of the adult population does not access the Internet.

2 Identify and explain three benefits of modern media technology.

3 Discuss the view that the evolution of media technology is leading to new forms of inequality and new sets of social problems.

Round-up

The media affect all aspects of our lives; there is now media saturation. Moreover, the evolution of media technology has meant that it no longer matters where and when an event takes place; the mass media ensure that immediate coverage is beamed into our homes. In this sense, the modern media has 'shrunk' the world and consequently we now live in a 'global village'.

Do the owners of the mass media have too much power?

The Instrumental Marxist view

It is argued, mainly by Marxist sociologists, that the mass media act as an ideological state apparatus. They argue that the content of the mass media is deliberately manipulated by media owners in order to reproduce, continue and justify the inequalities of wealth and power produced by capitalism.

Marxists are particularly concerned about five trends that have occurred over the past 20 years in terms of ownership of the media.

Is the ownership of the mass media in the hands of a small élite?

- *Concentration* – Media ownership across the world was once evenly spread across a large number of relatively small and competing companies. However, takeovers and mergers have become common in recent years and **media conglomerates** have emerged that monopolise ownership of a range of different types of media. For example, nine corporate giants own the media in the USA, whilst six companies control 94% of newspaper sales in the UK.

Media conglomerates: Large-scale media companies that often have global economic interests.

- *Vertical integration* – Media companies often own all the stages in the production, distribution and consumption of a media product. For example, the media giant AOL-Time-Warner owns the film studios, the distribution companies and the cinema multiplexes in which its films are shown.

- *Cross-media ownership* – Many media conglomerates own more than one media form. For example, Rupert Murdoch's company, News Corporation, owns newspapers across Australia, the UK and the USA, as well as satellite television stations in Europe (i.e. Sky) and Asia (i.e. Star TV) and film and television studios (i.e. Twentieth Century Fox) and major publishing interests (i.e. HarperCollins).

- *Diversification* – Many media conglomerates have diversified their interests so that changing economic fortunes in one sphere may be counterbalanced by stability in another. A good example of this in the UK is Richard Branson's Virgin: in addition to its media interests (i.e. music, films, cinemas and publishing), it owns an airline, a train service and a mobile phone company, as well as providing various financial services, soft drinks, wedding outfits, etc.

- *Transnational ownership* – Thirty years ago, most media companies (apart from the Hollywood film studios) operated mostly within their own countries. Now, however, the bigger companies have established themselves as global operators by buying up smaller media producers across the world.

To investigate the ownership of the media, you could visit the websites of the key conglomerates. In the USA, these are AOL-Time-Warner, Disney, News Corp, Viacom, Sony, Seagram, AT &T/Liberty Media, Bertelsmann, Microsoft and GE. In the UK, check out Virgin, Pearson, Granada, Daily Mail and General Trust (DMGT), EMAP, United MAI, IPC, Polygram, EMI, and Hollinger.

Research issue The fact that media-owners are known to interfere with the product of the companies they own does not necessarily mean that they are engaged in some sort of joint conspiracy. Researching this issue would require some first-hand data collection. However, it is notoriously difficult to do first-hand research on the activities of the rich and powerful.

Marxists argue that if national governments fail to legislate to prevent cross-media ownership within their own countries, the control such companies have over the flow of information to the general public will become a problem for several reasons.

- Media owners can hold enormous power over the hearts and minds of the general public. This means that unelected individuals may have more influence than the normal democratic political process.

- Editors may learn that there are a number of 'sacred cow' issues, i.e. issues that owners feel very strongly about. Consequently, these may be avoided or dealt with very cautiously.

- Pressures from sponsors or advertisers could limit editors' freedom to cover issues of concern, e.g. if a story appears that is critical of a major advertisers' activities, it may be played down or excluded from the news process altogether.

- Media owners may view alternative media and new media technologies as a threat. Owners may use their economic and legal powers to close down new media that threaten its economic or political interests. For example, the free music downloading site, Napster, was the subject of a sustained legal attack by the music conglomerates.

- It is claimed that news and documentaries no longer encourage us to think critically about the state of the world. It has been suggested that news has been 'dumbed-down' – it is now presented as 'infotainment', whilst the number of serious investigative documentaries on British television has declined by 50% in the past five years.

Important studies

James Curran, in *Power without responsibility* (Curran and Seaton, 1991), argues that, in the post-war period, owners of newspapers and other business corporations had similar educational and economic backgrounds and similar conservative ideologies. Since the 1970s, a new generation of mainly right-wing proprietors has emerged, with a more interventionist and personalised style of management. Curran argues that these proprietors have downgraded their coverage of serious political issues in the tabloid press by giving more space to human interest stories, entertainment features, sport, competitions, etc. In addition, coverage of public affairs has been simplified and reduced to the level of personalities, e.g. Blair versus Saddam Hussain.

The critique of the Marxist position

There are problems with the quality of the evidence for this Marxist argument. Much of it is anecdotal and speculative, rather than scientific and proven. For example, it is fairly easy to find stories that suggest interference by media owners (Mick Underwood's website, *see below*, is full of them!). However, this does not prove a sustained and deliberate attempt to align media content with the economic and ideological interests of the capitalist class or even the interests of owners. There is plenty of evidence to suggest that media owners have often failed to get their own way, e.g. in 1999 Murdoch failed to get control of Manchester United because the Government blocked his bid. The existence of a fierce newspaper price war does not suggest a united media class. In any case, even if media owners *are* influencing content, this does not necessarily mean they are influencing the *audience*.

New-media technologies

New-media technologies may have led to wider choice for consumers and more opportunities for audiences to influence the form and content of media. For example, the internet has provided access to unlimited information and therefore more choice, education and opportunities to be an active citizen. Recently, the internet has proved an effective means of co-ordinating international protest against global capitalism.

Think it through

We know which newspapers endorsed which political parties at the last election, although the extent to which they covered the campaign and the enthusiasm of these endorsements varied widely between them. To different degrees *The Guardian*, the *Independent*, *The Financial Times*, *The Mirror*, *The Sun* and the *Daily Star* recommended voting for New Labour in 1997. Equally and again with varying levels of enthusiasm the *Daily Telegraph*, *The Express* and the *Daily Mail* supported the Tories. Research suggests that there is a clear association between voting behaviour and newspaper readership. The majority of *Daily Mirror* readers voted Labour whilst the majority of *Daily Mail* readers voted Conservative. There are two possible explanations for this finding: either readers are following the endorsements of their favourite newspapers, or editors are carefully reflecting the views of their readers. If, as seems likely, both things are happening at the same time then clearly editors, or in some cases newspaper proprietors, are exercising real political power.

Adapted from: Whiteley, Professor Paul (2000), 'The Paper Chase', *The Guardian*, 9 May

1 What is the relationship between newspaper readership and voting behaviour?

2 How far do Whiteley's findings support the Instrumental Marxist theory of the media?

3 Outline and assess the view that newspaper proprietors exercise real political power.

www.cultsock.ndirect.co.uk *is an excellent 'sociology of the media' site maintained by Mick Underwood. It is excellent in its review of who owns what in the British media.*
www.sonoma.edu/projectcensored *is a website based on an annual research project undertaken at Sonoma State University, which documents major news stories that are ignored by the press.*

Round-up

Instrumental Marxism sees the mass media as playing a key ideological role, alongside the educational system, in making sure that the class inequality of capitalism remains largely undisturbed. This is because media owners, as part of the capitalist class, benefit from the way capitalism is currently organised. However, the evidence to support this view is not proven.

Do the mass media shape how we think about the world?

Cultural effects theory

Marxists argue that the function of media content is to disguise the true extent of economic and political inequality in capitalist societies and to keep the working class in a state of 'false class consciousness'. In other words, the media shapes how the working class thinks about the world and persuades them to be content with their lot. As we saw on pp. 92–3, Marxists see owners as playing an important role in this process.

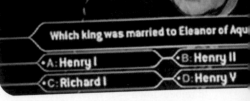

How the media affects its audience	
Media content	*Alleged effect*
The emphasis on entertainment on television, e.g. daily soap operas, sit-coms and reality shows.	People are not encouraged to think critically about important issues such as the organisation of society, inequality, etc.
Sex, scandal and sport in tabloid newspapers. Game shows such as *Who Wants to be a Millionaire?* and their focus on competition and material rewards.	The working class becomes committed to materialism, consumerism and competitiveness – essential values in the smooth running of capitalism.
Films and television programmes about crime and the police, which generally show criminals being caught and punished.	Viewers take in the message that society needs rules (i.e. laws) and that we should stick to them or face negative consequences.

Most of us have strong beliefs about wealth, politicians and who the bad guys are in the world. But where do such beliefs come from? Do we make up our own minds about these things or do we have our minds made up for us by the media?

Important studies

Morrison's analysis (1992) of the reporting of the 1991 Gulf War showed that politicians who were critical of the conflict were often given less access to television media.

Marxists therefore argue that the mass media has created a 'mass society' in which the working-class audience is mainly passive because it receives a media content focused on a superficial and uncritical popular culture. Consequently, such an audience rarely questions its position at the bottom of the socio-economic hierarchy.

The critique of the cultural effects model

The cultural effects model is criticised because it underestimates the audience's ability to interpret media content in a variety of ways or even to resist ruling-class messages. Past evidence of industrial action and working-class protest suggests that the British working class is neither passive nor easily manipulated.

Pluralism

Media professionals generally believe in the pluralist model of the media, which argues that the mass media do not shape the thinking of the population. Three distinct strands can be seen in this argument.

* *The market*
  Pluralists argue that the decisions of those who own and control the media are shaped by the market (i.e. by the need to make profit). They therefore argue that the content of the media depends upon the general public who buys the newspapers, magazines, etc. and who form the television and cinema audiences. Ultimate control therefore lies with the consumer. If the media does not give the public what it wants, the public will react by not buying or watching the product and consequently the newspaper, magazine, etc. will fail or the programme will be cancelled.

  It is also argued that this '**free market**' produces a competitive media that caters for a wide range of political viewpoints and therefore increases choice for media consumers (i.e. more television channels, newspapers, magazines, etc.). This is seen as being healthy for democracy.

* Some sociologists have observed a gradual decline in the time and space devoted to serious news both on television and in tabloid newspapers. The audience's lack of access to news and facts may mean their attitudes are easier to manipulate.

Free market: An economic system based on free competition between those willing to invest and/or take risks with capital.

- *The fourth estate*
  Pluralists argue that the mass media are the guardians of democracy, the watchdogs of public morality and the defenders of the public interest. As Underwood notes, the media presents itself as a fourth 'power' that checks and counterbalances the government, parliament and the judiciary (see www.cultsoc.ndirect.co.uk). It does this by scrutinising the political and economic élite and policing their activities through means such as investigative reporting. Pluralists note that such journalism has brought down US presidents (for example, Nixon and the Watergate scandal) and in the UK resulted in the resignations and even imprisonment of high-profile politicians such as Jeffrey Archer. Pluralists therefore argue that journalists and editors are motivated by professional **news values** that stress **objectivity**, **integrity**, **impartiality** and social responsibility.

- *State controls*
  Pluralists point out that owners and journalists are not free to act totally as they wish because they are governed by:
  - legislation restricting media monopolies
  - rules regarding the quality of programming, e.g. Channel 4 is required by its charter to cater for minority tastes and needs
  - the contempt-of-court and libel laws
  - watchdogs such as the Press Complaints Commission and the Broadcasting Standards Council.

  In addition, pluralists argue that the existence of public broadcasting organisations such as the BBC (see pp. 100–1) also ensures democratic pluralism because such organisations are not motivated by profit and are governed by rules of impartiality.

News values: What journalists think is newsworthy.

Objectivity: Without bias.

Integrity: Trustworthiness.

Impartiality: Neutrality.

Consensus: Broad agreement on basic values.

KEY QUESTIONS TO ASK A PLURALIST

- How much choice and diversity really exists in the media? Think about the range of choices transmitted to females via women's magazines (see p. 103) or how different types of media cater for minority ethnic groups (see pp. 106–7).

- How far is choice restricted to those who can afford to buy?

- Can journalists with mortgages and families afford to have principles?

- Do advertisers have too much power over media content?

Hegemonic Marxism

Hegemonic Marxists such as members of the Glasgow University Media Group (GUMG, 1993) believe that media content, especially news, often benefits ruling-class interests. However, this is not the result of owners manipulating media content. Rather, it results from the social background of media professionals – journalists and broadcasters (who tend to be white, middle class and male) usually hold a **consensus** view on most issues. For example, they genuinely believe that the UK does not require radical change and that dialogue and debate rather than conflict is the best way to bring about change if it is required. Those who suggest otherwise are likely to be labelled as 'extremist'.

There is also a market dimension to this consensus view of the world. Journalists and broadcasters aim to attract the largest possible audiences. It is assumed that the general public also believes in the consensus view and therefore journalistic news values (see pp. 96–7) assume that the public will approve of media criticism of so-called 'extremist' ideas.

Hegemonic Marxists argue that this emphasis on consensus results in ruling-class **hegemony** because capitalism is rarely critically analysed or challenged in the media. Consequently, media content sets an ideological agenda about what we should think about and how we should think.

Hegemony: Cultural domination, usually by an economically powerful group.

Think it through

The case is often put that where there are more channels, more programmes to choose from, diversity inevitably follows. However, LeDuc comments, in reference to claims of increased channel choice 'it resembles the degree of diversity in dining opportunities experienced when a McDonalds restaurant begins business in a town already served by Burger King'. More sometimes actually means less. Golding and Murdock argue that there may be a struggle between competing ideas in the media but this is not the amicable and equal free-for-all identified by pluralism. Some ideas are backed by greater material resources and have easier access to the major means of publicity and policy-making such as those of advertisers and conservative politicians backed by capitalist corporations.

Adapted from: Watson, J. (1998) *Media communication*, Macmillan, London

1 In your own words, explain LeDuc's critique of pluralism.

2 Identify and explain the two weaknesses of pluralism outlined by Golding and Murdock.

3 Outline and assess the view that the diversity of media in the contemporary UK ensures that audiences are exposed to a plurality of opinions.

Round-up

The Marxist case – that media content, whether deliberately or unconsciously, reflects ruling-class interests and shapes how we think about the world – is an attractive one. However, it is undermined by the fact that there is no proof that audiences passively accept what is being fed to them. Audiences are selective and are often critical (see pp. 112–13). However, the pluralist argument that audiences determine media content is no more convincing. How can we know what we want if the media don't present us with all viewpoints?

How is the news constructed?

The social manufacture of the news

The news is our main source of information about what is going on in the world. Most of us recognise that newspapers contain some degree of political bias. However, we tend to think of television news as neutral – a 'window on the world', reporting on what is going on in an impartial way.

However, critics of the media argue that 'news' is not impartial. Events happen but this does not guarantee that they become news because it is clearly not possible for every single event to be reported. The reality is that news is actually a socially manufactured product because it is the result of a process of selection. Editors and journalists, and sometimes proprietors – '**gatekeepers**' – make choices and judgements about which events are important enough to cover and how to cover them. In other words, media professionals are involved in agenda-setting – they prioritise events and select which ones will be defined as 'news'. There are three main influences on the process of selecting the news:

- organisational or bureaucratic routines
- the news values held by media organisations.
- **ideology** and bias.

Evidence from social surveys indicates that the general public trusts television news more than newspapers to give them an impartial view of the news

Organisational or bureaucratic routines

Newspapers and TV news programmes do not react spontaneously to world events. News coverage is affected by constraints that arise from how news gathering is organised.

EXAMPLES OF ORGANISATIONAL CONSTRAINTS

Financial costs
Sending staff overseas and booking satellite connections can be very expensive and may result in 'news' reports even when very little is actually happening. In 1989 ITN missed out on live coverage of the pro-democracy protests and subsequent massacre in China because its budget for covering foreign affairs had been exhausted.

Time or space available
News has to be cut to fit either the time available for a news bulletin or the column space in a newspaper. This telescoping of events can lead to ideas about the event being distorted.

Deadlines
Television news can bring us news as it happens, e.g. the destruction of the World Trade Center. Newspapers have to focus on yesterday's news; this is why they tend to have more focus on analysis.

The audience
The content of the news and how it is presented is a reaction to the type of audience that is watching or the social characteristics of a newspaper's readers. For example, Channel 5 news is characterised by short, snappy bulletins because it is aimed at a young audience. *The Sun* uses basic language because it believes this is what its readership wants.

Ratings and circulation
Commercial pressures can lead to the dumbing-down of news and less serious coverage in favour of human-interest stories and entertainment.

Gatekeepers: Media personnel who decide what counts as news.

Ideology: A set of ideas that offers explanations for the way things are or ought to be.

Primary definers: Powerful groups (e.g. the government) that have easier and more effective access to the media.

Power élite: The minority who control economic and political power.

Marginalised groups: Groups of people who are excluded from economic and political power, e.g. the poor.

*New Labour has been heavily criticised for its use of 'spin doctors' – one public relations specialist was forced to resign after she sent an e-mail advising that the media focus on the aftermath of September 11, 2001 meant that this was a good time to release bad news on government policy.

News values

News values refer to what journalists, editors and broadcasters consider as 'newsworthy', i.e. interesting enough to appeal to and attract a large enough readership or audience. What is regarded as newsworthy will vary from newspaper to newspaper because each is aimed at different types of reader. What television editors and journalists regard as newsworthy may also differ between channels, e.g. Channel 4 tends to focus on more social-policy issues than the BBC or ITV.

Ideology and bias

Marxists such as Stuart Hall argue that news supports capitalist interests and is therefore biased because those in powerful positions have better access to media institutions than the less powerful (Hall and Young, 1981). Hall argues that such bias arises naturally from the bureaucratic routines and news values that journalists use in their everyday practices, rather than because they share the same socio-economic backgrounds and are conspiring with the capitalist class. In particular, journalists subscribe to a 'hierarchy of credibility', i.e. they rank the views of politicians, police officers, civil servants, business leaders, etc. ('**primary definers**') above those of pressure groups, trade unionists, etc.

Manning (1999) argues that pressure on journalists to use primary definers as their main sources of news has probably increased. He points out that the Labour government, large corporations and financial institutions spend millions on 'managing' their public image. However, Schlesinger (1990) is critical of the concept of primary definition because it implies a united **power élite**. He points out that governments often contain politicians and departments that compete for media attention and, therefore, power structures change over time. Marxists also fail to clearly identify who these primary definers are. Finally, Schlesinger points out that Marxists imply that although the power élite shape the news, contemporary politicians are actually very careful about what they say to the media because they know that the media can shape public perceptions of their policies and practices.

Anderson (1993) argues that some new social movements like Greenpeace have cultivated good relationships with the media. However, Manning notes that it is powerful groups that still have the best access to news institutions, and that marginalised groups are still restricted to using a narrow range of media. They have access to broadsheet newspapers and the BBC but not to tabloids and commercial television. In order to get their message accepted by the media, these **marginalised groups** have to tone down anything extreme or radical in their message. In all, Manning concluded that powerful institutions are more newsworthy simply because they are big and powerful.

Think it through

Manning investigated the news coverage of trade unions in the 1990s and noted that trade unions employed press officers who shared a set of 'news values' with journalists and a common view of a 'good story'. Manning focused on the ambulance workers' dispute of 1989/90 and how the trade union attempted to use press coverage in order to keep the general public's initial sympathy with their cause. However, the union soon faced tabloid hostility as government ministers started using their power in stimulating media stories against the union. Readers were also rarely given a detailed analysis of the union's case. As unofficial strikes started to break out, the union found that its attempt to present itself as 'moderate' was undermined. Manning, therefore, concludes that the powerful retain significant advantages in dealing with the news media.

Adapted from: Manning, P. (1999) 'Who makes the news?', *Sociology Review*, September

1 Identify two ways in which trade unions attempted to ensure better news coverage.

2 Outline three reasons why the news coverage undermined the ambulance workers' case.

3 Outline and assess the relationship between journalists, editors and the powerful in the social manufacture of the news.

Important studies

Galtung and Ruge (1970) identified the following set of news values used by journalists.

WHAT MAKES NEWS?

Extraordinariness – unexpected, rare or surprising events.

Size – the 'bigger' the event, e.g. war, disaster, etc., the more likely it is to be nationally reported.

Involving élite persons or celebrities – the activities and opinions of élite persons are seen to be important, e.g. a minor operation on the Queen's knee may be ranked as more important than a rail disaster in rural India.

Involving élite nations – events in English-speaking nations, especially the USA, are regarded as more important than events in Africa or Asia, where events may only be reported when they involve Westerners.

Personalisation – Complex events and policies are often reduced to conflict between personalities.

Frequency – short-term events (e.g. murders) suit the nature of news reporting. Events that take a long time to unfold (e.g. inflation) may not receive the same degree of attention.

Negativity – bad news is regarded as more exciting and dramatic than good news.

Round-up

The news is not as impartial as we may think it is. A range of influences – agenda-setting, bureaucratic constraints, news values and primary definers – suggests that the news is a socially manufactured product that may reflect the interests and ideology of powerful groups. This may undermine democracy because audiences are not exposed to a full range of opinion and are therefore unable to make informed choices.

How do moral panics come about?

What is a moral panic?

The term 'moral panic' was made popular by the sociologists Jock Young (1971) and Stanley Cohen (1972). It describes the way in which the media over-reacts to certain social groups (particularly youth cultures) or to particular activities that are seen as threatening to social order. This media over-reaction, mainly found in tabloid newspaper coverage and occasionally in television news and documentaries, is shown in sensational and exaggerated headlines and language. This creates public anxiety and, as a result, pressure is put on the authorities to control and discipline the problem group or activity.

The characteristics of a moral panic

An analysis of American newspaper reporting by Goode and Ben-Yehuda (1994) suggests that moral panics have five distinct characteristics, as described in the following table.

The media sometimes focus on certain groups and activities and, through the style of the reporting, define them as problems worthy of public anxiety and official censure and control

MASS MEDIA

Characteristic of moral panic	Examples from sociological studies	Contemporary examples
Concern – that a particular group or activity is a threat to social order. This is picked up by the media and made more of through sensationalist headlines and reporting, which distort the importance of the group or event.	Stan Cohen's (1972) study of the media's reaction to youth 'disturbances' on Easter Monday 1964 shows how the media blew what were essentially small-scale scuffles and vandalism out of all proportion by using headlines such as 'Day of Terror' and words like 'battle', 'riot', etc. in their reporting.	In 2003, this concern is focused on the numbers of refugees and asylum seekers entering the UK and on their motives for doing so. Elements of the tabloid press, particularly the *Daily Mail* and *The Sun,* have created public anxiety by focusing on alleged links between asylum seekers and terrorism.
Hostility – the media engage in a campaign that makes the group appear to be the enemy of society, i.e. the group become 'folk devils'.	Young (1971) notes that the media stereotyped hippy dope-smokers as social misfits who were psychologically unstable and easy prey for 'wicked' drug pushers.	In 2002, the *News of the World* named and published the photographs of known paedophiles with their addresses. This led to their persecution by local people.
Consensus – influential people such as politicians, leaders of pressure groups, etc. are able to drum up public support for their beliefs. They become 'moral entrepreneurs'. Those people who take a more reasoned approach then find it difficult to be heard or are labelled as 'guilty by association'.	Cohen found that the consensus tended to simplify the causes of the so-called problem. He reports that the behaviour of the mods and rockers was seen as a symptom of the decline in morality and the growing disrespect of the young for the older generation and the Establishment.	In the case of asylum seekers, the moral panic of 2003 simplifies the motives of people wanting to enter the UK as being either terrorism, crime or to take advantage of Britain's Welfare State. The complex and genuine reasons why people come to the UK are ignored.
Disproportionality – the societal reaction, especially the official reaction, to the media coverage is excessive. A 'disaster mentality' is developed, based on exaggerated information, which predicts further problems if severe action is not taken.	Redhead (1992) notes that the moral panic regarding acid-house raves in the late 1980s led to the police setting up roadblocks and turning up at raves in full riot gear, and to the Criminal Justice Act (1990) which banned illegal 'assemblies'.	In 2003, a moral panic developed around black youth culture after two girls were killed by cross-fire in a gun fight between two gangs in Birmingham. Rap music was accused of encouraging and celebrating a culture of violence.
Volatility – moral panics tend to come in intense short bursts. Jones (2000) notes that it is difficult to keep up hysterical anger for any length of time and stories soon lose their newsworthiness. However, moral panics can have a lasting impact in that they may result in changes in social policy or legislation.	Moral panics tend to be shorter in length today than those studied by Young and Cohen in the 1960s, which lasted months rather than weeks.	Two current examples – paedophilia and black gun culture – confirm that today's moral panics tend to be short-lived. However, the moral panic regarding asylum seekers is likely to continue as long as there are fears about terrorism.

Cohen and Young's work includes an important aspect of moral panics that Goode and Ben-Yehuda tend to neglect – the reaction of the folk devils themselves. Thornton (1995) notes that the moral panic that surrounded rave parties in the late 1980s and early 1990s attracted more young people to an e-culture (one involving use of the drug Ecstasy) simply because it had been labelled deviant by disapproving media coverage.

Why do moral panics come about?

- Furedi (1995) argues that moral panics happen when society fails to adapt to dramatic social changes and it is felt that there is a loss of control, especially over groups such as the young.

- Some commentators argue that moral panics are the result of news values and the desire of journalists and editors to sell newspapers. They are a good example of how audiences are manipulated by the media for commercial purposes.

- Marxists such as Stuart Hall (1978) see moral panics as serving an ideological function. His study of the coverage of black muggers in the 1970s concluded that it had the effect of labelling all young African-Caribbeans as criminals and a potential threat to white people; it served the triple ideological purpose of:
  - turning the white working class against the black working class (i.e. 'divide and rule')
  - diverting attention away from capitalism's mismanagement
  - justifying the introduction of repressive laws and policing that could be used against other 'problem' groups.

- Left realists, however, argue that moral panics should not be dismissed as a product of ruling-class ideology or news values; moral panics have a very real basis in reality. The media often identify groups who are a very real threat to those living in inner-city areas. Portraying such crime as a fantasy is naïve because it denies the real harm that some types of crime inflict on particular communities or the sense of threat that older people feel.

Some examples of moral panics from the 1950s onwards

Mid-1950s	Teddy boys
1964	Mods and Rockers
Late 1960s	Hippies smoking marihuana; skinhead violence
Early 1970s	Football hooliganism; street crime, i.e. mugging
1976–77	Punk rock; heroin addiction
Mid- to late 1980s	Homosexuality and AIDs (i.e. 'gay plague'); illegal acid-house raves; hippy peace convoy; video-nasties
Early to mid-1990s	Child sex abuse; single-parent families (especially teenage mothers); ecstasy use; children, violence and video-nasties; dangerous dogs
Mid- to late 1990s	Welfare scroungers; boys' underachievement in schools
2002/2003	Paedophiles; black gun culture; asylum seekers

Think it through

Researchers such as Stan Cohen have demonstrated the role of the media in actively constructing reality for the general public by defining what counts as normality and deviance through the creation of moral panics. This approach was later adopted by Marxist critics of the media who demonstrated how the media helped to avoid wider conflict in society by focusing our attention on the supposedly deviant behaviour of 'outsider' groups such as youth cultures, welfare scroungers, etc. Moral panics have an ideological function, i.e. 'we' are encouraged to view 'them' as a threat and consequently we fail to see the real cause of our problems, i.e. the capitalist system.

Adapted from: www.cultsock.ndirect.co.uk

1 Identify three reasons for the creation of moral panics.

2 In what sense do moral panics perform an ideological function?

3 Outline and assess the view that societies often experience periods of moral panic started by the mass media.

Important studies

McRobbie (1995) argues that moral panics today are the creation of conservatives who fear that society is out of control. She maintains that moral panics are actually becoming less frequent and harder to sustain as folk devils now effectively fight back through pressure groups and new social movements.

These two websites contain excellent summaries of moral panic theory or articles focusing on the moral panics that resulted from the murder of Jamie Bulger and the discovery of paedophilia in the 1990s: www.cultsock.ndirect.co.uk and www.abu.co.uk.

Round-up

The study of moral panics shows the power of the media in defining what counts as normal behaviour and what counts as deviant. It also points out the effects of such media labelling on particular social groups and on how the public regards them. Most importantly, it reminds us to continually question our 'common sense' and media-influenced understanding of crime and social disorder.

What is the role of public service broadcasting in the contemporary UK?

Three types of provider dominate television broadcasting in the contemporary UK, as shown in the box on the right.

The role of Public Services Broadcasting (PSB), particularly the role of the BBC, has been debated in some depth in the past 20 years. Pluralist media sociologists and politicians have dominated this debate – as can be seen in the aims of PSB described in the box at the bottom of the page.

Pluralists see PSB as playing an important role in keeping democratic debate alive and making sure that powerful interests do not abuse their power and privileges. PSB acts as a counterbalance to the market forces that underpin commercial television.

 Visit the websites of the BBC **www.bbc.org.uk** *and ITC* **www.itc.org.uk** *and compare their corporate aims with the ideals of PSB, as outlined below.*

* Ninety-eight percent of homes in Britain possess at least one TV, with almost half having two or more. Each viewer on average watches television for 25 hours per week. Many of us now have a choice of hundreds of channels.

TYPES OF TV PROVIDER IN THE UK TODAY

The BBC is state-owned and controlled by a Board of Governors, which is appointed by the Home Secretary. Day-to-day BBC policy is managed by a Director-General appointed by the governors. The BBC receives its funding from the government via the licence fee, although it adds to its income by exporting programmes abroad and marketing videos, etc. This non-profit-making type of television is known as Public Service Broadcasting (PSB).

Independent commercial television companies such as Granada, Carlton, etc. compete for the rights to broadcast in particular areas. The Independent Television Commission (ITC), whose members are appointed by the Home Secretary, regulates these companies. Commercial television is mainly financed through advertising revenue. There is a PSB element apparent in independent television, e.g. the Charter that set up Channel 4 in 1982 states that C4 is required to cater for tastes, interests and audiences not served by ITV and to devote a proportion of its airtime to educational programming.

Subscriptions to satellite television have increased dramatically in recent years. Companies such as Rupert Murdoch's BSkyB are funded by both advertising and subscriptions.

THE IDEAL AIMS OF PUBLIC SERVICE BROADCASTING, i.e. THE BBC

Quality and standards – it is argued that PSB should compete to produce 'quality' programming, especially in providing the arts, drama and news rather than just producing programmes that attract the largest possible audience.

Impartiality and accuracy – PSB should keep its distance from **private capital** and government influence. Its focus should be on reliable and objective news, education and information.

Plurality and diversity – PSB should allow freedom of expression to all viewpoints so that proper debate and democracy can exist. Programme content should provide something for everybody so that all minority groups, interests and tastes are catered for.

Access – there should be universal and affordable access for all social groups.

Concern for national identity, community and common good – audiences should be addressed as citizens rather than as consumers. Public and national interest should be stressed above partisan interests. PSB should act as a cultural voice for the nation.

Private capital: Financial resources in the hands of private investors.

Terrestrial television: Broadcasting using land-based transmitters.

The Marxist critique

However, this view of PSB has been attacked by Marxist sociologists, who argue that:

- PSB broadcasters and journalists hold a set of shared values and attitudes that stress a consensus view of the world. Marxists point out that such ideas mainly serve the interests of the capitalist class. (See pp. 92–3 for a more detailed analysis of these ideas.)
- PBS is not detached from government influence. The government has sanctions that it can use to threaten the BBC, e.g. it has the power to freeze, increase or even remove the licence fee. In the 1980s, the Conservative government actually stopped some BBC programmes from being transmitted.
- the Boards of Governors of both the BBC and the Independent Television Council (ITC) are political appointments made from the ranks of the 'great and good', i.e. members of the ruling establishment.
- the values associated with PSB are conservative and even patronising, e.g. the BBC's emphasis on the arts, education and quality drama has been interpreted by some as an arrogant attempt to define what counts as culture. This is seen as being snobbish and value-laden. Viewing figures indicate that the BBC channels are more popular with middle-class viewers – working-class viewers have preferred ITV since it was launched in 1954.

However, in defence of the BBC, one could point out that the Corporation has been criticised by all political points of view about its political coverage. Both Conservative and Labour governments have questioned the BBC's impartiality by suggesting that particular programmes or commentators are biased against them.

Recent concerns

The Broadcasting Act (1996) blurred the difference between PSB and commercial television because the Act abolished many of the restrictions on them (i.e. it led to **deregulation**). In addition, this Act allows for the provision of an extra 30 channels. The BBC has responded to this and competition from satellite television by becoming more commercial, e.g. it has set up its own **digital channels** (BBC3 and BBC4) as well as going into partnership with commercial companies and setting up UK Gold.

Some people argue that public service broadcasting no longer actually exists because, in trying to compete with commercial and satellite television for mass audiences, the BBC has sacrificed quality, standards, the aim to inform and educate, and even impartiality. This argument suggests that the main BBC aim today is to provide entertainment for a mass culture. Consequently, PSB is no longer providing more choice, just more of what is already provided by commercial and satellite television.

So has the quality of PSB been 'dumbed down'? We certainly get more repeats, cheap imports and 'reality' programmes that make personalities out of unknowns, e.g. *Big Brother*, *Pop Idol*, etc. There are 50% less documentaries and many of those are 'docusoaps'. There has been a growth of 'infotainment', a mix of news and light entertainment, e.g. breakfast television often focuses on personalities and the life-styles of the rich and famous rather than on political issues.

However, there is a danger that claims about 'dumbing down' may be exaggerated. The concept depends on interpretation and there is a danger of implying that only particular forms of programming (e.g. those that appeal to middle-class audiences) count as culture.

A new concept for PSB?

Some commentators have suggested that we should redefine the concept of PSB. The new digital market is expensive and there is a danger that a digital underclass denied access to this market could emerge. PSB may need to focus on ensuring that the poorer sections of the community continue to access information, education and culture. On the other hand, critics have argued that PSB may become 'ghettoised' in the future as the masses watch commercial **terrestrial** and satellite TV, whilst the middle classes watch the BBC. If this happens, the licence fee will become unjustifiable and PSB principles may well be abandoned as the BBC travels down the commercial road and introduces advertising.

Think it through

Eyre (1999) argues that public service broadcasting will soon be dead because it relies on the notion of an active broadcaster and a passive viewer, and in the era of wider choice, many viewers will pass on the wholesome, healthy and carefully crafted programmes provided by PSB in favour of the easily digestible, pre-packaged and undemanding provided by commercial channels. Increased consumer choice in the form of hundreds of television channels will also be impossible to regulate. Regulation is also rapidly being outpaced by technological and commercial developments. If **convergence** of digital media technologies continues at its present pace, we will use the box in the corner to watch movies, read the paper, play games with people on the other side of the world, e-mail friends, buy goods, video-conference with relatives, etc. In what sense is that a television, and how can it be regulated?

Adapted from: Mick Underwood, 'Mass media: broadcasting systems' on www.cultsock.ndirect.co.uk

1 Identify four ways in which our use of television has changed.

2 Describe, in your own words, the reasons why Eyre sees PSB as being in decline.

3 Outline and assess the view that there is no need for public service broadcasting in the contemporary UK.

Deregulation: The removal of legal restrictions and rules on broadcasters.

Digital channels: TV channels only available via digital, satellite or cable.

Convergence: The coming together of different types of media, either in one company or one technology.

Round-up

The role of PSB is the subject of lively debate today. Pluralists argue that it plays an important role in a democratic society by ensuring that the population continues to have access to information in an otherwise entertainment-orientated television culture. Marxists argue that the impartiality of PSB is a myth and that it actually supports capitalist interests. Other critics suggest that PSB is now virtually redundant because of the range of consumer choices provided by commercial television.

How does the media help construct feminine identity?

Feminine identity

Bob Connell (2002) argues that feminine identity in the UK is still the product of hegemonic (culturally dominant) ideas of how the sexes should be socialised and how they should behave as adults. Women are still given very distinct roles, including the traditionally main domestic one, i.e. women as mothers, housewives and emotional caretakers. In addition, young women are often seen as sexual objects, and viewed in terms of their physical attributes, size, shape, etc. Connell points out that all agents of socialisation are involved in creating these expectations about femininity but that the mass media has played a particularly important role in reinforcing these traditional ideas about women.

The role of the media

Media representations of females often do not reflect the reality of their lives. Media images today largely restrict women to a narrow range of social roles. In particular, television advertising, newspapers, magazines and even the music industry show women as either seeking fulfillment in the home as wives, mothers and consumers, or as sexual objects for men to look at. Social changes such as girls outperforming boys at all levels of education, the feminisation of the workforce and the fact that women are increasingly choosing to use divorce to escape unhappy marriages are generally not included in the way the media represent females.

Some media representations seem to be very positive. For instance, TV shows such as *Prime Suspect* and *Cold Feet* include assertive female lead characters, as do soap operas such as *EastEnders*. However, on closer examination, many of these 'strong' female characters are shown as having problems, i.e. they are incapable of maintaining successful relationships or unstable and neurotic.

Although the way women are portrayed in the media has changed over the past decade, media representations still mainly focus on stereotypes such as busy housewives, contented mothers and sex objects

Important studies

Guy Cumberbatch's (1990) study of television commercials concluded that such adverts reflected an 'unacceptable face of sexism' and also contribute to the idea that women exist in what is essentially a man's world. His study showed that youth and beauty were the main features of women in commercials, and that women occupied a decorative role far more often than men. Men were more than twice as likely to be shown in paid employment while women were more than twice as likely to be shown doing things like washing and cleaning.

Research issue Much of the research into images of women in the media is based on content analysis (see page 135). If possible, try to read Cumberbatch (1990) and see if you agree with the categories he used and his analysis (see p. 173 for full details of this work).

Women's magazines

The women's-magazine industry has stressed that a primary goal of women's identity should be the mother-housewife role. Ferguson (1983) carried out a content-analysis study of such magazines between 1949 and 1980 and concluded that magazines like *Woman*, *Woman's Own*, etc. were like an apprentice manual for training women in domestic skills such as childcare, keeping a husband happy, self-improvement, etc. These magazines, Ferguson claimed, socialise their audiences into a 'cult of femininity', i.e. into being 'good' wives and mothers, and looking 'good' for men. These conclusions are fairly similar to Angela McRobbie's (1982) study of teenage magazines. She argued that such media encouraged girls to see romance and marriage as primary goals and to value themselves only in terms of how they are valued by boys.

Feminist research carried out over the past 10 years suggests that some changes have occurred in magazine images of femininity. During the past 30 years there have been new women's magazines available such as *Cosmopolitan*, *Marie Claire* and *Options*, which have focused on serious issues such as domestic violence, careers for women, sexual freedom, etc. In other words, these magazines seem on the surface to reflect social and economic change. Winship (1986) argues that such magazines have helped create new feminine identities based upon self-confidence, competitiveness, career aspirations, sexual frankness, materialism, etc. However, Ballaster *et al.* (1991) note that such magazines contain conflicting messages. For example, they often encourage women to behave radically in terms of careers and sexual relationships, yet they also contain conformist messages about staying thin, losing weight, looking good, how to get involved with men, etc. This reflects the contradictory messages that women experience in their daily lives, i.e. they are encouraged to have careers and independence yet society still expects them to see marriage and motherhood as their main goal.

Representations of the ideal body

It is argued by Wolf (1990) that women's bodies are presented by various types of media as 'projects' in need of improvement in terms of size, shape, weight, etc. In 2000, the British Medical Association claimed that, through the use of abnormally thin models, fashion advertising and women's magazines promote impossible 'ideal' body shapes that can trigger and perpetuate eating disorders. Their research also showed that female actresses and news presenters on television are thinner than average. In addition, women's magazines put great pressure on young women to be thin by containing articles and adverts on diets and slimming, and various types of cosmetic surgery. It is argued that this particular type of representation has become part and parcel of the socialisation process – girls and young women are strongly encouraged to see their identity as bound up with achieving this 'ideal' body.

Sex objects

The pressure to conform to a particular physical type is reinforced by traditional sexual objectification in some sections of the media. The 'Page 3 girl' daily feature found in *The Sun* presents women as objects to be enjoyed by men, in the same way as the images commonly found in lads' magazines such as *FHM* and *Arena*. Recently studies of rap and heavy metal music have commented on how these genres of music tend to demean women by overemphasising their sexual attributes.

Journalists such as Kate Adie and Anna Ford have complained that, if you are a woman, the qualifications needed to be a journalist or newscaster on prime-time television news are youth, physical looks and sex appeal rather than intellect, ability and experience.

Think it through

The objectification of women's bodies in the media has been a consistent theme in the analyses of how women are represented. Mulvey (1975) argues that the female body is displayed for the male gaze in order to provide erotic pleasure (voyeurism) and ultimately a sense of control over her. Women are often represented as victims of physical attacks in movies for the benefit of men and this extreme violence reinforces female fear. However, masculine control is not always the outcome of media representation. In the video for her song 'Open Your Heart', Madonna performs in a 'peep show' for a variety of male voyeurs, but the gaze is reversed so that the men are seen through Madonna's eyes – as pathetic and frustrated. Madonna is an example of a female media performer who is able to exercise greater control over look and image.

Adapted from: Sullivan, T. O. *et al.* (1997)
Studying the media, Edward Arnold, London

1 Identify two negative representations of females identified by Mulvey.

2 In what ways might Madonna symbolise the new feminine identities that are now being seen in the media?

3 Outline and assess the view that positive change in terms of how women are represented in the media has been very limited.

Round-up

There is no doubt that new feminine identities are starting to be seen in the media – and these reflect the new-found freedom of females today. However, these images and representations are still very much in the minority. Media messages about the role of women, through channels such as women's magazines, tend to lag behind reality and, at best, reflect the contradictions of being a modern woman in a patriarchal society.

Patriarchy: Domination by males in society.

 Visit **www.theory.org.uk** and read the student essays about *More magazine* and *Madonna*.

What messages does the media transmit about masculinity?

Images of masculinity in the media have tended to focus on a masculine myth that stresses strength, aggression and power. Recent images of masculinity have, however, suggested that men can be more in touch with their emotions and sexuality

Masculine identity

Bob Connell (2002) argues that expectations about gender roles in the UK are dominated by '**hegemonic masculinity**', i.e. traditional ideas about the role of men and masculinity that stress **individualism**, competition and ambition. Paid work is central to men's identity and role. Men are expected to be breadwinners and heads of households, responsible for the economic security of their dependants. They are not expected to show emotion. Connell points out that all **agencies of socialisation** transmit these expectations about masculinity to boys, but that the mass media has played a particularly significant role in doing so.

The role of the media

Until fairly recently, there has not been a great deal of analysis of how the media represent men and masculinity. However, Tunstall (1983), in an analysis of how the media over-represented women as wives and mothers, pointed out that although similar numbers of men are fathers and husbands, the media has much less to say about these roles. Rather, male family-roles are presented as secondary compared with the primary representation of men as workers, high-powered businessmen and leaders. He points out that, while newspapers and television have often focused on the problems of motherhood (especially for working mothers) and on female-headed single-parent families, fatherhood or male promiscuity are rarely presented as causes of social problems. Moreover, Tunstall observed that, in contrast with women, men are seldom presented nude or judged by the media in terms of how well they match up to a feminine view of an ideal male form.

The masculine myth

Hopefully, you will have noticed that media representations of femininity (as described on pp. 102–3) are closely linked to media representations of masculinity.

Easthope (1986) argues that a variety of media, especially Hollywood films, transmit the view that masculinity based on strength, aggression, competition and violence is biologically determined and therefore a natural goal for boys. He notes that the Hollywood action hero of the 1980s, such as Bruce Willis in the *Die Hard* films, was the embodiment of this ideal. Easthope argues that most men cannot hope to achieve such a masculine image (i.e. it is a myth). However, he believes that they do take in from such films the idea that men have power in a variety of forms, i.e. physical, cultural and emotional, and that this is part and parcel of their male identity.

Hegemonic masculinity: Dominant and traditional ideas about the role of men that stress individualism, competition and ambition.

Individualism: A set of values that stresses the importance of the individual rather than groups or communities.

Agencies of socialisation: Institutions such as the family, education system, religion, mass media, etc. from which we learn the culture of our society.

Research task It would be interesting to do some research to see whether Tunstall's observations are still true today. For example, compare the language used by a broadsheet and tabloid newspaper to see how males and females are described. Compare the number of advertisements for slimming and cosmetic surgery to see how many are aimed at men and how many at women.

Men and magazines

Magazines show a clear gender breakdown. Traditionally, female magazines have tended to focus on interests centred on the domestic sphere and beauty or appearance. Men's magazines have tended to focus on a wider range of interests, e.g. cars, computers, sport, pornography, gardening, hobbies, etc. It can be argued that even serious current affairs magazines such as *The Economist*, *New Statesman*, *Newsweek* and *Time* were aimed at male audiences. This gender division reflected hegemonic definitions of male and female roles.

However, the 1980s saw the arrival of a new breed of glossy magazine aimed at middle-class young men, such as *GQ*, *Maxim* and *FHM*. Their content focuses on the male experience rather than on hobbies. They often suggest that men are emotionally vulnerable, that they are more in touch with their feelings, that they should treat women as equals, that they should care more about their appearance and that active fatherhood is an experience worth having. Some writers saw this as evidence of the emergence of a new type of masculinity – the new man – who is more sensitive and more in touch with his feminine side, while still having certain masculine qualities. Television advertising in the 1980s and 1990s also focused on this idea, with a series of commercials showing lots of caring, sharing men.

This led sociologists to consider whether masculinity was responding to the growing economic independence and assertiveness of women. The media focus on male fashion and hygiene in these magazines was a sign that men realised that they could no longer simply take for granted that women would find them attractive.

In criticism of these ideas, Collier (1992) notes that these magazines are often contradictory in how they represent masculinity. He notes that they continue to define male success in terms of work, salary and materialism while women are treated as sexual objects. Some of these magazines (particularly *Loaded*) actually reject behaviour associated with the 'new man' and actively re-assert traditional masculinity by celebrating 'birds, booze and football'. Some feminist sociologists see this as part of an anti-feminist backlash. However, as Sharples (updated webpage) notes, it is unlikely that these magazines set out to be **misogynist** – just that they simply promote masculinity in what their editors and journalists see as positive ways.

Changing images in the media

There can be no doubt that the mass media are gradually reacting to men's changing perception of masculinity. Three examples illustrate this.

- The media, especially in the field of television entertainment and music, has encouraged the social acceptance of gay men (and women), e.g. Graham Norton.

- Westwood (1999) notes that we are seeing more programmes on television that experiment with traditional gender roles. For example, in *The X-Files* the female character, Scully, represents the 'masculine' world of science, rationality and facts, whilst the male character, Mulder, is emotionally open and vulnerable – traits normally associated with femininity.

- Whannell (2002) notes that mass-media representations of the footballer David Beckham have challenged some of the dominant assumptions of masculinity. Media representations of Beckham are fluid. His good looks, football skills and considerable competitive spirit and commitment mark him out as a 'real man' but this image has been balanced with alternative images that suggest he is happy to modify his masculinity. For example, in 1999, Beckham said that having a child meant more than his football achievements. The positive media coverage of David Beckham as a father may help to shift popular notions of how men should behave.

Misogynist: Hating, demeaning and devaluing women.

Visit www.theory.org.uk and download material on changing masculinities and representations of masculinity in contemporary men's magazines.

Think it through

Nixon (1996) claimed that the concept of the new man can be traced back to a television commercial shown in late 1985 that showed a male model stripping down to his boxer shorts in a launderette. This advert showed that it could be 'cool' and acceptable for men to take the same amount of care over their personal appearance and clothes as women do. Frank Mort (1988) argued that the rise in men's fashion magazines and the advertising and consumption of male toiletries and designer-label clothing for men reflected changes in social attitudes towards masculinity. He goes as far as suggesting that men's bodies were sexualized in this period by the media – they became subjected to a 'female gaze'. However Tim Edwards (1997) argues that Nixon and Mort exaggerate the influence of social changes in masculinity. He argues that the new man was quite simply a product of advertisers invented to sell products to both men and women.

Adapted from: Abbott, D. 'Identities and new masculinities', *Sociology Review*, September 2000

1 Identify three changes in masculinity identified by Nixon and Mort.

2 What is Edwards' attitude towards changing masculinity?

3 Outline and assess the idea that the media continue to transmit traditional expectations about how men should behave.

Watch out

In an exam answer, be careful not to make too much of the changes that are taking place in how men are portrayed in the media and the extent to which men's identity and behaviour may be changing. Deep-rooted cultural traditions take a long time to change.

Round-up

There are signs that media representations of masculinity are moving away from the emphasis on traditional masculinity. Representations now include new forms, such as those symbolised by homosexuality and those that value fatherhood and vulnerability. However, we must take care not to exaggerate the extent of these changes.

How does the media transmit ethnic and national identities?

The media and identity

There are three main ways in which the media can influence minority ethnic identities.

1 Newspapers, television and especially cinema (Bollywood) and Asian satellite channels can keep minority groups firmly in touch with their countries of origin and cultural norms. Newspapers such as *Eastern Eye*, *The Voice* and the *Indian Times*, magazines such as *Snoop* (dedicated to gigs and Asian music), the BBC Asian digital network and programmes such as *Ebony* and *Café 21* and the website www.Brasian.co.uk all contribute to the transmission of various minority ethnic cultures.

2 The white mass media also contributes – positive role-models of black and Asian sports, music and film/television stars may encourage positive self-esteem in minority ethnic cultures.

3 However, such representations can also be negative. People of African-Caribbean origin are often stereotyped as criminal and minority ethnic concerns and anxieties, especially about racism, are marginalised (i.e. defined as unimportant) or excluded altogether. Images of feminine beauty tend to overemphasise whiteness, e.g. Naomi Campbell has complained about the relative lack of black and Asian models because it is assumed that Anglo-Saxon blondes have the ideal feminine look. These negative representations can lead to strong cultural reactions among some sections of minority ethnic culture. For example, the slogan 'Black is beautiful' was adopted as a means of asserting black identity in a society where definitions of beauty focus almost exclusively on white people.

Although television and the music industry have produced many positive minority ethnic role-models, other forms of media have tended to focus on degrading, unsympathetic and negative stereotypes of a range of minority ethnic people

Evidence for unsympathetic stereotypes

Stereotype

Newspapers over-emphasise the criminality of minority ethnic groups e.g. African-Caribbean culture is presented as dominated by a drug and gun culture celebrated by 'gangsta rap'.

During 2002 and 2003, the tabloid media reported that illegal immigration was out of control. It suggests that the country was becoming swamped with asylum seekers who were potential terrorists, criminals (especially from Eastern Europe) or workshy scroungers taking advantage of the British Welfare State. In other words, minority groups were presented as a 'threat'.

Minority groups are often shown as being abnormal because of their cultural practices, e.g. it is claimed that some Asian women in the UK are oppressed by having to wear a veil, when in reality they may choose to wear it.

Stories about the developing world are almost entirely negative in their focus on famine, starving refugees, over-population, AIDS, corruption and war. They suggest that areas such as Africa are over-dependent on white Western help. There are few positive stories about 'normal' life in the developing world.

Representations of black people in the media are often limited to sport and music.

Think it through

National Union of Journalists guidelines on race reporting
- Only mention someone's race if it is strictly relevant. Would you mention race if the person was white?
- Think carefully about the words you use. Ask people how they define themselves.
- Do not make assumptions about a person's cultural background – whether it is their name or religious detail. Ask them.
- Remember that black communities are culturally diverse.
- Do not sensationalise race-relations issues.

Media stereotypes of minority ethnic groups

Sociologists have identified a number of negative and unsympathetic stereotypes of minority ethnic groups – see the table below.

Sociological observation

Van Dijks (1991) noted that unconscious racism can be found in the language used in a news story. The reporting of inner-city disturbances in the 1980s frequently described these as 'riots'. This implies irrational, criminal and rampaging mobs that need to be controlled by justifiable use of police force. Journalists very rarely used the word 'uprising', which means rebellion against injustice.

Many sociologists agree that this media representation has all the hallmarks of a classic **moral panic** (see pp. 98–9). A problem group has been identified and sensationalist language employed by the media. This has created anxiety among the general population, especially in areas where refugees have been re-located, and pressure has been put on the authorities to act. The idea that the vast majority of such refugees may be genuinely escaping political persecution, torture and poverty in their home country is neglected or ignored. This type of moral panic is not new; in the 1960s and 1970s, it focused on Asian immigration.

British news reporting is ethnocentric, i.e. shaped by the view that British white culture is superior in its values and norms compared with other cultures. Consequently, the activities of other cultures can be reported as inadequate, inferior, strange, etc. in ways that devalue other societies.

The Glasgow University Media Group (GUMG, 2000) found that there has been a drastic reduction in factual programming (i.e. 50% in ten years) about the developing world. One third of coverage was devoted to war, conflict, terrorism and disasters, while much of the remaining coverage was about sport or visits by Westerners to developing countries. For example, some countries were only featured because Richard Branson's balloon had floated over them! Little time was devoted to analysing why countries were under-developed and poor, or to the role of the West in relation to domination of world trade, debt and multinational exploitation.

The constant images of blacks as athletes and musicians restricts the role-models open to young blacks and reinforces stereotypes in white people's minds.

The representation of minority ethnic groups on television

A BBC report in 2000 showed that minority ethnic groups make up 5.5% of the UK population yet 7.5% of people who appear on television come from minority ethnic backgrounds. A disproportionate number of black presenters appear in children's programmes or drama such as soaps. A significant number of news presenters are from minority ethnic backgrounds. Some, such as Sir Trevor McDonald, are in positions of considerable authority.

Research carried out in 2002 by the Broadcasting Standards Commission (BSC) concluded that the minorities should be better represented both on screen and behind the scenes in decision-making roles. The BSC found that Asian audiences were unhappy at how certain cultural practices were presented on television, e.g. they felt that the way arranged marriages were shown was often inaccurate and did not reflect how this system has changed over time. Nearly all participants from minority ethnic groups felt that their country of origin was negatively portrayed or was not represented at all.

Akinti (2003) argues that television often reflects an inaccurate and superficial view of black life. It focuses almost exclusively on stereotypical issues such as gun crime, AIDS in Africa and black underachievement in schools. At the same time, it ignores the culture and interests of a huge and diverse black audience and their rich contribution to UK society.

Other critics have suggested that television programmes dedicated to minority issues actually **ghettoise** such issues because:

- the fact that mainly minority audiences watch these programmes means that the white mainstream audience rarely gets to access or understands minority culture
- the mainstream media assume that certain issues are being dealt with by minority programming; mainstream news and documentaries may therefore be less likely, and willing, to report them.

It is argued that minority ethnic issues and interests should be integrated into mainstream programming. This would reinforce the view that all interests, whether they are rooted in the white majority or minority ethnic cultures, have equal status and importance.

Moral panic: Exaggerated social reaction to a group or issue, amplified by the media, with consequent demands for action.

Ghettoise: To imply that a group or issue should not be a mainstream concern.

Important studies

1 Identify three negative representations of minority ethnic people that could result if these guidelines were not followed.

2 Identify three examples of how race-relations issues are, or have been, sensationalised.

3 Outline and assess the view that mass-media representations reflect the multicultural nature of UK society.

Adapted from: Branston, G. and Stafford, R. (1996) *The media student's book*, Routledge, London

Douglas Kellner's *Media culture* (1995) notes how rap music is a means of expressing black identity in what is perceived by African-Caribbeans to be a hostile and racist environment.

Round-up

With some exceptions, media representations of minority ethnic groups continue to be mainly negative and misleading. Such representations may not change until members of minority ethnic groups can increase their participation and influence in the production of television programmes, newspapers, etc.

How does the media represent social class?

Representations of the upper class

 The Government's own statisticians estimate that four million children are living in poverty in 2003.

 Some Marxists would argue that this is because the media are owned and controlled by the wealthy and aim to 'cover up' inequalities by focusing on entertainment, trivia etc (see pp. 92–3). Media professionals, on the other hand, would argue that the facts about wealth and poverty are not 'newsworthy' (see pp. 96–7).

Republican ideas: Set of ideas opposed to hereditary power, e.g. arguing that the Queen should be replaced by an elected Head of State.

Marxists would argue that the upper class (the monarchy, the aristocracy and the wealthy), who live off their wealth rather than work for a living, symbolise a UK society that is characterised by extreme inequalities in wealth and income.

However, the UK mass media hardly ever show the upper classes in a critical light, nor do they draw serious attention to these inequalities. Sociological observations about media representations of the upper classes suggest that popular films and television costume drama tend to portray members of this class either in an eccentric or nostalgic way. They often paint a rosy picture of a ruling élite characterised by honour, culture and good breeding.

Representations of the monarchy

Nairn (1988) noted that the monarchy has successfully won over much of the modern mass media to its side. In the 1960s and 1970s, it was rare to see any criticism of the idea of an inherited monarchy, or specific criticism of individual royals, or support for **republican ideas**.

Nairn argues that this is because after World War II the monarchy, with the help of the media, re-invented itself as a 'Royal Family' with a cast of characters, not unlike our own families, who stood for national values such as 'decency' and 'ordinariness'. This idea that the Queen is just an 'ordinary' person doing an extraordinary job resulted in a national obsession with the royal family. This was reflected in media coverage that focused positively on the trivial detail of their lives. Newspapers, magazines and television turned the Queen and her family into stars and celebrities. However, this is a two-way process – for the past 50 years, royal features and gossip have been vital to the media in selling newspapers and magazines, and both the BBC and ITV employ Royal Correspondents to report specifically on royal news.

Mass media representations of social classes tend to focus on celebrities and stereotypes. They rarely reflect the social conflicts that some sociologist see as underpinning society.

Although there was some criticism of the royal family in the 1980s, it was not until the death of Diana, Princess of Wales in the late 1990s that the monarchy started to attract real criticism from the media and lost some popularity with the general public. However, the positive reaction to the Queen's Jubilee in 2002 suggested that the royal family had again succeeded in convincing the media (and consequently the general public) that Britain's identity depends upon the Queen continuing to be Head of State.

Jones' (1998) analysis of public reaction to the death of Diana suggests that the public grief that followed was 'substantially shaped and sustained by media responses to her life and to her demise', especially their construction of Diana as a celebrity and **icon** as the 'Queen of Hearts'. Such media representations made it very difficult to be critical of Diana's privileged lifestyle or even to be indifferent to her death.

Representations of wealth, poverty and inequality

Icon: Figure to be worshipped or admired.

The popular media have not shown much interest in the fact that wealth in the UK is concentrated in so few hands. Apart from a period in the mid-1990s when there was some media concern about the ever-increasing pay of so-called 'fat-cats', (i.e. people who ran recently privatised industries), the popular media have shown little concern about the unequal distribution of wealth or income.

Research issue

There has not been much sociological research into how the mass media deals with class issues or how particular social classes have been represented on television or in newspapers and magazines. Why do you think this might be?

Representations of the middle classes

Some sociologists argue that the middle classes (i.e. professionals, managers, white-collar workers) and their concerns are over-represented in the media. There is not a great deal of British sociological research in this area but four broad sociological observations can be made.

1   A large number of British newspapers, (e.g. the *Daily Mail* and the *Daily Telegraph*) and magazines are aimed at the middle class and their tastes and interests.
    There is a wide range of magazines dedicated to quite expensive activities
    (e.g. computers, music, cars, house and garden design) that can only be afforded by those with a reasonable standard of living.

2   The content of newspapers such as the *Daily Mail* suggests that the journalistic view of the middle classes is that they are anxious about the decline of moral standards in society. It also suggests that they are proud of their British identity and heritage but see this as threatened by alien influences such as the Euro, asylum seekers and terrorism. Consequently, newspapers like the *Daily Mail* often crusade on behalf of the middle classes and initiate moral panics on issues such as video-nasties, asylum-seekers, etc.

3   Television sit-coms that focus on the middle-class family often stereotype members as being over-concerned with manners and social respectability, worrying about what the neighbours think, etc. One example is the character Hyacinth Bucket in the TV sit com *Keeping Up Appearances*, who insists that her surname be pronounced 'Bouquet' in order to gain her greater social cachet.

4   Most of the creative personnel in the media are themselves middle class. In news and current affairs, the middle classes dominate positions of authority – the 'expert' is invariably middle class.

Representations of the working class

Adams (1985) notes how television drama, especially soap operas and comedy drama, stereotypes northern working-class culture. The stereotype of the two-faced northern woman, (i.e. outwardly friendly to your face but gossiping about you as soon as your back is turned), is common. So also is the eccentric but harmless and lovable rogue found in serials such as *Heartbeat*, *Last of the Summer Wine*, *The Royle Family*. etc.

However, it is also argued that some soap operas show working-class life in a positive light, as supportive communities in which strong working-class women deal realistically with the problems thrown up by working-class life. However, critics of these representations argue that such working-class communities have largely disappeared with the decline of traditional industries and slum clearance and re-housing programmes, so the soap operas do not actually reflect working-class life today.

Some media, particularly film, have presented working-class life more realistically. The 'kitchen-sink' British cinema of the 1960s, including films such as *Saturday Night and Sunday Morning* and *Kes*, television drama such as *Our Friends in the North* and more recent films such as *The Full Monty* and *Brassed Off* have shown working-class life and problems in a dignified way, and even commented upon class conflict and exploitation.

However, it can also be argued that tabloid newspapers aimed at working-class audiences tend to suggest that the working-class are not interested in politics, only in celebrity scandal, sex, sport and entertainment.

Think it through

The media often represents working-class life in a problematic way. Working-class groups, e.g. youth subcultures such as mods, skinheads, etc. are often subjected to moral panics while reporting of issues such as poverty, unemployment or single-parent families often suggest that individual inadequacy is the main cause of these social problems, rather than government policies or poor business practices. Studies of representations of industrial relations reporting by the Glasgow University Media Group suggest that the media portray 'unreasonable' workers as making trouble for 'reasonable' employers.

1   Identify three negative media representations of the working class.

2   Outline two reasons why the media may represent working-class groups in negative ways.

3   Outline and assess the view that media representations of the powerful are more positive than those of the powerless.

*   Do similar stereotypes exist about the southern working-class in sitcoms such as *EastEnders*?

Watch out

Postmodernists argue that class is no longer important. They say that representations in the media today focus on people who are classless, i.e. they are identified by their choices in fashion, style, etc., rather than by their social class.

Round-up

Despite the lack of empirical research in this area, it can be argued that media representations of the powerful, i.e. the upper class and the middle class, tend to be more positive than representations of the less powerful working class.

Does violence in the media lead to violence in real life?

Throughout the twentieth century, comic books, radio programmes, television, cinema, videos, pop music, computer games and the internet have all caused social anxiety and sometimes moral panics about their 'effects' upon the younger generation. It is generally suggested that the media offer inappropriate role-models, that they encourage forms of anti-social behaviour that can easily be imitated, (particularly violent behaviour) and that they generally corrupt morals.

✳ The Columbine High school massacre in the USA (1999) was blamed on violent computer games such as 'Doom' and the music of the American pop star Marilyn Manson. The recent film *Bowling for Columbine* (2002) is worth seeking out in your local video shop because it critically examines these assumptions.

✳ In January 2003, the Culture Minister Kim Howells noted that the 'constant diet of death and destruction in modern film and television has created a "pornography of violence" appealing to viewers' lowest urges'.

Screen violence

Most of the concerns about media content have focused upon screen violence, i.e. that found in the cinema, on video and DVD, and on television. Moral entrepreneurs such as the late Mrs Mary Whitehouse (founder of the media watchdog The National Viewers and Listeners Association, now known as Mediawatch), MPs such as David Alton, and editors of national newspapers, have claimed that there is a direct and almost immediate link between violent crime and films/videos.

Models of media effects

The hypodermic-syringe model

These views are linked to the 'hypodermic syringe' model of media effects, which sees rising levels of violent crime as directly linked to increased exposure, at ever-younger ages, to screen violence. This model states that children and impressionable adults are 'injected' with a 'fix' of sex and violence, which results in copycat behaviour or imitation. Popular opinion has tended to mirror this model; for example, the film *Child's Play 3* is firmly associated in the public's mind with the murder of Jamie Bulger in Liverpool in 1993 although there is absolutely no evidence that his young killers had seen it.

Could this influence a child?

The drip effect

Elizabeth Newson (1994), using evidence from the USA, argues that imitation as an effect of screen violence is probably less important than '**desensitisation** by systematic repetition'. She argues that children in the early socialisation years are constantly exposed via films and videos to violence and cruelty in the context of entertainment and amusement (i.e. a constant drip). As a consequence, children grow up believing that violence and aggression offer an acceptable answer to all human problems.

Desensitisation: Becoming immune to having feelings or to showing emotions as a result of over-exposure to, for example, violent images.

> **Research issue** There are serious ethical issues in researching this area. Exposing participants, particularly children, to screen violence, even for research purposes, may have distressing or damaging effects.

Important studies

Belson (1978) conducted a survey of 1565 boys aged between 13 and 16 over the period 1959–71 and concluded that boys who were 'high viewers' of violent TV were 49% more likely to commit acts of aggression than 'low viewers'.

Philo (1997) interviewed 10 children from a large comprehensive school in Glasgow who had seen the 18-rated film *Pulp Fiction*. Most of the children had seen the film more than once. Philo's research concluded that films like *Pulp Fiction* resulted in children adopting value systems in which violence was perceived to be 'cool' and 'being in control'. However, Philo does note that children's values systems are also very influenced by parental controls, legal sanctions, education and peer groups and this means that children do not necessarily copy or identify completely with any single source of influence.

CRITICISMS OF THE HYPODERMIC-SYRINGE MODEL

The hypodermic-syringe model has attracted a lot of criticism.

- Researchers such as Belson often fail to make sure that the participants in their research share the same definitions of violence as the research teams.

- We have to be careful about generalising from the American experience because audiences in the USA have access to a greater range of media compared with the UK, and gun violence is far more widespread there than in the UK.

- Key concepts are poorly operationalised by the hypodermic model. David Gauntlett (2000) notes that it is often unclear:
  - what media content is being defined as 'violence' (i.e. real violence in the news is often omitted)
  - whether very minor or extremely serious acts of 'violence' shown in the media lead to trivial or major acts in the real world
  - whether the 'effects' are short-term or long-term.

- The model ignores possible positive effects of exposure to media content such as 'sensitisation', e.g. Jock Young (1987) argues that television can inhibit violence by showing its consequences in terms of pain, suffering and the grief that it causes the relatives of victims.

- Murdock and McCron (1979) argue that the model looks at media influence in isolation and fails to consider other important social influences on violence such as gender-role socialisation, family background, peer group pressure, social class, the experience of unemployment, drugs, etc.

Think it through

The view of a powerful media seducing children away from their better nature is part of a Western ideology that sees children as essentially innocent, vulnerable and in need of protection from the potentially harmful influences exerted by the media. Theorists from both the left and the right have tended to see children as a passive, **homogeneous** audience who are unable to see the difference between mediated (on screen) and situational (lived) reality. Clearly, children do imitate what they see on screen, from the actions of Power Rangers to the pro-social activities of Blue Peter. However, research shows that different people experience excitement, violence, horror and power – as well as other media and cultural contexts – very differently, need it differently and attach different meanings to it.

Source: Kitzinger, J. (1997) 'Media influence', *Sociology Review*, April

1 How does Western ideology view children in general?

2 What positive effects might the media have for children?

3 Evaluate the view that audiences experience screen violence in different ways.

Homogeneous: Sharing the same social characteristics.

How much censorship is there in the UK?

- The Independent Television Council (ITC) has agreement from all television companies in the UK to show sex and violence only after a 9pm watershed.
- The Video Recordings Act 1985 made the video rental and sale of some films illegal, i.e. video nasties.
- The Broadcasting Standards Commission monitors complaints about the content of television programmes.
- The British Board of Film Classification gives certificates to films and videos on the basis of their sexual and violent content.
- Both terrestial and satellite television stations cut films even further and warn audiences about sexual and violent content and bad language.

www.mediawatch.com – this is the official website of a pressure group that strongly subscribes to the hypodermic-syringe model.
www.theory.org.uk – In particular, you should visit the page on this website where David Gauntlett is extremely critical of the hypodermic-syringe model.

Round-up

The hypodermic-syringe model, despite its methodological weaknesses, has had a major influence on the debate about the effects of screen violence and censorship. Sociologists are generally sceptical of the model because they believe that it assumes passive audiences and underestimates their active response and intelligence. The next section will examine research into how media-literate audiences really are.

Are people passive or active users of media?

The active audience

Many media sociologists argue that the audience is far more active than the hypodermic-syringe model of media effects accepts. J.T. Klapper (1960), for example, argues that such models ignore the three selective filters that audiences use in order to make sense of media content.

Klapper's theory recognises the importance of the active audience. He argues that we should be thinking about what people do with the media rather than what the media do to people. Generally, people use the media to reinforce attitudes that they already have.

KLAPPER'S SELECTIVE FILTERS MODEL

1 **Selective exposure**
People are exposed to media content in different ways. They make different decisions about what to watch or buy depending on their existing tastes, values and experiences. These are based on influences such as social class, gender, age, education, etc. People do not generally choose media that will change their attitudes.

2 **Selective perception**
People interpret media content in different ways. If people are exposed to a media message with which they are unsympathetic, they may adapt it so that it fits in with their beliefs.

3 **Selective retention**
People tend to remember what they want to remember, i.e. usually those aspects of media content that fit their belief system.

The uses and gratifications model

This model of media effects believes that human beings have particular social needs, e.g. the need for social contact, personal relationships, community, status, excitement, etc. Media sociologists such as James Lull (1990) argue that different types of audiences use different types of media to meet these needs. The media can have a number of functions in relation to this, as shown in the table below.

The uses and gratifications model focuses on the active use of media by audiences. However, it has been criticised for failing to explain why people have particular needs or why people choose particular types of media to satisfy themselves.

The media and social needs

Social needs	Audience use/gratification
Isolated individuals such as the elderly and housebound mothers may have a need for community, i.e. interaction with others.	Television and radio, especially soap operas such as *Coronation Street* and *The Archers*, may compensate for the lack of real human contact by encouraging identification with a fictional community.
Some groups, e.g. the working class, who do not have formal qualifications or power at work may have a need for status.	Giving the answers to questions on game shows in front of family and friends may result in people being given status and respect.
Some social groups, e.g. young people, may have a need for excitement.	Violent films may have a cathartic effect, i.e. people can get rid of pent-up feelings by watching and as they do so feel they are participating in films and televised sport.
Family relationships need to be stimulated and maintained.	Media content may be a social lubricant – it can initiate and encourage family interaction, e.g. talking about a particular news story or drama storyline.

Important studies

David Morrison (1999) showed violent scenes from films to a range of social groups, e.g. women over 60, single men aged 18–24, retired male war veterans, etc. He discovered that factors such as the use of humour, or how realistic the situation is, reduce the impact of violence but that the key criteria for judging the level of violence in a scene is that it is 'fair'. For example, few viewers saw as shocking a scene in *Pulp Fiction*, in which a man accidentally has his head blown off, because it was dealt with in a humorous manner. However, scenes of domestic violence from the film *Ladybird, Ladybird* caused distress to most groups because of the realism of the setting, the strong language and the unequal power between the male and his female victim. Morrison's study therefore supports Klapper's view that audiences use the media to reinforce values and prejudices that they already have – the impact of violence depends on the context in which it is shown and something like domestic violence is regarded as being a very real and unjust phenomenon.

David Buckingham (1996) looked at how children respond emotionally to screen violence. He concluded that children use a range of coping strategies that enable them to deal with the content of horror and violent films. Their main strategy involves questioning the reality of the media portrayal using their own experience, as well as evidence and logic. Buckingham concludes that media that cross the boundary between fact and fiction are the most likely to cause confused and emotional responses from children.

Early research into media effects on audiences often assumed that they all passively received media messages in the same way; recent research shows that audiences often select, interpret and react to media messages in active ways according to their own social backgrounds and prejudices

Postmodernist analyses: Analyses based on the theory that suggests industrial society has been superseded by a media-saturated society in which the old indicators of identity – e.g. social class – have been replaced by new forms of identity based on consumption of style, fashion, etc.

Reception analysis

From the 1980s onwards, studies of the media focused on how particular audiences 'received' media messages, i.e. how they actively interpreted and acted upon media content in its variety of forms.

David Morley (1980) is typical of this reception analysis approach. His work is particularly critical of Klapper's selective filters model. His research agrees that audiences can interpret media messages in a variety of ways but he argues that there is a dominant or preferred interpretation (or 'reading'). This dominant reading is shaped by cultural expectations and the way media institutions structure particular stories. A good example of this was the death of Diana, Princess of Wales. The dominant reading focused on national loss and grief. It was therefore difficult at that time to have a different view (or 'reading'), e.g. that her death, whilst sad, was no more important than the death of anyone else.

Postmodernist theory

In the late 1990s, **postmodernist analyses** of the media have suggested that audiences create their own meanings from media texts. Postmodernists argue that there is no such thing as 'shared interpretation' because there is no such thing as fixed 'truth' or 'reality'. They believe that truth and reality are relative. Therefore, media messages are 'polysemic' (i.e. they mean different things to different individuals and audiences).

Critique of postmodernist theory

Philo (2001) and the Glasgow University Media Group (GUMG) are critical of the 'complacent relativism' of postmodernist ideas. They suggest that newspapers, magazines and television news contain particular messages (Morley's 'preferred readings') and that audiences are aware of this and can clearly see these media perspectives. However, how audiences interpret these messages depends upon their:

- specific belief systems about particular subjects (although these beliefs could be weakened by the nature of the media text, e.g. by the images used)
- direct experience
- use of logic and evidence.

Philo argues that people do not simply interpret media content on the basis of pre-existing belief systems; they are willing to accept or to reject media messages, and even to accept new ones. In particular, television messages are most likely to be accepted because television images were more 'immediate' and 'stuck more'. Philo refers to this as 'seeing is believing'.

 Visit the GUMG at: **www.gla.ac.uk/departments/sociology/media.html** to see their latest research on audiences. Visit **www.cultsock.ndirect.co.uk** and look up what Mick Underwood has to say about the various models of media effects.

Think it through

People often assume that they are immune to media manipulation. They accept that the media have power to influence – but only to influence other people. Consider the following examples. A film-maker defends himself from accusations of glorifying sexual violence. It is only a film, he says, just entertainment. The audience is intelligent enough to know this. Viewers know the difference between fact and fantasy. Besides, the rape scene is 'ironic'.

Tobacco companies argue that media messages have very limited influence. They state that their adverts only encourage people to switch brands, not to take up smoking in the first place. A soap-opera shows a scene of two men kissing. A right-wing moral campaigner complains that this could 'corrupt' young viewers.

Adapted from: Kitzinger, J. (1997) 'Media influence', *Sociology Review*, April

1 Identify three views about the audience contained in this extract.

2 Some sociologists argue that the media-effects debate is very political. Using the extract as illustration, explain what that statement means.

3 Outline and assess the view that people are immune to media manipulation.

Round-up

The relationship between media institutions and their audience is complex. What Morley and Philo, in particular, show us is that audiences are engaged in constant interaction with dominant messages that are apparent in media content. They may reject these but they may also use them to add to and reinforce their existing stock of beliefs and attitudes.

What is the role of the mass media today?

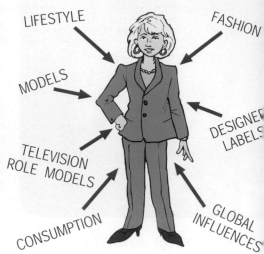

21st-century identity

The postmodernist view

Postmodernist sociologists argue that UK society has undergone such fundamental change in the past decade that we are now living in what they call a 'postmodern age'. They base this conclusion on their observations and interpretations of economic and cultural changes.

Postmodernists argue that postmodern societies are 'media-saturated'.

- Economically, it is suggested that industrialisation and the manufacture of goods is in decline. In the postmodern age, service industries concerned with the processing and transmission of information and knowledge have become more important than factory production.

- In cultural terms, the mass media have more influence on our lives than traditional influences such as family, community, social class, gender or ethnicity.

This has a number of consequences for culture and identity.

- The globalisation of media means that we now have more cultural influences available to us in terms of lifestyle choices and consumption.

- The media often provide most of our experience of social reality. Postmodernists argue that the media often define our lifestyles and identity for us – i.e. how we should dress and look, how we should organise our homes and gardens, what we should think, how we should be feeling, etc. are shaped by a variety of media such as lifestyle magazines, television documentaries, advertising. If we don't like any aspect of ourselves, all sorts of media can advise us on how we can make-over our bodies, relationships, lives, etc. Moreover, we no longer belong to real communities – the online communities of internet chat-rooms and the imagined communities of television soap operas have replaced real relationships with neighbours and extended kin.

Do you know more about the characters from soap operas than about the people living in your street?

- In the postmodern world, the media inform us that the consumption of images and signs for their own sake is more important than the consumption of the goods they represent. We buy the designer labels rather than the clothes and goods themselves, and we judge people on how 'cool' they look or behave rather than on the basis of ability, skill or personality.

Postmodernists conclude that there has been a radical revolution in the way we think about the social world as a result of these postmodern influences. It is suggested that we no longer look to grand theories (postmodernists call these 'meta-narratives') such as science, Marxism, etc. to explain the world and its problems. An increasingly media-literate society is now aware of how diversity, plurality and difference can provide us with greater choice in terms of values, belief systems, solutions, etc. Identity is now organised around consumption and lifestyle choices rather than traditional sources of identity such as class, gender, ethnicity, occupation, community and nation.

Think it through

The internet is often used by activists such as the anti-globalisation movement as a means of communicating information that the giant corporations who own and control the world's media are unlikely to want to report. It is argued that the internet is 'a loose and anarchic confederation of millions of users around the world who communicate in perhaps the freest forum of speech in history'. From the point of view of global media-conglomerates, the internet, which is essentially a body of people exchanging information and communication largely on a 'gift' basis, is an annoyance because these companies are unable to obtain exclusive commercial rights over websites. They can control some points of entry, i.e. internet service providers such as AOL and the bigger service sites such as Amazon, but the distribution of information on the web is largely outside their control. Governments, too, have confined their efforts to attempting to monitor and control pornography, especially paedophilia, and to closing down sites that promote race hate and terrorism.

1 Identify and explain three reasons why media corporations and governments may attempt to control internet content.

2 In what ways can the internet promote freedom of speech and democratic practices?

3 Outline and assess the view that the benefits of new media technologies outweigh the costs.

The cultural optimist perspective (the neophiliacs)	The cultural pessimist perspective
The digital revolution in television offers consumers greater choice. Competition between media institutions will result in more high-quality media output.	Increased choice leads to an inevitable decline in quality of television. Harvey (1990) notes that television is about transmitting a 'candy-floss culture', which speaks to everyone and to no one in particular. A survey conducted by the British Broadcasting Standards Commission (BBSC) in 2003 showed that television viewers feel that the existence of more channels has led to a decline in the standard of television programmes.
Convergence in media technologies (i.e. interaction between computers, television services and music, e.g. MP3 technology) will also increase consumer choice.	The poor are excluded from this information superhighway because they cannot afford to plug into the new media revolution. They are a 'digital underclass' who cannot keep up with the middle-class technological élite.
New media technologies offer opportunities to people to acquire the education and information they need in order to play an active role in democratic societies and to make politicians more accountable to the people.	Increasing concentration of ownership undermines both democracy and freedom of speech. Owners of the media exercise powerful influence both over government and over the flow of information required for people to effectively participate in democratic societies.
The Labour government intends to control the media by setting up an independent 'super-regulator' known as the Office of Communications (OfCom), which brings together the BSC, the Independent Television Authority, the Radio Authority, etc. Its main task will be to protect the interests of citizens by maintaining standards in media content and balancing freedom of speech against the need to protect against offensive or harmful material.	The newspaper and satellite television industries will not be regulated by OfCom. Some see this as the government giving in to the power of media barons such as Rupert Murdoch.

The critique of postmodernism

Postmodernists are criticised for exaggerating the degree of social change. Evidence from attitude surveys indicates that many people see social class, ethnicity, family and religion as still having profound influence over their lives and identities. Media influence is undoubtedly important but it is not the main factor in most people's lifestyle choices. Postmodernist analyses also tend to be rather naïve because they ignore the fact that many people are unable to make consumption choices (and thereby define themselves through these) because of the continuing inequalities caused by unemployment, poverty, racial discrimination, patriarchy, etc. Traditional forms of inequality remain a crucial influence and access to the internet, digital television and so on is denied to many people in the UK because of their poverty.

The future of the mass media in the UK

According to Curran and Seaton (1991), two perspectives dominate the debate about the future of the media in the UK:

- the 'neophiliacs' are optimistic about the spread and influence of media technologies, whereas
- the 'cultural pessimists' are particularly concerned about the digital revolution in television – which has brought about the appearance of more choice, but in reality has led to a decline in standards.

For a more detailed comparison of these perspectives see the table above.

Mick Underwood's **www.cultsock.ndirect.co.uk** *contains excellent discussions on the range of new media technologies, and especially the internet. The Campaign for Press and Broadcasting Freedom* **www.presscampaign.org** *monitors ownership of media and government regulation of the BBC and new media technologies.*

The future of public broadcasting

A great deal of sociological attention will be focused on the role of the BBC in future years. Cultural pessimists see it as the last means through which quality and cultural standards can be maintained. However, the BBC's unique role in the media may be under threat for the following reasons:

- Critics of the BBC are critical of the licence fee – they refer to it as a 'cultural poll tax' and argue that the general public should not have to pay for BBC services that they do not use. However, the 2003 BBSC survey into television viewing habits suggests the BBC is actually now preferred for the first time in 34 years by audiences because it is seen as producing quality television in contrast to that on commercial channels.

- Commercial television sees the licence fee as giving the BBC an unfair advantage in the marketplace, e.g. Disney and Viacom fiercely contested the BBC's decision to launch digital channels for children because it would eat into their market.

Round-up

Postmodernists and neophiliacs are optimistic about the future role of new media technologies. However, cultural pessimists remind us that we need to be cautious about ways in which the new media may be used and also how old media, particularly the BBC, might be undermined.

Mass media: summative review

The media revolution

The past twenty-five years has seen a revolution in the use of mass-media products in our everyday lives. In the 1950s, your grandparents' use of media was probably restricted to reading newspapers, magazines and comics, listening to BBC radio programmes and '78' gramophone records and going to the cinema. Television didn't really take-off in popularity until the late 1950s, and until 1982 choice was limited to three terrestrial channels, BBC1, BBC2 and ITV.

Compare this with your own experience of the mass media. If you or your parents subscribe to BSkyB or a digital service, it is likely that you have access to hundreds of television channels. Some of these will be beamed into your home from outside the UK. Some of these channels will be interactive – you can choose the camera angles for live football matches, participate live in quizzes such as *Who Wants To Be a Millionaire?* and vote for your favourite *Pop Idol* or inhabitant of the *Big Brother* house. If you enjoy music, you can choose from literally hundreds of BBC and commercial radio stations, many of which occupy specific consumer niches, i.e. they specialise in things like sport, classical music, reggae, chat, etc. Moreover, you can choose to buy your music in a range of formats – vinyl, tape, CD, CDVD, or minidisk or you can download it in MP3 format from the internet. You may have a huge music collection but actually own no records, tapes or CDs. Rather, your music is stored on your computer or on an iPod. If you're bored with current releases, you can 'burn' your own CDs with music of your choice or get an internet site to do it for you.

The twenty-first century

The advance of media technologies and products shows no signs of stopping. The twenty-first century looks like it will be the age of media convergence as media conglomerates look to bring digital television, DVD, computer technology, telecommunications, e-mail, video-conferencing, mobile phones and the internet together in integrated formats. Moreover, these media conglomerates are increasingly moving towards vertical integration, i.e. owning all the stages in the production of a media product, and using parts of their media industry (e.g. newspapers, magazines, television, etc.) to promote their other media products such as music or films.

Thinking positively about the media

Some sociologists are very positive about these developments. Pluralists see audiences as well served by the media and the professionals that make up its ranks. It is argued that media content reflects the values, attitudes and interests of those who use the media – in this sense, the media is a mirror on society. Other sociologists argue that audiences actively use the media to gratify their own particular social needs. Postmodernists are in general agreement – they argue that our global, media-saturated society provides us with more choices than we have ever experienced before and that we can use these to construct our identities. Consequently, we can see that traditional sources of identity such as social class, community, gender, etc. are no longer important. Rather, the media (especially advertising) makes us aware that personal identity can be shaped by consumption of style and fashion, e.g. buying the 'right' car, drinking the 'right' drink, etc. Whatever the perspective we go with here, the media is generally portrayed as a force for good in our lives.

Thinking negatively about the media

However, critical sociologists take exception to this view of the media. Marxists argue that 'information is power' and whoever has control over the flow of news and education wields tremendous power over the hearts and minds of the general public. They believe that societies can only be truly democratic if all members of society have equal access to all information available – the media is obviously a major source of such information.

Instrumental Marxists are particularly concerned about the increasingly concentrated nature of media ownership. They argue that media owners deliberately abuse their position and put pressure on their employees such as editors and journalists to manufacture a news content that generally supports the interests of the capitalist establishment to which media owners belong. It is argued therefore that concentration of media ownership and the trends towards conglomeration are undermining democracy because members of the public are not given the full facts and may even be diverted altogether from the 'truth' about how capitalist societies are organised.

However, not all Marxists agree with this analysis. Hegemonic Marxists reject the conspiracy element, although they agree that media content generally supports capitalist interests. However, they suggest that this is a product of the generally middle-class backgrounds of most journalists, which means that they reject extreme or radical ideas in favour of those that support the mainstream. This consensual worldview, alongside their desire to attract the largest possible audiences, results in them subscribing to news values that produce stories generally uncritical of the existing social order. As a result, the inequalities that underpin the economic system largely go unaddressed and capitalist wealth and power are not seriously challenged.

Some aspects of the sociology of the media have focused on the role of the media as an agency of social control. Moral panic theory, in particular, notes how the media may function on behalf of society to reduce the social anxieties brought about by social change and particularly groups perceived as a threat to social order, e.g. adolescents. It is argued that the public anxiety generated by the tone of media reporting often leads to harsher policing and legislation.

Thinking about the audience

Many of the above approaches assume that audiences are somehow 'influenced' by media content. They tend to take a deterministic approach. For example, Marxists clearly believe that media content operates to divert the working class from the 'true' nature of their exploitation by encouraging the 'dumbing down' of both newspaper and public service broadcasting. This assumption can also be seen in discussions of 'media representations' of particular groups such as men, women, minority ethnic groups, particular social classes, etc. Feminists, for example, often argue that the way that women are portrayed can have negative consequences for them – images of 'thin' models have been connected to eating disorders whilst it is believed that media representations of women that focus exclusively on the mother-housewife role may assist in the lowering of women's aspirations in regard to work and careers. These views are, of course, not dissimilar to those held by the hypodermic-syringe model of media effects, which suggests that screen violence may be responsible for violent crime and anti-social behaviour. What all these views of the media have in common is the assumption that audiences are generally passive and are incapable of making their own decisions about media content. Recent research by reception analysts suggests that this view of the audience is patronising and does not take account of the way much of the audience actively engages with media content in an intelligent and media-literate way.

New media technologies

Finally, some sociologists are concerned about the direction the new emerging technologies are taking. Marxists, in particular, are concerned about inequalities in access to computer technology, the internet, etc. and the possible emergence of what has been termed a 'digital underclass'. They point out that middle-class access to the world-wide web is likely to increase already wide educational inequalities in the UK. It is also noted with alarm that much of this new technology is in the hands of the media conglomerates, who may use it to further their own political and economic interests.

Media commentators are particularly worried about the future role of the internet, which at the moment is regarded as the most democratic of all media outlets because there is no control over what can be posted on the world-wide web. Consequently the internet has been used to promote a wide variety of political views, many of which are critical of the existing world political and economic order, and to organise and coordinate anti-globalisation campaigns. However, there are signs that governments are now looking for ways to 'control' such sites and that the commercialisation of the internet is underway as the conglomerates buy up internet service providers and use the courts to shut down sites that threaten their profits.

Mass media: self-assessment questions

1 What percentage of British households in the contemporary UK is connected to the internet?
   a 83%
   b 63%
   c 42%
   d 22%

2 What percentage of internet users are female?
   a 15%
   b 50%
   c 60%
   d 30%

3 What is the 'digital underclass' denied access to according to sociologists?
   a Satellite television
   b The information superhighway
   c Digital radio
   d Newspapers and magazines

4 What is 'conglomeration'?
   a Ownership of all of the stages in the production, distribution and consumption of a media product.
   b Ownership of more than one media form, e.g. newspapers and television.
   c Ownership of media in foreign countries.
   d Monopoly of media institutions in one large company.

5 Which theory of the media argues that media owners manipulate media content?
   a Hegemonic Marxists
   b Instrumental Marxists
   c Pluralists
   d Postmodernists

6 Which theory of the media do journalists and editors tend to subscribe to?
   a Cultural effects theory
   b Instrumental Marxism
   c Structuralism
   d Pluralism

7 What group of sociologists argues that media content reflects the social backgrounds of journalists?
   a The Glasgow University Media Group
   b The Centre for Contemporary Cultural Studies
   c Instrumental Marxists
   d The Goldsmiths College Media Group

8 The process by which events are prioritised and selected as news is known as what?
   a Gate-keeping
   b Agenda-setting
   c Sub-editing
   d Primary definers

9 Which of the following is not a bureaucratic constraint on news-gathering?
   a Deadlines
   b Costs
   c Extraordinariness
   d Ratings

10 What do journalists use to work out whether a story or event is newsworthy?
   a A hierarchy of credibility
   b Primary definers
   c Owners
   d News values

11 Why do moral panics come about, according to Furedi?
   a They are the product of real fears of victims of crime in the inner cities.
   b They are deliberately caused by capitalists in order to divide and rule the working-class.
   c They are the product of news values.
   d They are caused by social anxieties brought about by social change.

12 Which of the following is the public service broadcaster?
   a ITV
   b Sky
   c BBC
   d C5

13 What does Wolf mean when she accuses the media of perpetuating a 'beauty myth'?
   a They portray women mainly as sexual objects.
   b They portray women's bodies as constantly in need of improvement.
   c They portray women mainly as mother-housewives.
   d They rarely portray women in leading roles in television drama.

14 What does Westwood mean when she says that television is now beginning to show males and females in 'transgressive' roles?

a Programmes often show men and women in traditional roles.

b Some programmes now show females with male characteristics and males with female characteristics.

c There are now more programmes with females only.

d Women now play more lead roles.

15 Gary Whannell argues that the portrayal of which male role-model indicates a media acceptance of new forms of masculinity?

a Graham Norton

b Des O'Connor

c Bruce Willis

d David Beckham

16 What form of media does Kellner argue is a major means of expressing black identity?

a Reggae music

b *The Voice* newspaper

c The Cosby Show

d Rap music

17 What percentage of people portrayed on television come from minority ethnic backgrounds?

a 7.5%

b 5%

c 10%

d 1%

18 Which argument is based on the hypodermic-syringe model of the media?

a People are unaffected by violence on television.

b People should have the choice to watch what they want on television.

c Some people imitate the violence they see on television.

d Television is not responsible for crime.

19 Which of these effects does screen violence have according to Elizabeth Newson?

a De-sensitisation

b Catharsis

c Sensitisation

d Gratification

20 What social factors are ignored by the hypodermic-syringe model according to their critics?

a Family background

b The influence of the peer group

c Drugs

d All of these

21 Link each of the following sentences to the following four media sociologists; Lull, Morley, Klapper and Philo.

a Television audiences are willing both to accept and reject media messages, and even accept new ones.

b Audiences use the media in order to confirm their existing prejudices.

c Audiences use the media to satisfy needs that they have.

d Audiences are often strongly encouraged to follow the media's interpretation of an event.

22 Which theory argues that we now live in a 'media-saturated' society?

a Pluralism

b Postmodernism

c Marxism

d The hypodermic-syringe model

23 What is the most important source of identity in the postmodern world?

a Social class

b The mass media

c Community

d Globalisation

24 What is the name of the new super-regulator of the media set up by the Labour government?

a The Broadcasting Standards Council

b OfCom

c Oftel

d The British Board of Film Classification

25 Which of these statements is not a 'cultural pessimist' view of the future of the media?

a The digital television revolution will bring about a decline in standards.

b The digital television revolution will increase choice for everyone.

c Concentration of ownership undermines democracy.

d The Internet is yet another engine of inequality.

Mass media: a timeline

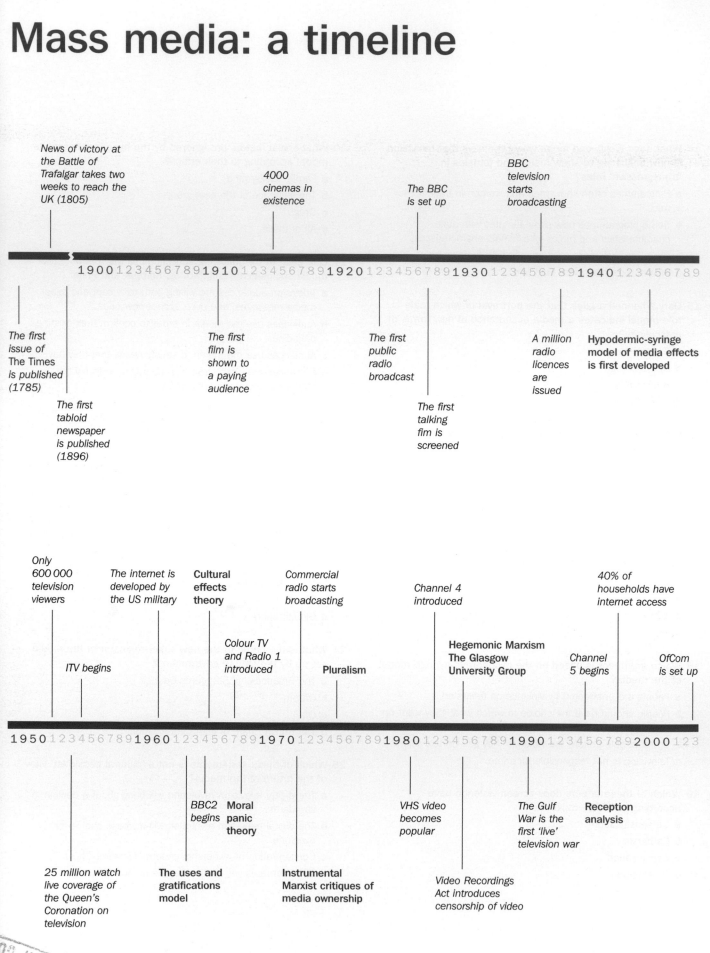

News of victory at the Battle of Trafalgar takes two weeks to reach the UK (1805)

4000 cinemas in existence

The BBC is set up

BBC television starts broadcasting

1900 1 2 3 4 5 6 7 8 9 1910 1 2 3 4 5 6 7 8 9 1920 1 2 3 4 5 6 7 8 9 1930 1 2 3 4 5 6 7 8 9 1940 1 2 3 4 5 6 7 8 9

The first issue of The Times is published (1785)

The first tabloid newspaper is published (1896)

The first film is shown to a paying audience

The first public radio broadcast

The first talking fim is screened

A million radio licences are issued

Hypodermic-syringe model of media effects is first developed

Only 600 000 television viewers

The internet is developed by the US military

Cultural effects theory

Commercial radio starts broadcasting

Channel 4 introduced

40% of households have internet access

ITV begins

Colour TV and Radio 1 introduced

Pluralism

Hegemonic Marxism The Glasgow University Group

Channel 5 begins

OfCom is set up

1950 1 2 3 4 5 6 7 8 9 1960 1 2 3 4 5 6 7 8 9 1970 1 2 3 4 5 6 7 8 9 1980 1 2 3 4 5 6 7 8 9 1990 1 2 3 4 5 6 7 8 9 2000 1 2 3

BBC2 begins

Moral panic theory

VHS video becomes popular

The Gulf War is the first 'live' television war

Reception analysis

25 million watch live coverage of the Queen's Coronation on television

The uses and gratifications model

Instrumental Marxist critiques of media ownership

Video Recordings Act introduces censorship of video

Section 4 Research methods

Research methods: a mindmap

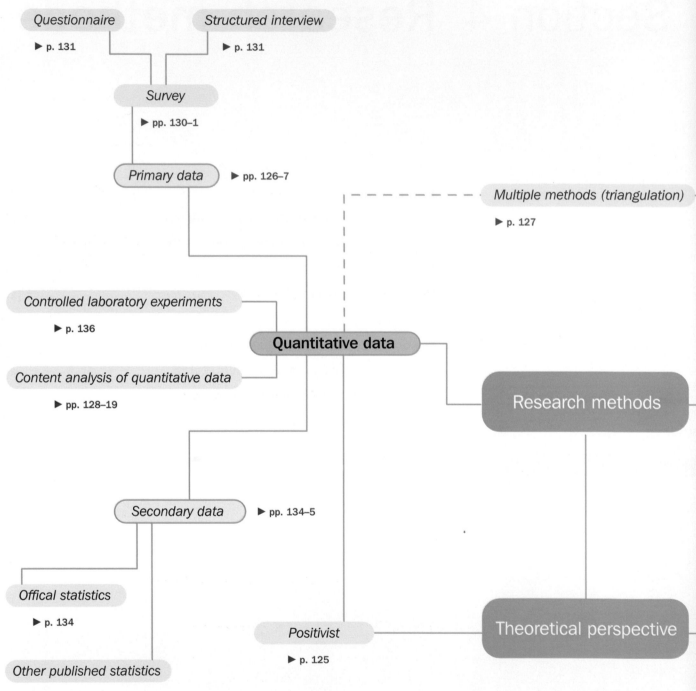

Questionnaire
► p. 131

Structured interview
► p. 131

Survey
► pp. 130–1

Primary data   ► pp. 126–7

Multiple methods (triangulation)
► p. 127

Controlled laboratory experiments
► p. 136

Quantitative data

Content analysis of quantitative data
► pp. 128–19

Research methods

Secondary data   ► pp. 134–5

Offical statistics
► p. 134

Positivist
► p. 125

Theoretical perspective

Other published statistics
► p. 135

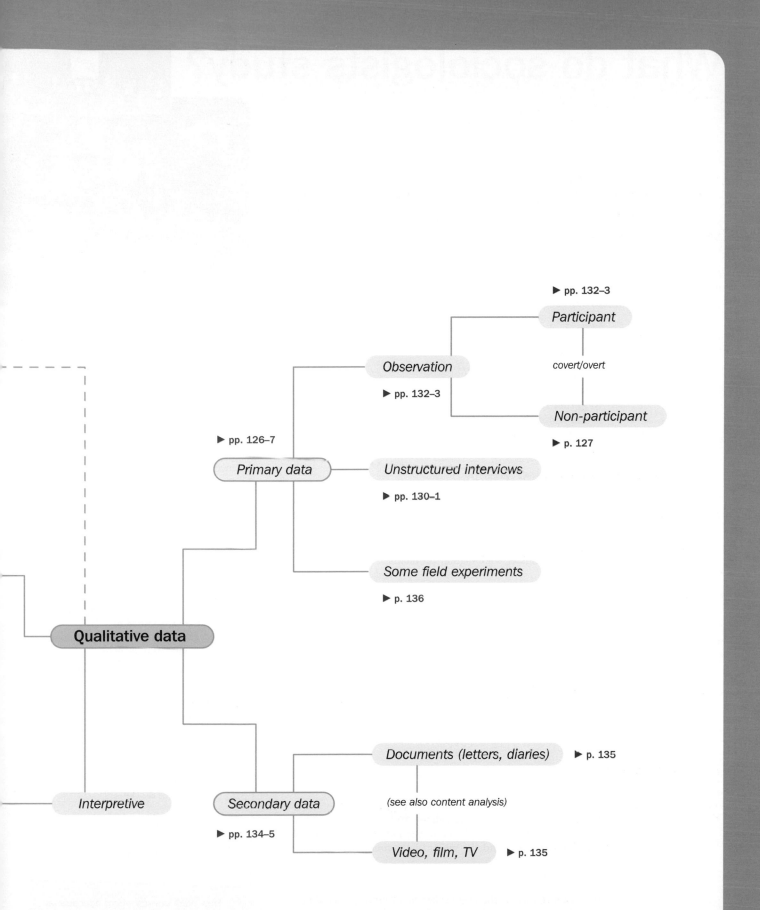

▶ pp. 132–3

Participant

covert/overt

Observation

▶ pp. 132–3

Non-participant

▶ p. 127

▶ pp. 126–7

Primary data

Unstructured interviews

▶ pp. 130–1

Some field experiments

▶ p. 136

Qualitative data

Documents (letters, diaries) ▶ p. 135

(see also content analysis)

Interpretive

Secondary data

▶ pp. 134–5

Video, film, TV ▶ p. 135

What do sociologists study?

S ociologists are inquisitive. They want to know and understand about society, social institutions, organisations and how people interact with each other. If we want to find out about something in everyday life we can ask questions about it, read about it, or maybe take part in a social activity. Sociological researchers do much the same but, as social scientists, they do it more systematically.

Good sociology is based on good **empirical** evidence that has been collected using reliable research techniques. The evidence and the conclusions drawn from it are published so that others can judge it.

What's going on here?

Empirical: Relating to observation or experiment rather than theory.

Why do sociologists do research?

Descriptive research

Some research aims simply to describe what is being studied, to gather information and to increase our knowledge of the social world. It asks questions such as 'How do the exam results of boys compare with those of girls?' or 'How do husbands and wives share household tasks?'

Explanatory research

Phenomena: Anything that can be seen or perceived.

This starts with description but goes on to look for the causes of social **phenomena**, such as 'Why do boys do less well than girls in exams?' and 'Why do women still do most of the housework?' It looks for the causes of problems, which may be social problems or sociological problems.

Cause and effect

Correlate: To show the relationship between two variables; may be positive or negative.

Trying to explain something raises the question of cause and effect. If factors A and B occur together, and B changes when A changes, these factors are **correlated** but it does not follow that A *causes* B. There may be no causal link between them; it may be that B causes A; it may be that a third factor, C, influences them both.

 In natural sciences (chemistry, biology and physics), researchers often use experiments to try to identify which 'independent variables' (causes) result in which 'dependent variables' (effects). See p. 136.

For example, a researcher might find (descriptive research) that young people who watch violent videos (factor A) are violent towards other young people (factor B). It could be that:

- there is no causal link between video-watching and violent behaviour
- video-watching causes violent behaviour
- violent behaviour causes video-watching
- a third factor (e.g. violence in the home) causes both the video-watching and the violent behaviour.

Action research

In action research, the researcher is actively involved in planning and introducing some change of policy and practice in a particular setting (e.g. a school, a hospital, a social work team) and then in studying the impact of the change as it happens in order to evaluate its effects.

SOCIAL PROBLEMS AND SOCIOLOGICAL PROBLEMS

Sociologists are not only concerned with explaining deviant behaviour or solving social problems such as juvenile crime or family breakdown. Many sociologists are interested in trying to explain 'normal' behaviour. For example, it is just as much of a problem to explain why most marriages last for a lifetime as it is to explain why some end in divorce.

Think it through

For each of the following research topics, identify the concepts that a researcher would need to operationalise. How could this be done and what are the problems?

We have made a start on the first question, as an example.

1 Why do children from working-class families get in trouble with the police more than children from middle-class families?

Concept	Operational definition	Problems/ weaknesses
Child	Person aged between 10 and 16 years	
Working-class		
Get in trouble with the police	Receive a formal caution or be convicted of an offence	
Middle-class		

2 How does poverty affect educational achievement?

3 What importance do people of Asian origin attach to their ethnic identity?

RESEARCH METHODS

What do sociologists think they are studying?

In studying the natural world, scientists assume that it exists independently of the observer and that stones, weather, chemical elements, etc. have no self-awareness and do not act with purpose. Scientists use observational and experimental techniques that produce objective information.

In this context, 'objective' means 'independent of the scientist'.

But sociologists study social phenomena and people rather than the natural world, and therefore need to ask the question 'What methods are appropriate for studying social phenomena?' The answer depends on how we view social phenomena. If we think they are similar to natural phenomena, then we can borrow the research methods of the natural scientists. But if we think social phenomena are different from natural phenomena, we should use different research methods. This is the basis of the debate between **positivist** and **interpretivist** approaches to sociology.

- A positivist approach to sociology argues that social phenomena are as real and objective as phenomena in the natural world. It argues that sociologists should study only what they can objectively see, measure and count and use methods that produce **quantitative** data, aiming to arrive at social laws that can explain the causes of events in the social world – and even to make predictions, as **natural science** has done. The researcher should avoid personal involvement and produce value-free evidence. The positivist view was taken by some early sociologists, mainly in the nineteenth century when sociology was striving to be regarded as the equal of the natural sciences.

Blundell and Griffiths (2002) includes summaries of 25 recent research studies, with commentaries.

Positivist: The belief that knowledge must be based on observation or experiment.

Interpretivist: An approach in sociology that focuses on the meaning that social phenomena have for the people involved.

Quantitative: Research that concentrates on collecting statistical data.

Natural sciences: These include chemistry, biology and physics.

Qualitative: Research where the sociologist aims to understand the meaning of social action.

- An interpretivist approach to sociology argues that social phenomena are different from natural phenomena. It argues that people are active, conscious beings who act with intention and purpose because of the way they make sense of the social situation they are in. For example, a family is not just a group of people with a biological relationship but a group of people who perceive themselves as a family and act accordingly. Social phenomena do not exist independently of people, as plants or birds do, but are created by people who share an understanding of the situation. Social researchers therefore need methods that enable them to get at these shared understandings. These methods generate **qualitative** data, i.e. data that express how people make sense of social situations. This view, although developed by Max Weber at the end of the nineteenth century and taken up by anthropologists in the 1920s and 1930s, did not become widespread in mainstream sociology until the 1960s and 1970s.

Operationalising concepts

Operationalise: To define something so that it can be measured or counted.

All researchers have to 'operationalise concepts'. This means defining the phenomenon being studied so that it can be counted or measured in a way that is clearly understood and that can be used consistently. This may be straightforward. For example, if we want to study changes over time in the age at which women give birth to their first baby, it is easy to agree on what is meant by 'age', 'women' 'birth' and 'baby' and to express these in objective, quantitative terms. However, what if we want to study changes in health and illness over time? We have to decide what we mean by 'healthy' – that is, we have to operationalise the concept 'healthy'. Do we mean:

- a state where the individual says they feel well, or
- a state where a doctor can find nothing wrong, or
- a physical condition where the individual can lead the sort of life they want to lead?

And should we include mental health as well as physical health in our definition? Clearly, how we define and operationalise 'health' will affect how many healthy people we find   and, to make comparisons over time, we must always use the same definition.

Watch out

It is a mistake to suggest that sociologists, or sociological research, fall neatly into one of two camps called 'positivist' and 'interpretivist'. For many years, researchers have recognised that different approaches suit different subject matter and that most social phenomena are best studied using a combination of objective quantitative methods and subjective qualitative methods – see pp. 130–3.

Round-up

Sociological research takes a systematic approach. It seeks to describe or explain social phenomena using a variety of methods that draw on both positivist and interpretivist approaches. Researchers must be clear about how they are defining and using concepts, especially when there may be disagreement about what they mean.

Coursework advice

If you do any research yourself, always make sure that you operationalise your concepts.

How do sociologists conduct research?

Choosing what to research

The first step is to choose a topic to research. The choice will be influenced by:

- *The interests and values of the researcher* – obviously, any researcher will want to study topics they find interesting but the question of 'values' raises some questions. If a researcher thinks a topic is important enough to research, perhaps because it raises moral or political questions, they may have strong feelings about it and there must be a risk that these feelings will affect how they perceive the situation and do their research.

- *Current debates in the academic world* – sociologists, like anyone else, will be drawn to study topics that are creating interest and controversy among their colleagues.

The choice will also be influenced by practical issues.

- *The time and resources needed* – first-time researchers often underestimate how long it takes to collect data, analyse it, and write the report. A lone researcher, perhaps studying part-time for a qualification, will only be able to do a small-scale study (maybe a **case study**). Large-scale studies need a team of professional researchers and can take years to complete.

- *Access to the subject-matter* – some areas of social life are more available to researchers than others. For example, the private life of a family is much harder to study than the public life of a school classroom. Rich and powerful people can deny access to a researcher more easily than poor and powerless people can.

- *Whether funding is available* – large-scale research projects are expensive: salaries, equipment, living expenses, travel, computer resources, secretarial help and a thousand other items have to be paid for. Individuals and organisations can bid for funds from sources such as the government-funded Economic and Social Research Council, or from charitable trusts, but there is stiff competition for this money. Many researchers have very limited resources.

Reading around the subject

The next step in any research project is to read what others have already published on the subject. This saves repeating the same work, and may provide some initial data. It will also give the researcher some ideas about how to approach their own project.

* Many sociologists are interested in social inequality in all its forms (eg class, gender and sexism, ethnicity and racism). Some critics say that this makes sociology politically biased.

Case study: The study of a single example of a phenomenon

* This is one reason why we know more about the lives of poor people than about the lives of the rich and powerful.

RESEARCH METHODS

Formulating a hypothesis or research question

Hypotheses

It is all very well to be interested in a topic but the research must be focussed on a specific issue. If the researcher already has a hunch about something, or wants to test an idea, they should formulate a hypothesis. This is simply a statement that can be tested. It is a prediction of what the research will find. For example: 'Students who study AS level Sociology watch the TV news more often than students who do not study AS Sociology' is an hypothesis. It can be tested by collecting evidence about the TV news-watching habits of the two categories of student. This will confirm or reject the hypothesis, or suggest what further research is needed.

Research questions

Researchers doing descriptive research do not usually start with an hypothesis. They will have a general question that has prompted the research but they don't make any predictions. However, they may develop an hypothesis as they learn more about what they are studying.

> ### Coursework advice
> **It is absolutely essential that you have a clear focus for your coursework. Be realistic about how much research time you have.**

Think it through

Imagine that you have been asked to produce the outline of a research design to study how A level students decide which university courses they are going to apply to.

1 When would be a good time of year to do this research? Explain your choice.

2 How might you collect primary data?

3 What sources of secondary data would you use?

4 Would you start with a hypothesis or a research question? And what would it be?

5 What problems can you foresee in collecting the data? How would you overcome them?

Preparing the research design

Primary data: Data collected by the researcher.

Secondary data: Data collected by others and used by the researcher.

What research methods do sociologists use?

First, there is the choice of whether to base the research on primary data (i.e. data collected by the researcher), or on secondary data (i.e. data that is already available). In either case, the data will have to be analysed and interpreted by the researcher.

✳ In natural science, hypotheses are tested by experiments. We will consider experiments in sociology on pp. 136–7.

PRIMARY DATA

The most common methods of collecting primary data are:

- by survey (see pp. 130–1), usually involving questionnaires (perhaps sent by post) and/or interviews; this generates mainly quantitative data
- by observation (see pp. 132–3), which may be participant (where the researcher joins in the life of the group being studied) or non-participant (where the researcher remains detached from the group); this generates mainly qualitative data.

Pages 130–3 examine these methods and techniques but it is helpful to have an overview of how they compare with each other. Figure A provides such an overview.

The Figure shows how the methods vary according to how many people can be studied and how closely the researcher is involved with the people being researched. It also shows how the methods produce more or less quantitative or qualitative data, and are therefore more or less appropriate to a positivist or interpretive approach.

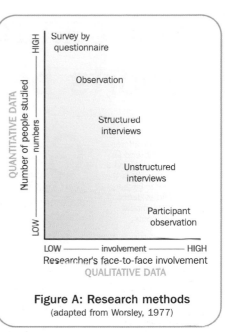

Figure A: Research methods
(adapted from Worsley, 1977)

SECONDARY DATA

Many kinds of data are already available to sociologists:

- Official statistics collected by government agencies (quantitative)
- Reports in newspapers, TV and radio (mostly qualitative)
- Historical documents (quantitative and qualitative)
- Personal letters and diaries (qualitative)

For a discussion of secondary data, see pp. 134–5.

Triangulation and multiple methods

The *research design* sets out how the researcher will collect evidence and what methods and techniques will be used (see Figure B). Some research designs may use only one method of data collection (for example, a survey using a written questionnaire). Many research designs use more than one method, perhaps combining observation with interviews, together with a study of documents or history, to look at the subject matter from several angles and gain a more complete picture. This is sometimes called 'triangulation' or 'multiple methods' and illustrates how sociologists should not be pigeon-holed into 'positivist' and 'interpretivist' categories.

Watch out

In the exam, don't suggest that triangulation is a method. It is a way of designing a piece of research.

 The Economic and Social Research Council (www.esrc.ac.uk) 'aim to provide high quality research on issues of importance to business, the public sector and government [including] economic competitiveness, the effectiveness of public services and policy, and our quality of life.'

 The internet has made it much easier to search for previous publications using sources such as JANET (Joint Academic Network) at www.ja.net . Many FE colleges have links to JANET.

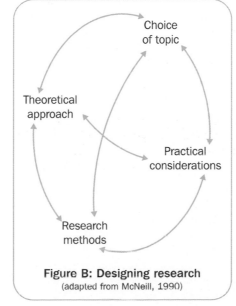

Figure B: Designing research
(adapted from McNeill, 1990)

Important studies

Researchers will, understandably, tend to write up their research as though it had all gone smoothly and in accordance with approved procedures. This is as true of natural science as it is of social science. Of course, life is seldom like that. There are several accounts of what doing the research was 'really like'.

- Bell and Newby (1977) *Doing Sociological Research*
- Hammond (1964) *Sociologists at Work*
- Bell and Roberts (1984) *Social Researching*.

(For full details, see the references list on pp. 158–60.)

Round-up

Choice of topic, choice of research methods, theoretical approach, and practical considerations are interrelated, as shown in Figure B.

Sociological researchers use whatever technique or combination of techniques is appropriate to the subject of the research, rather than being committed to quantitative versus qualitative data or positivist versus interpretive perspectives. In large-scale studies, many researchers will use one technique to check or confirm the findings of another.

How can research reports be evaluated?

But are any of these books any good?

Good sociology is based on good evidence. That's easy to say but it prompts the question: 'What is the difference between good evidence and poor evidence?' There are three main questions to be asked about any piece of sociological research:

1 Is the method of data-collection reliable?
2 Is the data valid?
3 Are the people or the social setting representative?

Reliability

To say that a method of collecting data is '**reliable**' is to mean that anybody else using this method (or the same person using it on another occasion) would produce the same findings. Take a simple example from the natural world. If one person measures the acreage of a farm on one day, using surveying equipment that is in good condition, and another person measures it again a week later using another set of equipment that is in equally good condition, the only reason why their results might differ would be that one of them had made a mistake in using the equipment or in doing the calculations. They have operationalised the concept of area by using 'acre' and used this as the unit of measurement. The method is reliable.

A survey using a well-designed questionnaire is reliable. The same results should be gained, regardless of who is asking the questions. By contrast, research that involves a researcher working alone and relying on their own interpretation of what they see, like much participant observation research, must be suspect as to its reliability.

Validity

For data to be regarded as **valid**, it must be a 'true' picture of what is being studied. Or, to put it another way, is it really evidence of what it claims to be evidence of?

For example, suppose we wanted to investigate racist attitudes in the teaching profession. If we designed a questionnaire that asked teachers about their attitude to ethnic minorities, we would certainly get some data that could be expressed statistically. But would this data be a measure of teachers' attitudes to ethnic minorities, or a measure of what teachers will say when they are asked about their attitudes?

A questionnaire may be well designed and produce reliable data but, if the data is invalid, it is no use to the researcher. The data is a product of the research method. Questionnaire-based research may collect data about how people will answer questions rather than about what they actually believe or how they actually behave.

The strength of participant observation is that, when done well, it produces **valid** data that reflects the reality of a situation, unaffected by the research method that is used. In this example, the researcher might get a more valid picture of teacher attitudes to ethnic minorities by joining the staff of a school (see pp. 132–3)

Representativeness

This is about how far the individual, group or situation being studied is typical of others. If they are typical, then what is true of them is also true of others. We can therefore generalise from this sample.

Researchers who conduct quantitative surveys have developed sophisticated statistical tools to assess how far a sample is **representative** of the whole population (see pp. 130–1). However, very small-scale research must always be questionable as to its representativeness.

The problem of objectivity

Science should be **objective** – that is, its methods and its findings should not be influenced by the personal interests or bias of the researcher. It is supposed to discover 'facts' and be value-free. There are major debates about the supposed objectivity of natural science but the problem of value-freedom is even greater in sociology. The more that sociologists study topics that they feel strongly about, and the closer they get to the people they are studying, the greater the risk of bias creeping into their research. We will look at the issue of values and value-freedom on pp. 136–7.

Watch out

You will often be asked about reliability and validity in sociology exams. Make sure you know which is which and what the difference is.

In practice, good sociological research makes a trade-off between reliability, validity and representativeness. This is often done by collecting data in several different ways. Thus Barker (1984), in her study of the Moonies, used written questionnaires and face-to-face interviews, joined a group of Moonies (at their invitation) in their everyday life and for religious meetings and ceremonies, and read all she could about their beliefs. She also compared the attitudes of the Moonies she worked with to the attitudes of a group of non-Moonies.

Watch out

Be careful to observe these ethical principles when you are planning research of your own.

The ethical research principles of the British Sociological Association can be found on their website at **www.britsoc.org.uk/about/ethic.htm**

Ethics in sociological research

Ethics is the study of what is morally right or wrong. There are ethical issues in social research just as there are in the natural sciences.

The main ethical principles of social research are that:

• no one should suffer any harm as a result of the research
• participants' rights to privacy and confidentiality should be protected
• researchers should be honest and open about what they are doing.

Harm

Obviously, sociological research should not risk physical harm to anyone. This is seldom a problem. However, there may be a risk of harming someone:

• emotionally – for example, by asking insensitive questions
• socially – for example, by damaging their reputation, or exposing them to ridicule or punishment.

Ethical research is designed to avoid these risks.

Think it through

A student made the following coursework proposal.

> For my research, I want to study the effects on families of a father serving a long prison sentence. To do this, I will interview some mothers with husbands in prison and then go to the prison to interview the fathers. I will then compare their answers. I can get in touch with some families like this because my father works at the magistrates' court.

Write a response to this proposal, paying particular attention to problems of:

• ethics
• operationalising concepts
• reliability
• validity
• representativeness.

Privacy and confidentiality

All research **participants** have a right to their privacy. They have a right to know what the research is about and to refuse to take part in it or to answer particular questions. If they do take part, they must be sure that whatever they say cannot be traced back to them as individuals.

Confidentiality means that the information an individual gives to the researcher cannot be traced back to that individual. Ethical researchers are careful to disguise the identity of individual participants when they write up their research. This is easy in the context of a survey, where individuals may be anonymous in the first place and where individual responses are merged into totals. It is more difficult when a small group of people have been studied through participant observation and where particular characters are described or quoted. Simply changing the name of a location or an individual may not be enough to preserve their anonymity.

Honesty and openness

Ethical researchers seek the informed consent of participants, ensuring they know:

• that the research is going on
• who is doing it
• why it is being done
• how the results will be used.

It is not always a simple matter to gain informed consent. For example, very young children or people with learning disabilities may not be able fully to understand what the researcher is doing.

Round-up

Good sociology is based on good research methods and good evidence. Evidence and methods can be evaluated in terms of their reliability, validity and representativeness. Sociological research should be free from bias and should follow ethical principles, particularly that of the informed consent of participants.

Social surveys

The survey method is widely used in sociology because it can obtain large amounts of data:

- in a statistical form
- from a large number of people
- over a wide area
- in a relatively short time.

A survey is sometimes used on its own as the complete research design and sometimes in association with other methods, as part of a larger design.

Survey research is about asking questions. The researcher has first to decide:

- who to ask
- what questions to ask
- how to ask the questions (e.g. by post or face to face).

HOW TO CARRY OUT A SURVEY

- Formulate the research question or hypothesis.
- Identify the population.
- Draft the questionnaire/ interview schedule.
- Pilot the questionnaire/ interview schedule.
- Finalise the questionnaire/ interview schedule.
- Select the sample.
- Collect the data.
- Process / analyse the data.
- Write the report.

Who will be included in the survey?

Surveys are usually carried out on a sample (i.e. a small proportion) of the **population** in question. The first task therefore is to identify the population, which may be made up of individuals, or households, or schools, or whatever other social unit is being studied. The next step is to select a sample, which should be representative of the population – what is true of the sample should be true of the population as a whole.

Random sampling

In random sampling, every member of the population has an equal chance of being included in the sample. For this, a **sampling frame** (i.e. a list of the population) is needed.

Once the sampling frame is known, the sample can be drawn randomly (e.g. by taking names out of a hat, or using random numbers generated by a computer), or quasi-randomly (e.g. by taking every tenth name from the list). Statistical checks can then be made that the sample is representative of the population.

Stratified random sampling

If the researcher has a sampling frame that shows the main characteristics of the population, it is possible to ensure that the sample includes the right proportions in each category. For example, if the researcher knows that of 1000 pupils in a school, 55% (550) are boys and 45% (450) are girls, a sample of, say, 10% can be drawn from each group (55 boys and 45 girls).

Quota sampling

In this case, rather than identifying individuals and then contacting them, the researcher establishes how many participants are needed in each category and goes looking for them. For example, if a researcher wants to interview 50 men aged 40–55 who have mortgages and live in Hertfordshire, he or she can go to where such people are likely to be found and ask each one if they are willing to be interviewed until the quota is filled. It does not require a sampling frame and is not truly representative.

Purposive sampling

In this method, the researcher selects individuals or cases that appear suitable for the research. The sample is not statistically representative. For example, when Goldthorpe and Lockwood wanted to research whether highly paid working-class people were becoming more middle class, they studied a group of workers in a car factory (Goldthorpe and Lockwood, 1969).

Snowball sampling

Here the researcher interviews an individual and then asks them to suggest who else might be interviewed. The sample can grow as large as the researcher wants. It will not be representative in the statistical sense.

Population: All the people, or other unit, relevant to the research.

Sampling frame: The list of people, or other unit, from which a sample is drawn.

Methods of asking questions

	Questionnaires (by post or telephone)	Structured interviews (face to face)	Unstructured interviews (face to face)
Potential advantages	• can reach large sample • relatively quick and cheap • personal influence of researcher is slight • produces quantitative, reliable and representative data	Similar to questionnaires, but: • higher response rates • can 'probe' the participant's responses by asking follow-up questions • can assess truthfulness of participant	• can create rapport with participant • can follow up responses in depth • produces valid qualitative data
Potential disadvantages	• response rates may be low • answers may be incomplete • data may not be valid, or even truthful • cannot be sure who completed the questionnaire • limits possible answers the participant can give	• 'interview effect, e.g. participant may wish to impress or please the interviewer • 'interviewer effect': age/gender, etc. of interviewer may influence participant's answers • time-consuming, so fewer participants and less representative • limits possible answers participant can give	• personal bias of interviewer • data may be less reliable • time-consuming

Asking questions

Questionnaires

These are simply lists of questions written down in advance. They can be administered face to face, by telephone, or by post (when the respondent will write the answers).

Questions may be:
- *Closed* – the range of possible answers is fixed.
  Example: Did you vote at the last general election? Yes/No
- *Open-ended* – the respondent can answer however they like.
  Example: Why did you vote at the last general election?
- *Multiple-choice*
  Example: Did you abstain from voting because:
  - you didn't think it would make any difference
  - you thought none of the candidates were worth voting for
  - you forgot
  - you were away from home
  - other reason?
- *Scaled*
  Example: How do you rate Tony Blair's performance as Prime Minister?
  Excellent – Good – Satisfactory – Unsatisfactory – Poor

Closed, multiple-choice or scaled questions can produce statistical data but limit the answers the respondent can give. Open-ended questions enable the respondent to express themselves but produce data that is difficult to express statistically.

Interviews

In a structured interview, the researcher reads out a list of questions (the **interview schedule**) and writes down the respondent's answers. An unstructured interview is more like a guided conversation, where the talk is informal but the researcher asks questions to ensure that the participant keeps to the subject of the research. Many sociological interviews are a mix of the structured and the unstructured. Responses in structured interviews can be expressed quantitatively; responses in unstructured interviews have to be analysed.

Piloting

Questionnaires and interview schedules should always be tried out on a small group of people to check that the questions asked are clear and unambiguous, that they don't upset or lead the participants, and that they will produce the kind of data that is wanted.

Response rates

However carefully a sample is identified, the results will be unrepresentative if not enough people agree to take part in the research. Postal questionnaires tend to have low **response rates**.

Longitudinal surveys

Most surveys provide a snapshot of the social context that is being studied. They do not provide a sense of change over time. Longitudinal surveys are a way of addressing this problem. They can be panel surveys (where the same group of people is interviewed at intervals over a period of years) or can be surveys that are repeated at intervals with different groups of respondents. (e.g. the British Social Attitudes Survey, the British Crime Survey and the Census).

Important studies

Most published reports of sociological surveys, including government-sponsored surveys, include a description of how the sample was drawn and of the questionnaire. The following may be of particular interest to AS-level Sociology students.

- Edgell (1980) *Middle class couples*
- British Crime Survey 2000 downloadable from www.crimereduction.gov.uk/statistics12.htm
- Park et al. (2001) *British social attitudes*; the 18th Report
- Mack and Lansley (1985) *Poor Britain*

Interview schedule: The list of questions used by the researcher.

Response rates: The percentage of the sample who return completed questionnaires.

Think it through

A researcher is interested in how success at school influences the early stages of a person's career. This is the first draft of their face-to-face interview schedule.

> 1 What is your name?
> 2 Are you male or female?
> 3 Are you aged: 15–20; 20–25; 25–30; 30–35; over 35?
> 4 When did you leave school?
> 5 What exams did you pass when you were at school?
> 6 What exams did you fail when you were at school?
> 7 What jobs have you had since you left school?
> 8 Do you think doing well at school has affected your career so far?

For each question, ask yourself:

1 Does the question make assumptions about the participant?

2 Is the question asking for information that is necessary to the research?

3 Is the question worded so that it will gain exactly the information the researcher needs?

4 Could the question be understood in more than one way?

5 Will it be easy to group the answers into categories for analysis?

Whenever the answer to one of these is 'No', draft a better question for the interview schedule.

Round-up

The survey method is widely used in sociology and other kinds of social research. It can be used on its own or as part of a wider research design. Using a questionnaire or an interview schedule, a survey produces quantitative data about a sample of the population. The data should be reliable and representative but may lack validity. Longitudinal surveys can track social change over a period of time.

Participant observation

Participant observation is the main research method used in ethnographic sociology. '**Ethnography**' simply means 'writing about a way of life'. Many writers do this, of course, but the ethnographic tradition in sociology is rooted in the work of **anthropologists** such as Malinowski, Evans-Pritchard and Radcliffe-Brown who worked mainly in the 1920s and 1930s.

Malinowski studied the people of the Trobriand Islands. He believed that the only way to get a valid picture of their way of life was to study them at first hand by living among them and learning their language, taking notes and recording his observations on a day-to-day basis. This is the research method that has become known as 'participant observation'.

> * Ethnographic research is sometimes called 'field research'.
>
> **Anthropology:** the study of the culture of small pre-industrial societies.
> **Macro:** Large scale.
> **Micro:** Small scale.

It is important that the participant observer is as inconspicuous as possible

Participant observation

The method of participant observation took a while to be adopted by sociologists who, in the 1920s and 1930s, were still mainly concerned with studying the structure of societies from a **macro** perspective rather than looking at the intricacies of everyday life from a **micro** perspective. The Chicago School of researchers in America in the 1930s was the exception to this. The leader of this group, Robert Park, encouraged his colleagues to take part in all aspects of the life of the city and to 'go get the seats of your pants dirty in real research' (Park, 1927). This approach was continued in the 1950s and 1960s by Howard Becker and his Chicago colleagues.

In a participant observation study, the researcher joins the group or social situation that is being studied. The aim is to understand what is happening from the point of view of those involved, to 'get inside their heads' and to understand the meaning that they give to their situation. The research is 'naturalistic': it is done in the natural setting and is not based on the artificial situation created by an interview or questionnaire. The research may take many months, or even years.

STRENGTHS AND WEAKNESSES OF PARTICIPANT OBSERVATION

Strengths
- Participants behave as they normally do, so evidence is valid.
- It takes the viewpoint of the participants rather than the researcher.
- It can 'dig deep' into social interaction.
- The researcher is open to new insights (questions are not fixed in advance).

Weaknesses
- It studies small groups, so may not be representative.
- It cannot be checked or repeated, so may not be reliable.
- It is time-consuming.
- The researcher's presence may change the behaviour of the group.
- The researcher may be biased, or even 'go native'.

If covert:
- It raises serious ethical issues.
- The researcher may be 'at risk'.
- The researcher may not be able to ask questions.

How participant?

How far the researcher participates varies from one research project to another, and at different stages of the same piece of research. The researcher may be a:

- complete participant – concealing the fact that they are doing research
- participant as observer – actively involved with the group but known to be researching
- observer as participant – present in the group but taking little active part.

Covert or overt?

If a sociologist conceals the fact that they are doing research, they are doing 'covert' research. If they tell group members who they are and why they are there, the research is 'overt'.

Covert research goes against the principle of informed consent (*see* p. 129), and so may be considered unethical. A researcher might argue that the research would be impossible if the group members knew they were being studied (for example, if they are involved in criminal activity), but this may simply mean that some sorts of sociological research should not be undertaken.

Important studies

Whyte (1955) is still the classic participant observation study. It contains a clear account of how the research was done.

Other studies of interest to AS sociology students include:
- Sewell (1997) Black masculinities and schooling
- Hey (1997) The company she keeps: an ethnography of girls' friendships.

> * In some studies, the researcher is only an observer, watching a group and recording their activities in an 'observation schedule' to produce quantitative data. This is an important research method but is not participant observation.

The stages of participant observation

Choosing the topic and group

The reasons for choosing a topic will be much the same as those listed on p. 126. However, participant observation is particularly appropriate for studying deviant groups such as street gangs who would be unlikely to respond to a questionnaire (not truthfully anyway). There are also several studies of occupational groups (e.g. police, factory workers), many of whose activities are invisible to the general public.

Joining the group

Occasionally, the researcher is already a member of the group being studied (e.g. Holdaway, 1983, on the police). The researcher may be invited to do the research (e.g. Barker, 1984, on the Moonies). If the group has a formal membership, the researcher can join it (e.g. Festinger, 1956, on religious sects). Very often, the researcher has to find a way of joining the group they want to study. This is usually done by befriending an individual who then introduces the researcher to the group. This individual typically becomes the researcher's 'key informant' (e.g. Tally in Liebow (1967) or Doc in Whyte (1955)).

Taking part in the life of the group

In the early stages, the researcher will tend to keep quiet, listening to and observing what is being said and done and gaining the trust of the group until their presence is taken for granted. From the start, the researcher will take notes and keep a field diary, as inconspicuously as possible.

After a while (sometimes a long while), ideas will begin to crystallize in the researcher's mind and it will be possible to start asking questions, particularly of the key informant. How far this is possible will depend largely on whether the group members know that the research is being done, i.e. whether the research is overt or covert.

Towards the end of the research, there may be an opportunity to conduct unstructured interviews.

The researcher must strike a balance between getting involved with the group and remaining an observer. If the researcher gets too involved ('goes native'), they will lose the detached perspective (objectivity) that a researcher must have.

Leaving the group

Eventually, the researcher must leave the group and begin writing up and analysing the notes and other material they have collected. Leaving the group may raise ethical questions. Will friends feel let down? Has the group come to depend on the researcher for advice or help? Has the researcher simply been using the group for their own ends?

Writing the report

The research report should describe the group's behaviour, suggest reasons (hypotheses) for this behaviour, and, crucially, show how the evidence supports these suggestions. The researcher will have developed some tentative hypotheses about the group throughout the research, but the report must show how far the evidence supports these hypotheses.

Think it through

The participant observer gathers data by participating in the daily life of the group or organisation he studies. He watches the people he is studying to see the situations they ordinarily meet and how they behave in them. He enters into conversation with some or all of the participants in these situations and discovers their interpretations of the events he has observed.

Becker, H.S. (1958) 'Participant observation and interviewing: a rejoinder', *Human Organisation*, vol. 17(2)

1 Why is participant observation considered to produce valid evidence?

2 Why is participant observation considered to be unreliable?

3 Imagine that you have decided to do participant observation research of your own group of sociology students. What practical, theoretical and ethical problems would you have?

Round-up

Participant observation is the method most commonly used in ethnographic or field research. The researcher, to a greater or lesser degree, joins in the day-to-day life of the group and learns to understand their social world from their point of view. Properly done, participant observation produces valid data but it may be regarded as unreliable and unrepresentative, and it raise important ethical questions.

The British Sociological Association has produced ethical guidelines on all these questions at www.britsoc.org.uk

Ethics in participant observation

We have already considered the ethics of overt or covert observation and the question of informed consent. However, participant observation raises particular problems in relation to the other ethical principles outlined on p. 129.

- How can the researcher protect the confidentiality and anonymity of the people who have been researched? Simply changing names and locations may not be enough.
- If the group or individuals can be identified, is there a risk of any harm to them, whether of ridicule or, more seriously, of arrest or reprisals?
- Is there any risk to the researcher if certain information is published? Is this a good reason for not publishing it?
- Are there any circumstances when a researcher should breach confidentiality (e.g. where a serious crime is being planned)?

Secondary data

Secondary data is data that is available to the sociologist because it already exists. There is a huge amount of this material, both quantitative and qualitative, about the present, the recent past, and the more distant past. The sociologist's task is to identify, select and analyse what is relevant to their research.

There is a mass of evidence already available to sociologists

Official statistics

Official statistics are the statistics that are produced and published by the government and its agencies. These are collected in three main ways.

Government surveys

The 2002 edition of *Social Trends* lists 26 major surveys regularly carried out by the government.

For details about the Census, look at the official website **www.statistics.gov.uk/census2001**

The best-known government survey is the Census of Population, which is carried out every 10 years. By law, every household in the United Kingdom has to complete a census form. The main questions (e.g. how many people there are in the household, their age, sex, relationships, occupation) are much the same for every Census. Other questions (e.g. about housing, ethnic origin, travel-to-work details) may vary from one Census to the next.

Registration

What effect might target-setting have on the validity and reliability of official records?

By law, all births, marriages and deaths, and certain illnesses, must be registered when they occur. The resulting data is published at least annually and provides a record over time.

Record-keeping

All government agencies, and many private organisations, are required to provide certain information to government at regular intervals.

- Schools have to keep records of their pupils and their achievements for the league tables.
- Doctors and hospitals have to keep records of how many patients they have treated and for what conditions.
- Employers have to keep records of how many employees they have and to make returns to the Inland Revenue (about income tax) and Customs and Excise (about VAT).

In recent years, many of the records kept by public bodies have been geared to assessing whether they have hit the targets they have been set by government.

Publications

The government publishes hundreds of booklets and leaflets containing official statistics. Of these, the most easily understood is the annual *Social Trends*, which contains statistics drawn from every area of public life.

The printed version of Social Trends is quite expensive but the contents of it are available on the internet at **www.statistics.gov.uk**

Think it through

ITEM A

Reporting rates vary according to the crimes committed. For example, a high proportion of car thefts are reported to the police as police involvement is required for insurance purposes. There is some evidence to suggest that shop theft is less likely to be reported to the police, with some thefts being absorbed by the businesses as overheads, and some shop owners either not wishing to attract publicity or else believing that reported crimes are unlikely to be detected.

Crime data collected by the police is a by-product of the administrative procedure of completing a record for crimes which they investigate... many crimes are never reported to the police and some that are reported are not recorded.

Police recording rates – whether a reported crime is considered of sufficient seriousness to go 'on the record' – depend to a certain extent on the discretion of the police officers concerned and will vary from force to force.

ITEM B

The official statistics list record crime in these categories:

- Theft and handling stolen goods, including theft of vehicles and theft from vehicles
- Criminal damage
- Burglary
- Violence against the person
- Fraud and forgery
- Drugs offences
- Robbery
- Sexual offences, including rape

Adapted from *Social Trends 32* (2002)

1. How likely is each of the crimes described in Item B to be:
   (a) reported to the police?
   (b) recorded by the police?

2. What factors will affect the reporting and recording of each type of crime?

How can sociologists use official statistics?

Some official statistics (for example, the number of babies born in a year) can be taken at their face value as valid, reliable and as accurate as can reasonably be expected. Other official statistics need to be treated with more caution, since it may be in the interests of the people who supply the data not to be entirely truthful (for example, data about income that is supplied to the Inland Revenue).

However, official statistic arc of special sociological interest, because they are the result not of counting or record-keeping but of the social process that created them. For example, the chart on the right is reproduced from *Social Trends 32* showing how many people committed suicide in the years between 1974 and 2000 per 100 000 of the population. The figures show how the trends vary between men and women and between age groups, and are based on suicides registered in each year. But, whereas a death is relatively easy to define, and a person's age and sex are usually known, for a death to be registered as a suicide requires a series of decisions to be made by:

- a doctor (whether or not to refer the death to the coroner)
- a coroner (whether or not to hold an inquest)
- perhaps a coroner's jury (what verdict to arrive at).

All these people will base their decisions on the information available to them (e.g. the age of the dead person, their circumstances, the cause of death), which they will interpret in the light of what they 'know' about previous suicides. The same kind of interpretive process produces health statistics, crime statistics and others. The point is not whether the statistics are right or wrong, but that they result from people making sense of, and *interpreting*, events. Sociologists can research this process using participant observation and interviews. The important point is that a suicide (or a crime, or a day off work through illness) is a different sort of 'fact' from the fact of a birth, or a three-bedroom house, or the number of 11-year-olds in the population.

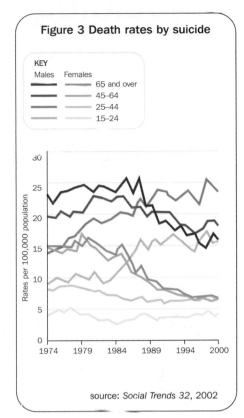

Figure 3 Death rates by suicide

KEY
Males Females
— 65 and over
— 45–64
— 25–44
— 15–24

source: *Social Trends 32*, 2002

Documents

Personal documents

Sociologists can also make use of personal documents such as letters and diaries. These are likely to be used by sociologists who take an interpretive or qualitative approach and want to understand more about the experience and world-views of people in the past. Such documents have not usually been produced with research in mind, though some researchers ask participants to keep diaries while the research is in progress. Care should always be taken to check the authenticity of personal documents (i.e. were they really written by the person who is claimed to have written them?). There may also be doubt about their representativeness. Extended writing is likely to be more popular among educated people, who may not be typical of the group being studied.

Public documents

These include school records, parish records, social work records, court records, hospital records, reports of government enquiries and a host of other resources. Published autobiographies may also fall into this category.

Mass media

Films, television programmes, TV news, newspapers, and even novels are rich sources of evidence for the sociologist. It is essential to remember that these accounts of events have been created by an author or journalist, rather than being factual objective descriptions of events. This is not the same as saying that they are biased (though they may be) but means that the account is an interpretation from a particular perspective.

Earlier research

Some sociologists revisit the data collected by earlier sociologists, either to add to what they have collected themselves or to check, and perhaps question, the conclusions drawn by the earlier research.

Content analysis

Most documentary data is qualitative, but it is possible to convert this into quantitative data using content analysis. Using this technique, the researcher classifies the content of the document into categories (e.g. in a newspaper, 'political news', 'economic news', 'sports news', 'advertisements') and then counts how much of the content falls into each category. This makes it possible to make quantitative comparisons between documents. Jagger (2001) used this technique to analyse lonely-heart adverts in newspapers.

 The Virtual Training Suite website has an excellent tutorial to help sociologists learn to evaluate what they find on the internet: **www.vts.rdn.ac.uk/tutorial/sociologist**

Round-up

Sociologists make use of a wide range of secondary data in their research. This may be quantitative or qualitative, private or public, official or unofficial. All this data should be assessed in terms of its validity, reliability, representativeness and objectivity. Official statistics can be used as a source of information or as a subject for research.

Is sociology more than just common sense?

ociologists would accept that there is good sociology and bad sociology (just as there is good and bad in any other subject) but would claim that good sociology is superior to common sense. As we saw on page 124, good sociology is based on good evidence that results from good research and draws logical conclusions based on that evidence. That is what makes sociology a social science rather than just common sense or journalism.

The question of whether sociology is a science like the natural sciences (e.g. physics and chemistry) was more important in the nineteenth and twentieth centuries than it is now. At that time, it was thought that natural science could be objective and unbiased, discovering the 'facts' about causes and effects in the world, and that it would be possible to develop a 'science of society' by, as far as possible, copying the positivist research methods used by natural scientists.

✳ The best-selling sociology textbook for A-level students in the 1960s was called *The science of society*.

Laboratory experiments

The classic scientific research method is the laboratory experiment, based on an hypothesis. Typically, this involves setting up a 'control group' and an 'experimental group', treating these groups in different ways, and then comparing the results.

Let's imagine a psychology experiment to test the hypothesis 'Having classical music playing in the background is a more helpful aid to students' exam revision than having pop music'. The scientist might:

- start by identifying the other variables that could affect the revision process, e.g. the age and sex of the students, the light, the temperature, the volume of the music, and what is being learned
- set up two groups (the control group and the experimental group), which are matched for variables such as age and sex. In other words, the scientist 'controls' these variables
- give the members of each group the same learning task in the same circumstances but with one variable (the independent variable) changed for the experimental group (e.g. playing pop music, whereas the control group is listening to classical music)
- measure the learning of each group.

If there was a difference in how much each group had learned (the dependent variable), the scientist might conclude, after many other experiments and changes to the variables, that the type of music affects learning.

How useful are laboratory experiments in sociology?

Laboratory experiments are widely used by psychologists but they have the following serious limitations in sociology.

1 The laboratory is an artificial situation; what happens there may have little relevance to the 'real world' (a validity problem).
2 Experiments can only be on a small scale and for a short time.
3 If the subjects (participants) in an experiment know that it is being done, they may not act as they usually do (the experimental affect – a validity problem).
4 If the subjects are misled about the nature of the experiment, they cannot give informed consent (an ethical problem).
5 It is not possible for a researcher to control all the variables that might affect the subjects' behaviour.

Field experiments

Although sociologists make very little use of laboratory experiments, there are several well-known examples of 'field experiments', where the researcher sets up a situation to observe in the 'real world'.

While field experiments may reduce some of the problems of laboratory experiments:

1 the researcher has even less chance of controlling all the possible variables
2 there may be greater problems about participants giving informed consent
3 the experiment may have adverse effects on participants' lives.

✳ See p. 81 for a description of Rosenthal and Jacobson's experiment about the effect of teachers' expectations on pupils' performance.

MAKING COMPARISONS

Experiments are of limited use in sociology but the basic principle of comparing one situation with another to try to identify causes (see pp. 114–15) lies behind a lot of explanatory research in sociology. For example, many attempts to explain why working-class children do less well than middle-class children in education have compared the variables in their home backgrounds.

Sociology and values: the problem of bias

Everyone has values – beliefs about what is morally right or morally wrong, but is it possible to keep these values out of the research process?

Sociologists have argued for years about whether sociology

- is value-free
- can be value-free
- should be value-free.

Values and bias can enter into sociological research at every stage of the research process:

- choosing what to research
- who pays for the research
- deciding what research methods to use
- deciding which questions to ask and which to leave out
- deciding who, what, where and how to observe
- deciding what secondary data to study
- choosing what data or information to record (from questioning, observation, or reading documents)
- interpreting data and observations, and reaching conclusions
- deciding what to include in the research report
- whether the report is published.

Most sociologists today would agree that sociology cannot be completely value-free but there is disagreement about how to respond to this.

- *Some would argue* (following Weber) that, while values will inevitably affect what topics a sociologist chooses to study (for example, a sociologist who feels strongly about domestic violence will be interested in studying it), the research methods should be as objective and value-free as possible. Personal bias and opinions should not affect the questions that are asked, the observations that are made, or the explanations that are offered.

- *Others would argue* that some degree of bias and value is inevitable and that value-freedom is a myth. The important thing is for the researcher to be open and honest about their values so that the reader can take this into account when assessing the work.

- *Yet others would argue* that sociologists should take a committed approach to their work, using it to defend the interests of the poor and the powerless and to challenge the authority and power of dominant groups. Feminists argue that sociology should challenge patriarchy. Marxists argue that sociology should reveal how the ruling classes maintain their power.

- *Some, including postmodernists, would argue* that there are no facts or objective truth anyway and that there is no way of deciding whether one 'account' is any better (more accurate, more objective) than another.

Avoiding bias

Sociological research is at risk of being biased and lacking objectivity. Research reports must therefore give a full account of how the research was done and the data collected must be available for other sociologists to check, along with the conclusions. Bias is not necessarily a bad thing; what *is* wrong is to claim to present 'objective facts' when in practice the work has been influenced by personal values or opinions.

Watch out

In the exam, don't just say that a piece of research is biased. Always explain why you think this. Was the sample biased? Or the questions? Or the conclusions drawn by the researcher? Or what?

 Many sociologists hope that their work will influence social policy in areas such as education, crime, or social welfare. Do you think this makes their work any more biased than the work of a natural scientist hoping to find a cure for disease?

In theory at least, natural science is unbiased. Supposedly, natural scientists take an objective approach to their work and do not allow their personal feelings or values to affect their work. It is 'value-free', in contrast to sociology – which is accused of being 'biased'. In practice, there is considerable argument about whether natural science really is, or should be, value-free.

Think it through

'A feminist sociology is one that is for women, not just or necessarily about women, and one that challenges and confronts the male supremacy which **institutionalizes** women's inequality. The defining characteristic of feminism is the view that women's **subordination** must be questioned and challenged... feminism starts from the view that women are oppressed.'

Abbott, P. and Wallace, C. (1990) (2nd edn, 1997) *An introduction to sociology: Feminist perspectives*, Routledge, London

1 Do you think it would be possible for a sociologist with these views to conduct unbiased research? Explain your answer.

2 What research methods do you think such a sociologist would prefer to use? Explain your answer.

3 What other social groups might claim that sociology should 'question and challenge' their 'subordination'?

Institutionalise: To reinforce something and make it permanent.

Subordination: Being in an inferior or powerless situation.

Round-up

What makes sociology superior to common sense is its research methods; these should aim to keep personal bias to a minimum. Natural scientists use laboratory experiments to control variables and minimise bias but they are not appropriate for sociology. Most sociologists would agree that it is important to keep personal values out of research as far as possible but that total objectivity is impossible.

Research methods: summative review

Most sociologists would claim that what makes sociology superior to common sense or journalism is that it draws relatively reasoned and rigorous conclusions from reliable, valid and representative evidence about its subject matter – people, social facts, social institutions and social processes. Furthermore, the evidence, how it was collected, and the conclusions drawn from it are all made available for others to check and scrutinise.

Whether interested in describing the social world or in trying to explain it (or both), sociologists have used, and continue to use, a variety of methods for obtaining evidence. In the past, particularly in the 1960s and 1970s, there were lively disagreements about theoretical perspectives in sociology and, hence, the merits of different methods. These disagreements were once called 'sociology's wars of religion', meaning that they aroused very strong and sometimes irrational feelings among the people involved. Today, however, it is generally agreed that it is sensible to use a variety of research methods, and sometimes a combination, according to the topic that is being studied.

However, this does not mean that the range of research methods can be treated as a kind of 'lucky dip' and that a researcher, whether an AS student or a full-time professional social researcher, can choose whichever methods they take a fancy to. It is important to take a systematic approach, to consider some of the issues that underlie the research process, and to understand why some methods, or combinations of methods, are more suitable in particular situations than others.

What is being studied?

This is the question that underlies the debate between positivism and interpretivism in sociology. Positivist approaches take the view that the only valid and reliable evidence is what we can observe, count and measure. Researchers should not speculate about processes that they cannot observe – for example, people's motives for behaving in a particular way. Positivism is a perfectly sound way of approaching most research in the natural sciences, where we can assume that the things being studied (e.g. plants, minerals, chemicals) are not self-consciously aware of their actions and do not choose to behave as they do. It is possible to observe them, to make comparisons between one situation and another (perhaps in a laboratory experiment) and to uncover the 'laws of nature'.

The positivist approach dominated nineteenth-century sociology. It was argued then that, by using the same methods as natural scientists, sociologists could produce objective and unbiased evidence, often in a statistical (quantitative) form, which would enable them to develop a 'science of society'. The quest for objectivity and value-freedom, in the context of 'grand theories' of society, tended to dominate mainstream sociology until the early 1960s.

However, this approach had first been questioned by Max Weber, whose work at the beginning of the twentieth century, though still firmly in the realms of 'grand theory', gave rise to the various forms of 'interpretivist' sociology. Interpretivists argue that the subject matter of sociology – people – is fundamentally different from the subject matter of the natural sciences, because people are self-consciously aware of what is happening in a social situation, give meaning to it and can make choices about how to act. Social reality and social phenomena exist because the people involved share an understanding of them and give them a similar meaning. So, to explain an event in the social world, whether it is two people interacting in the street or a major social change, we have to take account of how the people involved make sense of it and how this influences their actions. This view, developed by anthropologists in the 1930s, became more accepted in mainstream sociology from the 1960s onwards.

How do sociologists do research?

Today, most researchers would accept that it is sensible to use the research methods that are best suited to the subject matter. Using a combination of methods can help to balance the weaknesses of one method with the strengths of another.

A number of factors, including personal interests and current debates in the subject, will influence what a sociologist chooses to study and what methods to use. These can be summarised as the practical factors, the ethical factors and the theoretical factors. We have considered the theoretical debates above. Practical issues include:

- time (how much time has the sociologist got to complete the research?)
- money (can the sociologist get any financial support?)
- labour-power (is the sociologist working alone or in a team?)
- access (can the sociologist get access to the people or situation to be studied?).

All researchers should also take ethical factors into account, such as ensuring that the people being studied have given their informed consent to the work and that no harm will come to them.

Having taken all these factors into account, the researcher will produce a research design. This may involve a single research method, such as a survey or participant observation, or a combination of methods, and may make use of both primary data (collected by the researcher) and secondary data (already available because recorded by someone else).

Essentially, a researcher has three ways of collecting evidence:

- asking questions
- observing
- reading information that others have already recorded.

Each of these can be used to collect either quantitative data (in the form of numbers) or qualitative data (usually in the form of words, often quoted directly from the people being studied).

Whichever method is used, the researcher will have to operationalise the key concepts they are using. They will have to define these abstract concepts in such a way that valid and unambiguous empirical observations can be made about them.

Quantitative data

A researcher who wants to obtain primary quantitative data about how people live their lives, or their attitudes or beliefs, will usually carry out a survey on a representative sample of the population being studied. The questions may be in the form of a questionnaire, possibly delivered through the post, or a structured interview, where the researcher asks the questions face to face and notes the responses. The data collected should be reliable but may not be entirely valid.

Laboratory experiments, though they produce primary quantitative data, are seldom used in sociological research (unlike psychological research) because of problems of validity, ethics and scale.

For topics where a survey is not possible or appropriate, the technique of content analysis may be used. For example, a researcher studying the lives of people in the past might analyse in quantitative terms the content of old letters and diaries; similarly, a study of the content of the mass media might analyse how much time or space is spent on each topic in the news media.

A very large amount of secondary quantitative secondary data is available to sociologists from the official statistics that are published by the government and its agencies. Some of these (for example, the number of marriages that take place in a year) can be treated as reliable matters of fact. Others, such as crime or health statistics, are the outcome of social processes that can be studied in their own right.

Qualitative data

Sociologists who want to collect primary qualitative data, usually in an ethnographic study of the way of life of a group of people, will often use observation, which may be either participant or non-participant and either covert or overt. This ought to produce valid data but its reliability may be suspect and such studies are usually of small groups, which means that their representativeness may be questioned.

Many sociologists also use unstructured interviews, where the researcher has a relatively informal conversation with the research participant but asks a lot of questions and ensures that the discussion focuses on the topic that is being researched. The reliability of this method is often called into question.

Qualitative secondary data takes the form of letters, diaries and other personal documents, as well as film, video and TV. These can be analysed in terms of their meanings, symbols and use of language but also, as we have seen, in order to produce more quantitative data.

Evaluating research and research data

Some important questions that need to be asked about any piece of sociological research are as follows.

- Is the group or situation studied representative of any larger group or population?
- Is the data reliable? Would another researcher using the same methods, asking the same questions or making the same observations have come up with the same results?
- Is the data valid? Is it a true picture of what is being studied or has it been distorted by the research method used?
- Is the research objective? Does the research report claim to be free of bias? Does the researcher acknowledge how their values may have affected the outcome?
- Is the research ethically correct?
- Is there enough information in the research report for you to be able to answer these questions properly?

Research methods: self-assessment questions

1 **Who wrote Street Corner Society?**
   a Malinowski
   b Whyte
   c Barker
   d Booth

2 **Which of these approaches to research really existed?**
   a The Detroit School
   b The Washington School
   c The Chicago School
   d The New York School

3 **When was 'Family and Kinship in East London' first published?**
   a 1957
   b 1967
   c 1977
   d 1987

4 **When was the first UK Census of population?**
   a 1751
   b 1801
   c 1851
   d 1901

5 **Which research method was favoured by Howard Becker?**
   a Survey
   b Content analysis
   c Experiment
   d Participant observation

6 **Which of the following should produce a random sample?**
   a Snowball sampling
   b Quota sampling
   c Stratified sampling
   d Purposive sampling

7 **Match the word (a–c) to the correct definition (i–iii).**
   a Covert observation
   b Overt observation

   i observation done without the knowledge of the observed
   ii observation done with the knowledge of the observed

8 **Which of the following provides qualitative data?**
   a The census
   b A structured questionnaire
   c A laboratory experiment
   d A TV news broadcast

9 **Which of the following research methods did Barker use when researching for 'The Making of a Moonie'?**
   a Participant observation
   b Interviews
   c Secondary data
   d All of these

10 **Group these sources of data into 'primary' and 'secondary'.**
   a VAT returns
   b The results of a questionnaire
   c School registers
   d Letters written by soldiers in a war
   e The results of covert observation

11 **Which of the following did Charles Booth study?**
   a The Salvation Army
   b The people of London
   c The Trobriand Islanders
   d Symmetrical families

12 **Match the following (a–e) to their authors (i–iv).**
   a *Suicide*
   b *Family and Kinship in East London*
   c *Social Relations in a Secondary School*
   d *Poor Britain*
   e *The Company She Keeps*

   i Mack and Lansley
   ii Young and Willmott
   iii Hey
   iv Durkheim
   v Hargreaves

13 **Which of the following are ethical issues in research?**
   a Confidentiality
   b Representativeness
   c Informed consent
   d Validity

14 **Which of the following is correct?**

  a Content analysis can be used to convert qualitative data into quantitative data

  b Content analysis can be used to convert quantitative data into qualitative data

15 **Match the method (a–c) to its strength (i–iii).**

  a Written questionnaires   i Validity

  b Participant observation   ii Reliability

  c Random sample   iii Representativeness

16 **Which of the following influenced the researchers of the Chicago School?**

  a Marxism

  b The World War II

  c Statistical techniques

  d Anthropology

17 **Which of the following is funded by public money?**

  a The Census

  b The British Crime Survey

  c The British Household Panel Survey

  d All of these

18 **Match the word (a–d) to its definition (i–iv).**

  a Population

  b Sampling frame

  c Interview schedule

  d Response rates

  i The list of questions used by the researcher

  ii The percentage of the sample who return completed questionnaires

  iii All the people, or other unit, relevant to the research

  iv The list of people, or other unit, from whom a sample is drawn

19 **Which of the following is a natural science?**

  a Psychology

  b Biology

  c Physiotherapy

  d Philosophy

20 **Complete the following sentences.**

  a The difference between an opinion and a judgment is that a judgment is _____.

  b To say that a method of collecting data is _____ is to say that anybody else using this method, or the same person using it on another occasion, would produce the same findings.

  c For data to be regarded as _____, it must be a 'true' picture of what is being studied. Or, to put it another way, is it really evidence of what it claims to be evidence of?

  d _____ is about how far the individual, group or situation being studied is typical of others.

21 **Which of the following is correct?**

  a When variable A changes as variable B changes, we can say that B causes A.

  b When variable B changes as variable A changes, we can say that A causes B.

  c When variable A changes as variable B changes, we can say that A and B are correlated.

22 **To operationalise a concept is to:**

  a change it so that it suits the research you want to do

  b define it in a way that can be measured

  c put it to use in a piece of research

  d change its meaning after the research is finished

23 **What are the main factors that influence how a sociologist designs a piece of research?**

24 **What is the principle of 'informed consent'?**

25 **Put these research methods in order of how many research participants are likely to be involved, from most to least.**

  a Survey by postal questionnaire

  b Survey by unstructured interview

  c Case study

  d Participant observation

  e Survey by structured interview

Research methods: a timeline

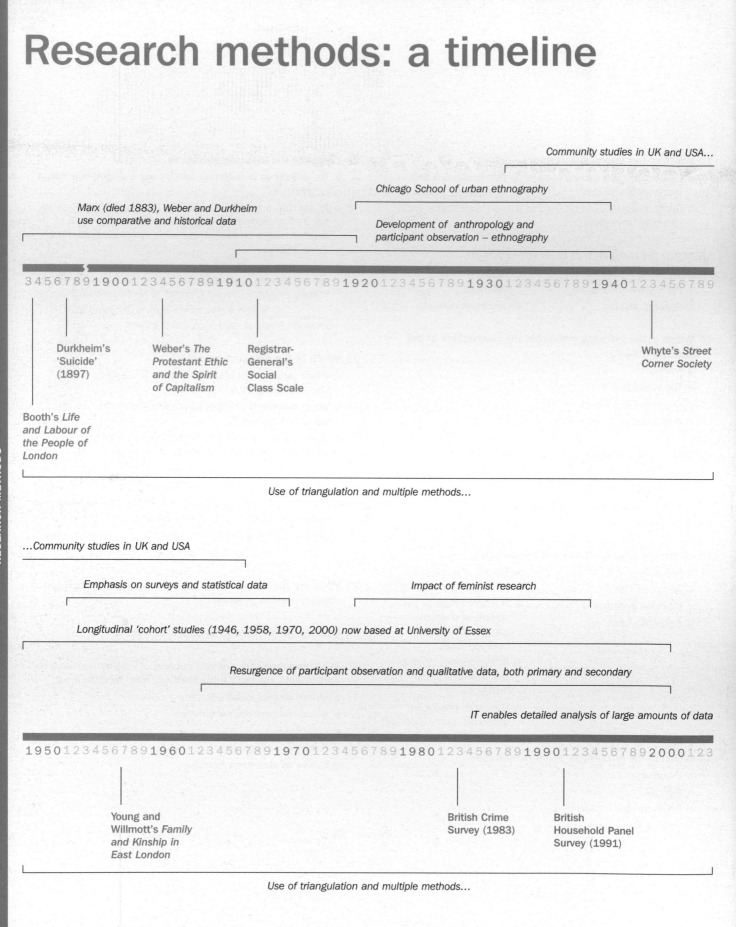

Community studies in UK and USA...

Chicago School of urban ethnography

Marx (died 1883), Weber and Durkheim use comparative and historical data

Development of anthropology and participant observation – ethnography

3 4 5 6 7 8 9 **1900** 1 2 3 4 5 6 7 8 9 **1910** 1 2 3 4 5 6 7 8 9 **1920** 1 2 3 4 5 6 7 8 9 **1930** 1 2 3 4 5 6 7 8 9 **1940** 1 2 3 4 5 6 7 8 9

Durkheim's 'Suicide' (1897)

Weber's *The Protestant Ethic and the Spirit of Capitalism*

Registrar-General's Social Class Scale

Whyte's *Street Corner Society*

Booth's *Life and Labour of the People of London*

Use of triangulation and multiple methods...

...Community studies in UK and USA

Emphasis on surveys and statistical data

Impact of feminist research

Longitudinal 'cohort' studies (1946, 1958, 1970, 2000) now based at University of Essex

Resurgence of participant observation and qualitative data, both primary and secondary

IT enables detailed analysis of large amounts of data

1950 1 2 3 4 5 6 7 8 9 **1960** 1 2 3 4 5 6 7 8 9 **1970** 1 2 3 4 5 6 7 8 9 **1980** 1 2 3 4 5 6 7 8 9 **1990** 1 2 3 4 5 6 7 8 9 **2000** 1 2 3

Young and Willmott's *Family and Kinship in East London*

British Crime Survey (1983)

British Household Panel Survey (1991)

Use of triangulation and multiple methods...

Note: Except for publication dates, all the dates and periods shown are approximate and open to discussion.

Section 5 OCR examination advice

What the examiner is looking for

How the OCR AS Sociology exam is organised

You will take *either:*
- three exam papers (Units 2532, 2533 and 2534) *or:*
- two exam papers (Units 2532 and 2533) plus coursework (Unit 2535).

The examination of the units is organised as follows.

Unit 2532: The Individual and Society

60 minutes

You have to answer 1 question from a choice of 2 four-part structured questions.

60 marks

See the sample question on p. 148.

AND

Unit 2533: Culture and Socialisation

90 minutes

You have to answer 2 two-part essay questions, chosen from the same or from different options.

90 marks

See the sample questions on pp. 152 and 156.

plus

Unit 2534: Sociological Research Skills

60 minutes

You have to answer one compulsory data-response question.

60 marks

See the sample question on p. 160.

OR

Unit 2535: The Research Report

This is a piece of coursework of no more than 1000 words.

60 marks

See pp. 164–6 for advice about how coursework should be organised.

Each unit demands a different combination of skills. The good news is that OCR offers you a variety of question types, which is useful because you're not stuck with one type of question that you may not be very good at. In addition, OCR will always use the same 'command' words and phrases to introduce questions. You should aim to become familiar with these command words and phrases because they tell you what skills are being assessed. (Examiners call these skills 'assessment objectives'.)

You need to demonstrate three skills at AS.

1 *Knowledge and understanding* – for this you have to recall and show understanding of key concepts, sociological studies (i.e. empirical evidence supporting particular arguments) and introductory theory relevant to the question. Command words such as 'outline' and 'explain' aim to test this skill, which is worth 53% of all marks available at AS-level.

2 *Interpretation and analysis* – for this you have to:
   - respond to the specific arguments contained in the question
   - present concepts, studies and theory that identify and address the issues raised in the question.

   Command words such as 'identify' and 'summarise' aim to test this skill, which is worth 27% of all marks available at AS-level.

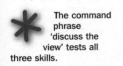

The command phrase 'discuss the view' tests all three skills.

3 *Evaluation* – for this you have to examine and comment on the strengths and weaknesses of relevant sociological arguments and the evidence, methods of data collection, concepts, etc. that underpin them. Command words such as 'evaluate' and 'assess' aim to test this skill, which is worth 20% of all marks available at AS-level.

EXAMINATION ADVICE

The questions

Unit 2532: The Individual and Society

Each of the two 4-part structured questions begins with a piece of data (Item A, Item B) which can take a variety of forms, e.g. a short piece of text, a photograph, a cartoon, etc., or sometimes a combination of these.

What is the item for?

The items may include a word that you don't understand. Don't panic – you can usually work out the meaning from the context, and you don't usually need to understand every word anyway.

The item is there to provide you with information to help you answer Question (a). This question tests your skills of interpretation and analysis. It will always use the command phrase '*Using Item A...*' (or B if it is the second of the two 4-part questions), '...*identify and briefly explain two...*' aspects of the data. To achieve all 8 marks for this question, you must:

- take most of the information you need to answer the question from the item
- clearly distinguish between the two points you identify
- explain their meaning clearly, using examples as illustration.

Question (b)

Questions (a) and (b) both stress 'briefly'. 'Identifying' should take you one sentence. 'Explaining' should take two or three sentences.

This is also worth 8 marks. It tests your knowledge and understanding of concepts central to this unit. It will always use the command words '*identify and briefly explain two*' things related to concepts used in the unit. It is important that:

- your response clearly distinguishes between the two things demanded
- you explain with reference to examples taken from sociological studies or theories.

Question (c)

This is worth 18 marks and requires you to demonstrate all three skills. It is broken down into:

- 10 marks for knowledge and understanding
- 4 marks for interpretation and analysis
- 4 marks for evaluation.

It will always use the command words '*outline and briefly evaluate two*' and is likely to focus on ways in which agents of socialisation transmit or reinforce norms, values, identity, etc.

'*Outline*' means 'describe'. Your description should be reasonably detailed and, if possible, should refer to relevant sociological studies.

However, the question also asks you to '*briefly evaluate*', so don't forget to assess each of the two points you are making, i.e. you will need to think about their strengths and weaknesses.

Question (d)

This is worth 26 marks and also requires you to demonstrate all three skills. It is broken down into:

- 14 marks for knowledge and understanding
- 4 marks for interpretation and analysis
- 8 marks for evaluation.

It will always use the command phrase '*discuss the view*' followed by a statement arguing a particular position. Essentially this is a mini-essay question. '*Discuss*' means you should outline the view in detail, examine its reliability and validity in terms of the evidence available, and outline and evaluate alternative views.

How much time should I spend on each question?

You have 60 minutes to do this question and 60 marks are on offer for it. However, you will need a few minutes to read through the data in Item A. Therefore, it is suggested that you adopt the following rules of thumb:

- 3–4 minutes should be used to familiarise yourself with the data.
- 6 minutes should be spent writing two succinct paragraphs for Question (a) – remember the question stresses 'briefly'.
- 6 minutes and two succinct paragraphs should also be sufficient for Question (b) – it, too, stresses 'briefly'.
- About 15 minutes should be spent on Question (c) – aim to write up to about a side of A4.
- You should devote about 25–30 minutes to Question (d). It is an essay question (there's more about the skills required for these below) and you should aim to write at least two sides of A4.

You will find an example of the four-part structured Individual and Society question on pp. 148–51.

Don't worry about the quality of your handwriting. It is very rare that a candidate's handwriting is so bad that an examiner cannot read it. You cannot afford to waste time making sure your handwriting is 'pretty'. However, your grammar and spelling have to be reasonably okay – more about this later.

Unit 2533: Culture and Socialisation

There are eight 2-part questions on this paper. You can answer any two. For example, you might answer both Family questions, or one question from the Family option and the other from the Mass Media option.

Part (a)

This part of each question is worth 15 marks and focuses exclusively on the skill of knowledge and understanding. It will always use the command words *'Identify and explain two'* of something related to the topic, e.g. the May 2002 questions asked for two *changes, reasons, ways, examples*, etc. You need to make sure that:

- your response clearly distinguishes between the two things demanded
- your explanation is illustrated with appropriate sociological studies and/or theory.

Part (b)

This part of the question is worth 30 marks and requires you to demonstrate all three skills. It is broken down into:

- 9 marks for knowledge and understanding
- 12 marks for interpretation and analysis
- 9 marks for evaluation.

It will always use the command words *'Outline and discuss the view'* followed by a statement that states a particular position in a sociological debate. This is essentially an essay question. 'Outline' means you have to describe the view in the question. 'Discuss' means you need to examine its strengths and weaknesses and, if appropriate, present alternative views or theories.

How much time should I spend on each part?

Each question is worth 45 marks, which is broken down into 15 marks for Part (a) and 30 marks for Part (b). You have 90 minutes, so you should be spending 45 minutes on each question – 15 minutes on Part (a) and 30 minutes on Part (b). Aim for a length of about two-thirds of a side for Part (a). Part (b) requires an essay response (see below for tips on how to organise these) and therefore you should aim for between two and three sides of A4.

You will find examples of the two-part Culture and Socialisation questions on pp. 152–9.

Unit 2534: Sociological Research Skills

This is a compulsory data-response question in four parts. It is organised around two pieces of data (Items A and B). Item A is likely to be a table, graph, chart, or piece of text.

Item B will start with a statement that reads:

'You have been asked to assess a research design in terms of its reliability, validity, representativeness and generalisability. The research is about… (Here there will be the name of a research topic such as 'the extent of joy-riding in urban areas'.) The research design consists of…'.

This will be followed by four bullet points listing various components of the research design, e.g. method(s) used, sampling technique, etc.

Question (a)

This is worth 6 marks and aims to test your knowledge and understanding of methodological concepts. It will always use the command words *'briefly explain the concept of'*. You will need to define that concept – and illustrate it if you can.

Question (b)

This is worth 8 marks and aims to test your interpretation and analysis skills in relation to Item A. It will always use the command phrase *'Using Item A, identify two'* aspects of the data in the item such as main differences, patterns, trends, changes, etc.

Question (c)

This is worth 16 marks, made up of:

- 8 marks for knowledge and understanding
- 8 marks for interpretation and analysis.

It will always use the command words *'Using Item B, identify and explain two'* (strengths, weaknesses, problems, etc.) *'of the research design'*. You will need to examine the four bullet points in Item B and, using the four concepts mentioned in the opening statement to Item B, evaluate the research design *in detail*.

Question (d)

This is worth 30 marks and is made up of:

- 18 marks for knowledge and understanding
- 12 marks for evaluation.

 Item A is likely to involve you looking at some type of statistical data. Don't worry if maths is not your strong point. You may be asked to explain what the figures mean, but you won't be asked to carry out any complicated calculations.

You should always look carefully at how the data is organised in terms of scale, proportion, percentage points, etc. Practise this skill whenever you can. Note, too, that you do not have to explain why the data is the way it is, nor do you have to evaluate it.

You have two choices of how to approach this question. You could focus on two bullet points and develop your response around these. However, a more effective approach is to choose two of the four key concepts, i.e. reliability, validity, representativeness and generalisability, and apply these to all or most of the bullet points. You will find an example of this approach on p. 162.

Revision tips

1 Start revising about six weeks before your exam.

2 Construct a revision timetable so that you know when you are revising particular topics and try to stick to it.

3 Make sure your notes are complete – your teacher should be able to help you do this.

It will always use the command words 'Outline and assess one sociological research method of collecting information about' a particular research topic, e.g. 'the relationship between teenage girls' smoking habits, dieting and self-esteem'.

This is essentially a mini-essay in which you need to select a research method that is appropriate to the subject of the research. You will need to discuss in some detail:

- the strengths of your chosen method, linking these to the research question
- how you would gain access to the research population
- the sampling frame and technique you intend to use if you decide to use a survey
- how you intend to manage interviews if you decide on this method
- how you intend to record data if you are using observation or content analysis
- potential ethical issues
- how you intend to operationalise the research question.

You can tackle the 'assess' component of this question in two ways:

- by clearly justifying, on sociological grounds, the choices you make
- by identifying potential problems that might arise from your choices.

How much time should I spend on each part?

The question is worth 60 marks in all and you have an hour to do it in. However you will need a little reading time and therefore it is suggested that you adopt the following rules of thumb:

- Spend 3–4 minutes examining the data in Item A – in particular, look at its organisation and work out what major trends, patterns, etc. it is describing.
- Spend about 3–4 minutes explaining the concept focused on by Question (a) – two or three sentences should suffice: the question does state 'briefly'.
- You've already spent some time looking at the data in Item A, so only spend about 5 minutes identifying the two things asked for in Question (b). Two brief paragraphs will suffice.
- Spend about 15 minutes on Question (c). It is important that you develop in detail the two things being asked for (e.g. strengths or weaknesses) and therefore it is worth writing up to half a side of A4 on each.
- Question (d) is essentially an essay and you should aim to write at least two sides of A4 in about 30 minutes.

You will find an example of the four-part data response Sociological Research Skills question on pp. 160–3.

Unit 2535: The Research Report

This piece of coursework involves writing a 1000-word report on a piece of sociological research of your choice, using a pro-forma booklet supplied by the Board. It is recommended that you choose a piece of research that is linked to either Unit 2532 or Unit 2533 and which might prove useful in answering a question in the exams for those units.

WHEN WRITING AN ESSAY...

- Read the title through at least twice and underline key words and technical terms that might assist your *de-coding* of what the question requires.
- Write out a plan – you might begin by '*brainstorming*', i.e. writing down everything you think might be relevant, and then organising it into a logical order.
- Write an introduction that sets the *context* for the essay, i.e. it should briefly explain what the debate is about, identify the key arguments or theories and define any key words or concepts used in the title.
- Set out the view contained in the title – summarise its key points and the supporting evidence into separate paragraphs.
- Each paragraph should finish with a concluding sentence that shows how the points you've made previously link to the essay title.
- Evaluate the view contained in the title by examining its specific strengths and weaknesses.
- Contrast the view with alternative views clearly showing how those challenge its conclusions – these counter-arguments should be set out in the same way, i.e. one paragraph per key point including supportive evidence and evaluation.
- Write a conclusion but don't just repeat what you have already said – make a direct reference to the view in the set question and either support it, attack it or ask questions about it – whatever position you take, however, must be explained and justified.
- Read over the essay – you will usually find at least one sentence that makes no sense and needs amending.

 If you plan to carry on to A2 Sociology, and to do the coursework option, you could use your AS report to start off your background reading.

The knowledge and understanding skill also rewards spelling, grammar and punctuation. This is important but don't get too worried about it – you will be judged primarily on the quality of your sociology.

---

4 Condense or reduce your notes onto index cards – one side could be made up of four or five key points of a particular theory, the other side could be made up of links to supporting evidence and some points of evaluation.

5 Alternatively, or additionally, use spider diagrams or flow-charts linking theories and evidence.

6 Ask your teacher for past papers and practise completing exam questions under timed conditions at home.

7 It is difficult and unproductive to revise for more than one hour at a time – do it in short concentrated bursts (e.g. 45-minute chunks) and then reward yourself with a drink, a short walk, a look at the newspaper, etc.

8 Switch to another topic when you feel that you are getting a mental block.

9 If you're not sure about something, talk to your teacher.

Unit 2532:
The individual and society

This section focuses on a typical examination question for Unit 2532 'The Individual and Society' and aims, through the use of a C-grade and an A-grade response, to give you some insight into the skills required to do well in this examination. Both responses are accompanied by commentary written by an experienced senior examiner.

It is important to note that the Grade-A answer is not a model or perfect answer. It simply achieves an A-grade. It is just one example of one particular successful style and approach. You must therefore not make the mistake of learning A-grade responses parrot-fashion. Your response to the same questions could be even better, i.e. it would be quite possible to take a different approach or use different material or come to a quite different conclusion and still get an A-grade. Flexibility, therefore, is all-important. The key to a good grade is to respond specifically to the command words and phrases in a question.

You may find it helpful to read the C-grade responses first, with the examiner's comments, and then to rewrite them, trying to improve them to an A, before you read the A-grade responses and comments.

Item A

Ms. Dynamite projects a frank personality; her lyrics are strident, defiantly female and well articulated. For example, she is critical of the macho world of hip-hop music, in which women are often relegated to the role of sexual objects and escorts. Her lyrics talk about how she likes to be challenged mentally and how a girl like her needs more than macho sexist posturing. She is also very proud of her black identity and argues that education should do more to promote pride in black history. In history lessons at school, she says 'I was told I was a slave. I was never told that black people contributed anything important to this world. We need to change that.'

Adapted from: www.observer.co.uk, 22 September 2002

(a) Using Item A, identify and briefly explain two aspects of identity that are central to Ms. Dynamite's sense of self.　　　　8 marks

(b) Identify and briefly explain two norms associated with traditional forms of masculinity.　　　　8 marks

(c) Outline and briefly evaluate two ways in which traditional forms of masculinity are being challenged in the workplace.　　　　18 marks

(d) Discuss the view that the social and economic changes of the last thirty years have led to few significant changes in female identity.　　　　26 marks

Total: 60 marks

Grade C answer

(a) Firstly, Ms. Dynamite is a very assertive female. Secondly, she is proud to be black.

(b) Men have been traditionally expected to be breadwinners, this means they have to earn money in order to look after their family and home. This explains why losing their job is so humiliating for some men.

Secondly, men are expected to be strong and brave.

(c) Unemployment is a threat to traditional forms of masculinity because men who believe that they should be the sole breadwinner in the family cannot find work and support their families. However, although this causes problems for men, i.e. a crisis of masculinity, women also suffer because they tend to have jobs and be mainly responsible for housework and childcare.

Secondly, lots of women are becoming managers and men may find themselves having to take orders from them, which may challenge their masculinity.

(d) There have been many big social and economic changes in the last thirty years. Lots of these have affected female identity. Traditionally, female identity was tied up with the mother-housewife role. Before the 1960s, few women got their identity from work or careers. However, feminist sociologists point out that female identity has changed a lot in the last thirty years because of economic changes like an increase in female employment opportunities and the feminisation of the workforce. Also, there have been social changes such as changes in attitudes towards divorce, cohabitation and sex.

Sharpe's survey of working-class girls in the 1970s showed that female identity was linked with family life. Boyfriends, marriage and having children came top of their priorities. Yet when she repeated her study with a sample of teenagers in the 1990s she found that these traditional priorities had changed to education, careers and economic independence. This showed that there was a new kind of assertive female identity. Wilkinson agreed, although she thought that it was middle-class not working-class girls who were benefiting from these changes. This was because economic opportunities for working-class girls are still limited.

The mass media has also had an effect on female identity by showing positive role-models such as the Spice Girls and women who have been economically successful.

Overall, however, women have more power today than ever and therefore more women are using divorce, rejecting marriage and choosing not to have children. This shows that female identity has significantly changed.

Overall this candidate scores 35 out of 60 marks This would usually be a basic grade C. Have a closer look at the answer and work out where you think the candidate could have gained more marks.

Grade A answer

Two aspects are identified. The idea of an assertive identity is clearly explained with three examples taken from the item. Similarly, black identity is explained in detail and yet the points made come entirely from the Item. Note, too, how the candidate puts these points into his or her own words. 8 out of 8 marks are awarded.

(a) According to Item A, Ms. Dynamite does not have a traditional female identity. Instead her gender identity is as an assertive young woman who doesn't like the sexism of hip-hop music (i.e. women being treated as sex objects), who values education and who 'likes to be challenged mentally' by men.

Secondly, she is very proud of her black roots and feels that both black identity and history should be made more of in schools. She feels that it would improve the self-esteem of black people if their achievements were praised more frequently.

(b) Bob Connell talks about hegemonic masculinity and this is a very traditional view of how men should behave. Firstly, this stresses that men should be breadwinners, which means that it is the job of men to be the major wage earner and to provide economically for their family dependents such as women and children. The fact that they do this gives them economic power and they therefore have the 'right' to make important household decisions and not to do a lot in terms of housework and childcare.

Secondly, another norm traditionally linked with masculinity is sexual freedom and promiscuity. It has usually been socially acceptable for a man to have lots of sexual relationships before he settles down and for this to be considered quite 'normal'. However, a woman who acts in a similar way is often negatively labelled and stigmatised as a slag, slut, etc. This is known as the 'double standard' by sociologists.

A clear identification of a traditional masculine norm with an excellent link to a concept (hegemonic) and a key sociologist. The explanation is detailed and intelligent.

A second norm is clearly identified and explained with reference to sociological concepts such as 'the double-standard', labelling, stigmatisation, etc.

The full 8 marks are awarded.

The candidate demonstrates a range of knowledge and understanding of how unemployment might affect masculinity. The response shows a clear understanding of what is meant by traditional forms of masculinity and illustrates it well. Relevant sociologists are referenced, although the response would have benefited from some specific examples from their work. The answer also convincingly illustrates the idea of the crisis in masculinity and its effects, with a range of issues analysed. Evaluation, too, is rewarded because despite its slightly assertive tone, this answer makes a valid feminist point.

(c) Firstly, both economic recession linked to globalisation and declining manufacturing have led to rising levels of unemployment for men in the 1980s and 1990s. This had a strong effect on masculinity because working-class men who had always seen themselves as the head of the household (because of being breadwinners and therefore having economic power) were challenged by the humiliation of being unemployed. Sociologists such as Faludi and Mac an Ghaill have described this challenge as a 'crisis of masculinity'. They believe the results of this crisis are social problems such as domestic violence, rising male suicide rates and underachievement by working-class boys at school (who cannot see the point of working for jobs that no longer exist). However, feminists argue that the crisis of masculinity has been exaggerated. Men have always had periods of unemployment and they therefore cannot use unemployment as a reason to beat up their wives.

Another so-called challenge to masculinity has come from the feminisation of the workforce. As manufacturing industry has declined, so the service sector (i.e. finance, retail, etc.) has grown. Most new jobs in this sector have gone to women. It is argued that women are now becoming major earners and in many cases, the major breadwinners within families. It is argued that this is challenging male hegemony and leading to a crisis of masculinity. However, this argument may exaggerate women's economic power. The latest research from the Equal Opportunities Commission (2003) shows that on average women receive 19% less pay than men and that men still dominate management and professional jobs. It also shows that a great number of jobs created for women are actually part-time and that women have a dual burden, i.e. they hold down jobs yet still take the major responsibility for childcare and housework.

A range of sociological knowledge and understanding is demonstrated in the discussion of the second way, e.g. feminisation of the workforce, the decline of manufacturing, women as breadwinners, etc., although some illustration was required in terms of statistical trends. The answer is let down a little by its failure to illustrate the effects of the crisis of masculinity. Analysis of the issues is therefore also a little disappointing. Evaluation, however, is first class and makes four excellent points.

8/10 marks are awarded for knowledge and understanding – two ways are focused on but knowledge of the first way was more convincing than the second. 4/4 was awarded for interpretation because most of the response was relevant and focused. Evaluation also scored 4/4. Overall, the candidate scored 16/18.

This response was about 300 words which is a good length for this section.

(d) Many sociologists, especially postmodernists, have argued that important social and economic changes have occurred in the last thirty years which have caused major changes in the role and identity of women. It is suggested that the choices available to females today have increased and therefore they are less likely to agree with hegemonic definitions of femininity, i.e. to see themselves primarily as mother-housewives. In addition, femininity has changed in other areas of social life such as the media, e.g. they are no longer presented mainly as sex objects, and positive female role-models of assertive and ambitious women appear in the media. However, not all feminists are convinced. Delamont, for example, argues that these changes and choices have been exaggerated and consequently hegemonic definitions are still firmly in place.

The argument that feminine identity has undergone major change is linked to the fact that the economy and work have become feminised in the last twenty years. The decline of the male-dominated manufacturing sector and the rise in the female-dominated service sector (especially retail and finance) has meant that women today have many more opportunities for careers especially in management and the professions. They are no longer expected just to have the mother-housewife role and work for 'pin-money'. It is argued by Helen Wilkinson (genderquake) that young women today are much more assertive and are increasingly expecting their identity to be wrapped up with their career and work rather than domestic roles. They are now more likely to be economically independent and may even be the main breadwinner in periods of high male unemployment. In education, females are out-performing males and surveys such as that conducted by Sue Sharpe in the mid-1990s suggest that female priorities have changed dramatically from the 1960s when they were focused on boyfriends, marriage and children. Also, surveys by Chandler suggest that some young women are choosing voluntary childlessness in order to concentrate on career development.

Sociologists such as Thornes and Collard note that in their personal lives women are demanding more from men in their relationships and marriage. They are less willing to put up with empty-shell marriages or domestic violence or partners who do not do their share of childcare and housework. They also want men who will listen to them and satisfy them both emotionally and sexually. Also, they are willing to use divorce to get their way.

However, although these changes sound significant, Delamont argues that they are exaggerated. In particular, although more women have moved into the workforce, men still dominate top jobs and a recent Equal Opportunities Commission report (2003) showed that women on average are paid 19% less than men. Boys still dominate high-status areas of education like the sciences, maths and IT, and higher education courses like the law, engineering, business studies and medicine.

Hakim and others argue that there is still a great deal of pressure on women to become wives and mothers. Women who choose to have careers rather than families are still seen as deviant and working mothers are often blamed for juvenile delinquency. Socialisation into gender roles in families is still very traditional, e.g. girls are still given dolls and domestic toys which helps prepare them for a very different future to boys.

There is not a great deal of evidence to support the view that media representations have changed for the better. McRobbie notes that young girls are strongly encouraged by teenage magazines to see their identity in terms of romance with boys and their appearance. Wolf points out that women are judged by the media in terms of their beauty, sexiness, size, shape, etc. and this may lead to some girls becoming anorexic or bulimic.

Finally, in conclusion, it has to be remembered that feminine identity is also affected by influences such as social class and ethnicity. Middle-class white women have probably experienced major changes as a result of the economic and educational changes that have happened. However, what postmodernists ignore is the fact that working-class white, Asian or African-Caribbean women may still find their choices restricted by poverty, tradition and religion. This probably means that their power to change their lives is limited and their identities are still shaped by hegemonic femininity. Finally, Delamont argues that women will find it difficult to change their lives for the better if men fail to change too.

Overall, this candidate scores the full 14 marks for demonstrating a range of knowledge and understanding about this debate and supporting studies and concepts.

The full 4 marks were scored for interpretation and analysis because the candidate remained focused on the question throughout and linked evidence convincingly to argument.

Finally, the full 8 marks were scored because this whole essay had an evaluative tone throughout. Argument and counter-argument were well constructed with supporting evidence. The candidate therefore scores the full 26 marks.

Overall, this candidate has gained 58 of the possible 60 marks. This puts the script in the top 1–2% of all scripts received. However, it could have scored 10 fewer marks (48 out of 60) and still have been likely to be awarded an A.

Unit 2533: Culture and socialisation – Families and households

This section focuses on a typical examination question for Unit 2533 Culture and Socialisation, Families and Households option. It aims, through the use of a C-grade and an A-grade response, to give you some insight into the skills required to do well in this examination. Both responses are accompanied by commentary written by an experienced senior examiner.

★ See p. 148 for notes on how to get the most from these sample answers.

Question

(a) Identify and explain two reasons for the increasing popularity of cohabitation.   **15 marks**

(b) Outline and discuss the view that the increasing diversity of family forms indicates a decline in family life.   **30 marks**

Total: 45 marks

Grade C answer

The candidate successfully identifies a reason, i.e. moral decline, and convincingly links it to a theoretical position, i.e. the New Right. He or she shows a range of knowledge in the explanation, which is well illustrated.

(a) The New Right say that people are cohabiting because society is in moral decline. They think that the popularity of cohabitation is a sign of the decline of marriage and the nuclear family. It shows that people are no longer willing to commit to long-term relationships because (the New Right believe) cohabitation is a temporary arrangement unlike marriage which is more permanent.

Secondly, cohabitation has become more popular because religion is less popular. Fewer people attend church today and therefore no longer believe that living with someone is wicked or living in sin.

A second reason is identified, i.e. the decline in religious belief. There is some attempt at explanation but it is a bit superficial compared with the previous paragraph. Some evidence is required here, e.g. church attendance data.

Overall, this candidate shows a good knowledge and understanding of two reasons for the growing popularity of cohabitation. However, the second reason lacked detail. The candidate scored 11 marks out of a possible 15.

This is a reasonable introduction, which aims at setting the scene for the essay. There is an attempt to define 'family diversity' and although it only focuses on family structures (and therefore ignores diversity in relationships and across factors such as social class, ethnicity, etc) it is related to the question. It also tackles head-on the central idea of the question, i.e. 'decline in family life', by using three very relevant examples.

This is a reasonable paragraph because implicitly it is about family diversity (i.e. divorce has led to the emergence of the single-parent family and a decline in the nuclear unit) and decline in family life (i.e. because of the easy availability of divorce, people are no longer committed to marriage).

(b) Society today has lots of different family forms. This is what is meant by family diversity. Some sociologists believe that this shows a decline in family life because they think that diversity comes from people being less interested in getting married and from a divorce rate which is out of control and single-parents failing to bring up their children properly.

Divorce is a major problem which is leading to more single-parent families and less nuclear families. Since the Divorce Reform Act (1972) divorce has gone through the roof because it has become a lot easier to obtain. People who want a divorce only have to separate for two years and if both agree, they can then have a divorce on the grounds of irretrievable breakdown of marriage. If they want a quickie divorce on the grounds of adultery, etc, they can sue their partner in the divorce courts after only one year of marriage. It is argued, as a result, that people are no longer committed to the idea of marriage, that they treat it too casually.

The candidate is evaluating the view that divorce is a bad thing but it is unclear how this criticism is relevant to the question that has been set. It requires an extra sentence saying that the resulting family diversity reflects women's new-found independence.

Critics of this view argue that divorce is a good thing especially for women. In the past, if a woman was unhappy in her marriage or was being beaten up by her partner, there was little she could do about it. Women did not go out to work and therefore were unlikely to have economic independence. They would have to put up with their lot. They were stuck in empty shell marriages.

There is a lot of interesting and potentially relevant material in this paragraph but it needs to be linked more effectively with the question. For example, the point made about women using divorce to escape from unhappy marriages needs to be used to deal with the idea of a decline in family life – it could have been used evaluatively to refute that idea. There is a danger that the material in this paragraph is wasted because it has not been made relevant to the question.

Again, the material is relevant but it is not clear how the points made link to the question set. The candidate misses the opportunity to develop the idea of a decline in family life – the idea of inferior family types could have been used to support this. It would also have helped to have added context – what theories argue these points? – and empirical studies.

This is changing because divorce is now easier. Feminism has contributed, too, because it has encouraged young women to see life beyond marriage. It has encouraged them to see careers and independence as an alternative. Even if they do marry, they have been taught by the media that they should not put up with abuse or unhappiness. Divorce no longer means shame or stigma. Therefore, women are using divorce to escape from unhappy marriages. This has resulted in an increase in single-parent families and a decrease in the number of nuclear units.

Critics of single-parent families claim that they are an inferior type of family because there is no father figure responsible for discipline. They say that boys in particular are more likely to grow up delinquent because of this. However, although children of divorced couples do suffer more problems at school and some depression, there is little evidence that divorce has a major effect upon the rest of their lives.

The view that different types of families means that family life is in decline is wrong. As postmodernists argue, more choice is actually good for us.

There is an overly assertive conclusion, which is unsupported by argument or evidence. The reference to postmodernism is relevant but far too brief, i.e. in what way, is more choice good for us?

Overall, this candidate demonstrated knowledge and understanding, which was generally relevant to the view that increasing diversity of family forms indicates a decline in family life. However, the candidate needed to consider a greater range of family types   the response never got beyond single-parent families. It was better on the idea of family decline and there was a reasonable attempt to address whether divorce was an indicator of such decline. There also needed to be a theoretical context, e.g. who argues the view described in the question? Studies and data (i.e. evidence) were absent too. The candidate, therefore, was awarded 5 marks out of a possible 9 for knowledge and understanding.

In terms of interpretation and analysis, the material used was relevant to the question but it needed to be made more clear about how it fitted into the debate. All too often, it was left to the examiner to work out how the material was answering the question. Consequently, the candidate was awarded 7 marks out of a possible 12.

Finally, evaluation in this response was disappointing. It lacked detail but most importantly, it lacked focus in relation to the question set. It evaluated aspects of the material used but because the candidate had not made clear how the material helped address the question, it was not clear how the evaluation addressed the question either. The candidate was therefore awarded only 4 marks out of a possible 9 for this skill.

This means that for Part (b) this candidate scored a total of 16 marks out of a possible 30.

The candidate scored 11 out of 15 for Part (a) making 27 out of 45 for the whole response.

Grade A answer

This is an excellent response because it clearly identifies a reason, i.e. changes in women's attitudes, and it presents detailed evidence to explain and illustrate that reason. The references to Sharpe and Thornes and Collard don't at first seem to be focused on cohabitation. However, the candidate cleverly links these changes in women's attitudes towards careers and marriage to cohabitation in the final sentence in a sociologically focused way.

(a) One reason has been the change in women's attitudes over the past twenty years. Surveys suggest that young women no longer want to conform to traditional ideas about marriage. Sharpe's survey of young working-class girls in the 1990s shows that they see education and careers as their priority today rather than marriage and families. Thornes and Collard argue that women have higher expectations of marriage today and are less likely to put up with empty-shell marriages. The combination of all these influences, i.e. careers, better employment opportunities and higher expectations of relationships, means that young women today are more willing to try cohabiting as a way of testing the potential success of the relationship. Cohabitation is a dress rehearsal for marriage.

Secondly, another reason for the increase in cohabitation is higher divorce. After the Divorce Reform Act was introduced in 1971, the number of divorces rose dramatically until the mid-1980s. That rise has now slowed down but the number of divorces granted in the 1990s is still significantly higher than it was before 1971. Divorce has resulted in more cohabitation because people who leave their husbands or wives for someone else cannot legally marry until they have undergone a legal period of separation. While they are waiting for this, they are likely to cohabit with their new partner. The more people who divorce, the more people are likely to be cohabiting. Another clue to this is the number of remarriages, which now make up one third of all marriages.

The candidate identifies another sociologically valid reason, i.e. the increase in the divorce rate, and supports this with a detailed explanation and illustration. However, it is slightly let down by its lack of supporting evidence. It requires some specific statistical data or a study to give it backbone.

Overall, the candidate demonstrates a range of knowledge and understanding of two reasons why cohabitation has become popular with clear and accurate reference to sociological concepts, studies and data. However the lack of supporting evidence on the second reason slightly lets it down. The candidate is awarded 13 out of 15 marks.

This candidate has provided an introduction that sets the context for the debate given in part of the essay question. The candidate identifies the theoretical position in the title and clearly and in detail outlines the position regarding the nuclear family, listing several relevant reasons why it has allegedly gone into decline. This candidate also explicitly addresses the question by identifying family diversity, with reference to alternative family types, and explaining why such alternatives are supposed to be inferior to the nuclear unit.

(b) The view that family life is in decline is a New Right idea. These thinkers believe in a very traditional view of family life, i.e. a nuclear family based on marriage and heterosexuality with traditional gender roles (e.g. father as breadwinner and mother as homemaker and child-rearer). They argue that the nuclear family is in decline because of social changes. These changes include easily available contraception (i.e. the pill), which has led to the sexual freedom of women, the reform of the divorce laws, which supposedly resulted in a rise of the number of single-parent and reconstituted families, the popularity of cohabitation and the feminisation of the workforce, which mean that women are no longer so committed to marriage and motherhood. The New Right think these changes show a general decline in morality and a rise in family diversity. Family forms such as one-parent families, cohabiting couples and reconstituted families are viewed as less effective in socialising and disciplining children compared with the traditional nuclear family unit.

However, if we critically examine aspects of this New Right argument, it can be argued that family diversity is a good thing for society. Divorce is a good example of this. It is generally assumed that divorce is always negative. However, Bernardes points out that divorce is less bad than domestic violence and empty shell marriages. Feminists such as Hart, and Thornes and Collard also point out that high divorce rates may show that women today actually value marriage and family life more than ever, rather than showing moral decline. Evidence suggests that younger women have high expectations of marriage and relationships and are no longer prepared to be dependent and over-burdened within marriage. They want men who not only share domestic and childcare tasks and roles but who also listen to their concerns and satisfy them both emotionally and sexually. There is evidence that they are willing to use both divorce (two thirds are initiated by women) and cohabitation to achieve these goals. The fact that a third of all marriages are re-marriages shows that people are still committed to marriage and family life.

The candidate addresses the question of a decline in family life in this section by refuting the notion that the processes that have led to family diversity (i.e. divorce, cohabitation, etc.) are necessarily a 'bad' thing. This is done convincingly, with accurate references to studies such as Bernardes, Hart, Thornes and Collard. The references to statistical trends, i.e. women's use of divorce and remarriages, are both relevant and accurate.

Another focused paragraph with accurate references to a study. The references to marriage after cohabitation and the majority of people still marrying would have benefited from evidence in the form of statistical trends but the points made are relevant to the debate. This paragraph is a good example of sustained evaluation.

Cohabitation is also not the threat to family life perceived by the New Right. Burgoyne points out that it often leads on to marriage and is just a way of postponing marriage rather than an alternative to it. Many cohabiting couples actually marry when they have children. Although marriage seems to be in decline, the fact is that the majority of people still marry and a majority of society still see it as a desirable goal.

In regard to one-parent families, the New Right have been negative about their value to society. Murray, for example, has gone as far as suggesting that such families are one of the main problems of a welfare-dependent and criminal underclass. He believes they are therefore both a cause and symptom of the decline in British family life. There is, however, little evidence to support the view that one-parent families are a major social problem. These families are scapegoated by politicians, and there are media moral panics about their growing numbers and the fact that many of them live in poverty. However, there are also sociological studies such as those by Phoenix and Cashmore which suggest that single mothers (who make up 90% of single-parent families) do a good job in bringing up children. Bernardes also argues that in spite of de-partnering (due to divorce) the relationships formed by fathers with their children after a break-up should be seen positively. Fathers are not deserting their children – instead they build healthy relationships with them and these children do not just survive family break-up but also gain from better relationships between ex-partners.

This paragraph is also focused on the question, as can be seen by the direct reference to decline in family life in the summary of Murray's ideas. As well as accurate knowledge and understanding of studies of one-parent families and concepts such as underclass, scapegoating, moral panics, de-partnering, etc. there is also focused evaluation. This paragraph also shows a healthy contemporary character.

Another type of family diversity is name-checked and the postmodernist ideas of Bernardes are intelligently used to make the point that it is richness rather than decline that should be seen in the character of these new types of families.

Reconstituted families, in particular, rather than being seen as inferior families, should be seen as a positive postmodern experience for most children. Re-partnering, as Bernardes calls it, can result in rich experiences for children because they can gain relationships with step-parents, step-brothers and sisters, half-brothers and sisters and the extended kin of their 'new' parents.

Finally, it can be argued that the New Right have exaggerated both the degree of family decline and family diversity. As Chester, and Abbott and Wallace argue, the majority of families in the UK today are still basically nuclear. Most children, despite divorce and cohabitation, are still brought up in nuclear families and although over a third of marriages break down, the majority do not.

An evaluative conclusion which uses the statistics in an intelligent fashion to suggest that the so-called problem of family decline, and even the movement towards family diversity, may be overstated.

Generally, this candidate is focused throughout on the question that has been set, i.e. the relationship between family diversity and family decline. Weaker candidates might have seen the phrase 'family diversity' as requiring a summary of the range of family types that exist in the UK. However, this candidate has very clearly seen the need to restrict the discussion to those types of families that supposedly have emerged out of the alleged 'causes' of family decline, e.g. divorce, cohabitation, women's attitudes. They have also have seen the need to examine the debate about the character of these so-called deviant families. Consequently, this candidate demonstrated an excellent range of knowledge and understanding in regard to the theoretical context of the debate, empirical studies and concepts relevant to the debate. There was a tendency to be a little too general at times but the candidate displayed breadth of knowledge, and was awarded 8 out of 9 marks for knowledge and understanding.

The candidate demonstrated focused interpretation and analysis skills throughout and all the material selected was appropriate to the debate, although at times there was a need for a little bit more evidence to add depth. The candidate was awarded 10 out of 12 marks for this skill.

Evaluative skills were shown throughout the response and were focused on the question. However, the candidate clearly took the anti-New Right side and as a result evaluation was a little unbalanced – you should always try to assess both sides of an argument. The candidate was awarded 8 out of 9 marks for this skill.

Overall for Part (b) the candidate scored 26 marks out of 30 and when added to the 13 marks awarded for part(a), they scored 39 marks out of 45.

Unit 2533: Culture and socialisation – Mass media

T his section focuses on a typical examination question for Unit 2533 Culture and Socialisation, Mass Media option. It aims, through the use of a C-grade and an A-grade response, to give you some insight into the skills required to do well in this examination. Both responses are accompanied by commentary written by an experienced senior examiner.

See p. 148 for notes on how to get the most from these sample answers.

Question

(a) Identify and explain two types of censorship of the mass media that exist in the UK today.　15 marks

(b) Outline and discuss the view that screen violence has direct and immediate negative effects on young audiences.　30 marks

Total: 45 marks

Grade C answer

The candidate's identification of a type of censorship is acceptable. The explanation includes a reasonable amount of detail – i.e. this type of censorship is informal, it's an agreement between TV companies and the regulators, it's about sex, violence and bad language, it was created following concerns from a pressure group, etc.

(a) Firstly, the 9pm watershed is a sort of censorship. This is an informal agreement between the television companies and the television regulators that started because of concerns by organisations like the National Viewers and Listeners Association (now known as MediaWatch) about the amount of sex, violence and bad language on television. The television companies agree that these things should not be shown before 9pm.

Secondly, censorship happens when films or television programmes are banned by the government because they disagree with them.

The second form of censorship (i.e. the banning of films) is fine but the explanation is inadequate. It is far too vague and gives no discussion about why this course of action might be taken. Overall, the candidate is awarded 10 marks out of a possible 15.

Unfortunately this essay begins with a statement that is not supported by any evidence. However, the writer then improves the situation by explaining what is meant by 'direct and immediate' effects (i.e. imitation) and describes one result of social anxiety about this (i.e. the banning of video-nasties).

This is sociologically focused and is addressing the question. The sociological perspective is outlined, although only briefly. The reference to Belson is both relevant and accurate.

This essay shows logical development. Newson's ideas are outlined reasonably well and the reader is made aware that it is not just behaviour that is supposedly affected, but attitudes too. However, the evaluation here, although relevant, is a little vague and could have done with some illustration.

The paragraph on reception analysis is very useful and here the candidate demonstrates a good understanding by accurately citing two very relevant studies. It was a shame that the Morrison study was not linked clearly enough to the debate – i.e. it needed to be made clearer that Morrison's findings show that effects depend upon the context in which the violence is set and how the audience interpret it.

(b) In the 1990s a young boy called Jamie Bulger was killed by two young lads after they had seen a film called Child's Play. This led to lots of concern that the mass media was affecting children because some kids were imitating the violence they had seen on television and in films. This led to the banning of some of these films called video-nasties.

The view that media violence causes violence in real life is called the hypodermic syringe model. This argues that children get an injection of media violence and go out and copy it, and this is the cause of crimes such as violence, drug-taking, etc. This is the view of a sociologist called Belson who carried out a survey of working-class boys. He found that the most violent of them spent much of their time watching violent television and films.

Elizabeth Newson also believes that if young children grow up always seeing violence they will think violence is a normal way of solving problems. She argues that young people today have aggressive attitudes and behaviour, and that television and video are responsible for this. However, she bases her views on American research which is not really relevant in the UK because we don't have the television shown in the USA or their gun culture.

Most sociologists are not very keen on the hypodermic syringe model. They argue that the media is blamed for social influences which are actually the result of the way society is organised or government policies. For example, violence might be caused by the ways boys are brought up to be tough and masculine, or the boredom of school or unemployment. It may also be due to family abuse or peer group pressure or drug use.

Reception analysis theory looks at how people use and interpret the media. Morrison found that when he showed the film 'Pulp Fiction' to various people of different ages they understood it in the humorous way in which it was meant. He found that audiences were much more upset by realist documentary style films which examine real issues such as domestic violence than Hollywood thrillers. Buckingham also said that the hypodermic-syringe model had probably exaggerated the effects upon children because he could see that they knew imitation to be wrong.

However, Greg Philo, although not agreeing that the media is completely responsible for our violent society, says that the media may cause crimes committed by some very vulnerable individuals. However, censorship of the media for all is not the answer to this problem.

The next paragraph is a reasonably good evaluation because it focuses on other possible causes of violence in society (i.e. the organisation of society, gender-role socialisation, peer-group pressure, government economic and social policies, etc.). This is a good list of alternative causes but the candidate should have cited some evidence or studies in support of these alternatives.

The conclusion is frustrating because although it rightly mentions a leading media expert, the point made needs to be explored in greater depth. The point about censorship also needs greater attention.

This candidate shows a reasonable understanding of the screen violence debate. He or she puts it in context by using references to the hypodermic-syringe model and the work of Belson and Newson. In addition, their knowledge of alternative perspectives was demonstrated by reasonably accurate references to Morrison, Buckingham and Philo. What lets this answer down is the fact that it is superficial. It needs to show more detail, especially in the section where it is argued that social and economic factors were more responsible for violence in society. The answer was therefore awarded 6 marks out of a possible 9 marks for knowledge and understanding.

In terms of interpretation and analysis, all the material selected was relevant but there was a tendency (especially in the latter half) for that relevance not to be made very obvious. The candidate needed to draw out the explicit links between the material selected and the debate being analysed. Consequently, the candidate was awarded 7 marks out of a possible 12 marks for interpretation and analysis.

The candidate mainly showed evaluation by putting ideas alongside one another. Although he or she raised some excellent alternative explanations for violence, these were treated too generally. There needed to be more evaluation of the actual hypodermic-syringe model. The candidate was therefore awarded 5 marks out of a possible 9 marks for evaluation.

Overall, for Part (b) the candidate scored 18 marks out of a possible 30.

With the 10 marks awarded for part (a), this candidate was awarded a total of 28 marks out of a possible 45.

Grade A response

The candidate successfully identifies a form of censorship (i.e. the Video Recordings Act (1994) and accurately outlines the powers such legislation gives to the BBFC. The context of such powers is also explained by reference to the Jamie Bulger killing and the moral panic that surrounded his death. The link to the hypodermic-syringe model of media effects is excellent. There is also very good knowledge and understanding demonstrated of the media-violence debates and ideas such as moral panics, imitation and de-sensitisation.

(a) In the 1990s after the Jamie Bulger murder the media created a moral panic around so-called 'video-nasties'. It was claimed by tabloid newspapers that the killing of Jamie by two boys had been inspired by the video Child's Play 3 although there was no evidence of this. This moral panic focused on the hypodermic syringe model idea that children were being emotionally damaged by such video violence and horror and therefore de-sensitised to violence and more likely to imitate it. The result of the moral panic was the Video Recordings Act (1994). This gave the British Board of Film Classification (BBFC) the power to censor and classify all videos using the same certificates as those used for films released to the cinema. That meant their content would be looked at and could be censored for things like violence and 'horrific' content, criminal behaviour and use of illegal drugs.

A second form of censorship in the UK is that which happens during war-time. During the Falklands War, newspaper and television correspondents found that news of the conflict was being censored by civil servants. Bad news, especially about British casualties, was generally held back until it could be released at the same time as good news. There is some evidence that such agenda-setting and news management still happens today, although nowadays it is called 'spin doctoring'. A New Labour aide was forced to resign in 2001 when she suggested that potential 'bad' news about the Labour Government's record could be released and 'lost' when the general public's attention was taken up by the events on September 11th.

A different type of censorship is identified here, i.e. news management or spin doctoring. This response is sociologically focused in its explanation, although it would have benefited from some reference to a sociological theory or study, e.g. the work of the Glasgow University Media Group. However, the candidate does compensate by using a good current example.

Overall, this candidate shows a perceptive understanding of censorship issues. The first example is clearly sociological and focused on theory and concepts. The second is also sociologically relevant but would be improved by referring to a relevant sociological study. The candidate was awarded 13 marks out of a possible 15.

A good introduction that places the debate in context. It explains that the view is based on a range of academic ideas, that it is very influential and that it has led to forms of censorship that are not found elsewhere in the world. It is also specific about what it means by screen violence, i.e. it focuses on cinema, video and television. A good introduction should set out briefly any alternative views and the student therefore name-checks three key studies here.

(b) The idea that screen violence has direct and immediate negative effects on young audiences has had a strong influence. It is generally the view of a group of media commentators, psychologists and some sociologists who believe in the hypodermic-syringe model of media effects. Although it has methodological weaknesses, this model has had a powerful effect on public and political opinion. It has been the reason why cinemas, videos and television in the UK have more censorship than any other country in the Western world. However, media sociologists such as Klapper, Gauntlett, and Newburn and Hagell do not believe that the mass media has the immediate effects in terms of imitation that the hypodermic model claims.

Psychologists such as Bandura, media commentators such as Medved and the pressure group, MediaWatch, and sociologists such as Belson claim that the media is a very powerful agency of secondary socialisation. It is argued that this is why advertising agencies spend billions of pounds advertising products and governments use media agencies as effective tools of propaganda. This hypodermic-syringe model claims that violent and anti-social media content such as drug-taking can trigger imitative delinquent behaviour amongst young people. This view has led to several moral panics about the effects of films such as Natural Born Killers, Reservoir Dogs, etc. and so-called video-nasties or horror films on children. It is claimed that such films have led to several copycat murders, most notably Jamie Bulger in the mid-1990s in Liverpool.

The candidate rightly focuses on the view in the question first. The reference to secondary agents of socialisation shows good understanding of concepts. This paragraph also mentions advertising and propaganda which are often cited in favour of the hypodermic-syringe model. The type of media content supposedly responsible is clearly identified and the phrase 'imitative delinquent behaviour' highlights the so-called effects. The influence of the model in terms of social anxieties, i.e. moral panics, is clearly outlined.

It is acceptable (indeed desirable) to refer to knowledge gained from reading other sociological sources.

Good use of two empirical studies as supporting evidence is demonstrated here. The candidate is clearly focused on addressing and answering the question.

The psychologist, Bandura claimed that after seeing a violent video of a man attacking a bobo (self-righting) doll, nursery-school children then treated the doll in a similar aggressive fashion compared with those children who had not seen the video. The sociologist, Belson, conducted a survey of 1,565 boys over a decade. He found that those boys who turned out to be violent watched more violent films than those boys who grew up with no criminal records.

However, Gauntlett is very critical of the methodology of both these studies. He points out that laboratory experiments like Bandura's are artificial situations and do not reproduce the natural environment of the home where parents are likely to have some control over their children's viewing habits. Also, people taking part in experiments may be influenced by experimenter effect, i.e. they work out what the researcher is after and give them what they want. Gauntlett is also critical of Belson because Belson did not make sure that the boys in his sample shared his interpretation of violence. Finally, Gauntlett points out that a correlation between two factors, i.e. violence and a preference for watching violent films, is not the same as a cause and effect relationship.

This is an excellent evaluative paragraph looking at the methodological problems of the two studies cited in the previous paragraph. It is clear and, most importantly, detailed in its explanation of the weaknesses of the evidence. The candidate then makes a very perceptive point about correlation.

The candidate realises the need to address the work of Newson and clearly explains it in a way that shows that he or she has a strong understanding of this whole debate and the concepts that underpin it.

This last point echoes another aspect of the hypodermic model argued by Elizabeth Newson. She now argues that imitation is less important an effect than inappropriate role-models and de-sensitisation. She believes that constant exposure to screen violence during childhood and adolescence can lead to young people acquiring anti-social and aggressive attitudes, and seeing violence as an acceptable way of problem-solving. She argues that children grow up to see violence as 'normal' – they are not shocked by it in real life because they have been conditioned to see it as a daily occurrence. Newson argues that this attitude contributes to general moral decline.

Sociological critics of this model argue that it ignores the social context of violence, i.e. some believe that there are other social influences on us that might trigger violence such as family experiences, peer-group pressure, drugs, social expectations about masculinity, etc. Secondly, the hypodermic model sees the audience as passive and incapable of interpreting media content on their own. However, a range of studies, including Buckingham, suggest that young people are actually media literate and therefore media has little effect on them.

There is some reasonable evaluation in this paragraph. However, it would have been even better if it had cited some specific sociological studies of how these social factors might trigger violence. The final point about Buckingham is pertinent but needed to make clear how exactly being media-literate leads to little effect from media content.

This final paragraph uses the work of Klapper to logically follow on from the reference to Buckingham in the previous paragraph. The candidate develops further the idea that media audiences are actually more sophisticated than the hypodermic-syringe model gives them credit for. This is an excellent evaluative point and is clearly related to the question that was set.

Finally, Klapper argues that the hypodermic model ignores the fact that we get some of our attitudes from social sources such as the family. When we engage with the media, he points out that we don't all watch or enjoy the same programmes (selective exposure) and we don't all interpret the content in the same way (selective perception) or remember the content of a lot of what we watch (selective retention). All in all, the audience is far more intelligent and sophisticated than the hypodermic model acknowledges.

This is a very good response which demonstrates some strong knowledge and understanding of the debate. Both sides of the debate are clearly laid out, and the studies that support and refute particular positions are discussed in very perceptive ways. However, on occasion the candidate was a little superficial and needed to supplement the excellent points he or she was raising with one or two more studies as supporting evidence. This candidate would be awarded 7 marks for knowledge and understanding out of a possible 9 marks.

In terms of interpretation and analysis, the candidate is focused on the debate throughout and every paragraph's contribution is very clear in how it fits into the debate. This is tightly written, although sometimes the brevity undermined the arguments outlined. The candidate would be awarded 10 marks for this skill out of a possible 12.

The essay is evaluative throughout – in particular, the candidate is aware of the need to be detailed, especially when exploring methodological weaknesses. However, a major concern about evaluation is the candidate's failure to cite problems with the alternative theories. However, he or she did acknowledge the contradictory nature of contemporary research. The candidate would be awarded 7 marks out of a possible 9 for this skill.

Overall, for Part (b), the candidate is awarded 24 marks out of a possible 30 marks.

With the 13 marks awarded for Part (a), this candidate scored a total of 37 marks out of a possible 45.

Unit 2534:
Sociological research skills

T his section focuses on a typical examination question for Unit 2534 Sociological Research Skills. It aims, through the use of a C-grade and an A-grade answer, to give you some insight into the skills required to do well in this examination. Both responses are accompanied by commentary written by an experienced senior examiner.

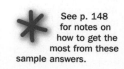

See p. 148 for notes on how to get the most from these sample answers.

EXAMINATION ADVICE

Item A

Identity in Scotland and Wales

	Scotland % (sample size = 1664 people)	Wales % (sample size = 656 people)
Think of self as Scottish or Welsh not British	37	28
More Scottish or Welsh than British	27	20
Equally Scottish or Welsh and British	25	30
More British than Scottish or Welsh	4	7
British, not Scottish or Welsh	5	14
None of these	2	1

Source: Brown, A., McCrone, D. and Paterson, L. (1996), *Politics and society in Scotland*, Macmillan, Basingstoke

Item B

You have been asked to assess a research design in terms of its reliability, validity and representativeness. The research is about the extent of racist prejudice in the white population. The research design consists of:

• selecting an urban area that has recently experienced conflict in the form of street disturbances between white and minority ethnic youth

• selecting a quota sample of shoppers outside a major supermarket on a Friday afternoon between 2pm and 4pm

• carrying out five-minute structured interviews with the sample testing their reaction to a series of racist statements

• setting up a focus group interview with a selection of concerned citizens recruited through newspaper advertisement.

(a) Briefly explain the concept of 'interview bias'   6 marks

(b) Using Item A, identify two main similarities between Scottish and Welsh people in terms of their attitudes towards being British.   8 marks

(c) Using Item B, identify and explain two weaknesses of the research design.   16 marks

(d) Outline and assess one sociological research method of collecting information about the social attitudes of council house tenants to asylum seekers moving into their areas.   30 marks

Total: 60 marks

Grade C answer

(a) Interview bias is when the interviewer puts off the person they are interviewing so that they don't tell the truth or don't trust the interviewer with the information.

(b) More Welsh people than Scottish people saw themselves as equally British. The Welsh were not as nationalistic as the Scots. Only 28% of the sample saw their Welsh identity as more important than their British identity.

This is not a precise definition but there is some sense that interview bias is about the effects that an interview may have on the interviewee. The reference to 'putting off the person they are interviewing' is not very sociological. This candidate would only be awarded 3 marks out of 6.

Note the error this candidate makes by using the word 'more' in the first sentence. He or she has not looked carefully enough at how the data is organised, i.e. 30% of 656 people is not more than 25% of 1,664 people. This first part of the response seems to be focusing on a difference, not a similarity. The second point is reasonably okay but would have benefited from some comparison with the equivalent Scots statistic. Overall, then, this candidate only shows the ability to select and analyse one main similarity and that was done rather vaguely. The candidate is awarded only 3 out of a possible 8 marks.

This is a fair response although for 16 marks, it needed a little more detail. However, the first weakness identified is sociologically relevant and focused on the context. The point about trust and rapport is relevant and the alternative method suggested, i.e. the unstructured interview, is appropriate. This response would, however, have benefited from more discussion about why the structured interview might not have established trust and why racism as a subject might not be suitable to that method.

(c) Firstly, racial prejudice is something that people probably won't admit to strangers, especially if an area has recently experienced some conflict and the police want to find people who took part in it. The design's ideas of using structured interviews is flawed. In order to get people to admit to racism, you need to either get their trust or rapport, or to fool them into thinking the questionnaire is about something else. However, that would be unethical so unstructured interviews are probably better.

Secondly, quota sampling is a non-random type of sampling technique. It may not gain a representative sample because not all types of people shop in supermarkets on a Friday afternoon. In fact, the sample will probably be made up mainly of women as most men will be at work. It is therefore not typical of the white population and this will make it impossible to generalise from the findings.

The second weakness is also sociologically relevant and uses the concept of 'representativeness' accurately. Again, the problem is lack of detail – other reasons why sampling outside a busy supermarket is not a good idea could have been discussed.

The candidate would be awarded 6 out of 8 marks for knowledge and understanding and 6 out of 8 marks for interpretation and analysis, i.e. 12 marks out of 16 in all.

(d) I intend to use a survey questionnaire to collect information about the social attitudes of council tenants. A survey is a kind of research which collects large amounts of data from a randomly selected large-scale sample. This sample will be sent standardised questionnaires through the post in order to collect large amounts of quantitative data.

A good start because the candidate chooses an appropriate method and the description of the method is conceptually accurate and detailed, i.e. there is good use of concepts such as random sample, standardisation, quantitative data, etc.

The candidate rightly discusses the reasons for not using other methods such as interviews in order to help justify their choice of the survey questionnaire. The focus on anonymity and confidentiality is an important point to make and is well linked to validity. This candidate is also aware of possible problems that might arise from adopting this strategy.

I have decided to use questionnaires because it may not be easy to find out attitudes towards asylum seekers through the use of interviews because people might not want to admit prejudice to a researcher's face. Instead questionnaires are better for seeking information about sensitive topics because I can assure anonymity and confidentiality by not asking for the names of my respondents. This may produce more honest and, therefore, more valid data. This might, however, create a later problem in that I will not be able to follow up responses in detail.

Questionnaire surveys are also useful because they will allow me to collect information nationally, i.e. from a geographically wide area. The larger the sample, the more representative it is likely to be so that I can generalise from my results.

Reasonably good use of conceptual knowledge is demonstrated in this paragraph, i.e. representativeness and generalisation.

Some sociologists think the type of survey I am carrying out is very reliable so long as I avoid loaded questions (i.e. 'are you prejudiced against asylum seekers?' is too direct and may result in an immediate 'no') and leading questions (i.e. 'don't you think asylum seekers are only here for the benefit system?'). Questions need to be more neutral and objective. My questionnaire ought to be highly reliable so that another sociologist should be able to repeat it and get similar results with a similar sample.

Some good practical examples of questions to avoid are used in this paragraph. Also, the questions are clearly related to the research situation. The reference to reliability shows, yet again, a good level of conceptual knowledge and understanding.

A reasonable range of practical problems are identified in these two paragraphs – all of which are relevant and focused on the research situation. The solution to problems of non-response is an interesting one, although the candidate does make a mistake in suggesting that it will result in more honesty – there is no guarantee of this.

There may be some problems. Questionnaires usually get very low response rates which may affect my ability to generalise. Also, the people who do reply (if the response is low) may be those who have a vested interest in the subject, e.g. as members of racist organisations. My results might therefore be biased.

Finally, I cannot be sure that the person I wanted to fill in the questionnaire actually did so. However, I plan to include a chance of entering a prize draw in order to motivate people to be honest and send them back.

Overall, this is a fair response. The candidate has chosen an appropriate method and discussed its strengths and weaknesses with the research situation always at the centre of their thinking. Also, this candidate handles the concepts of reliability, validity, representativeness and generalisability very well throughout. However, the candidate lets him- or herself down by not discussing the process of research, especially the sampling technique that they might use. They also neglect the concept of operationalisation – they really needed a brief discussion of how attitudes towards asylum seekers might be turned into questions and whether they were hoping to allow for such possible influences as gender and social class on answers given.

Evaluation, on the whole, was reasonable. Key problems were identified throughout, as were key strengths. However, some aspects of evaluation were neglected, e.g. especially potential problems of interpretation of questionnaires, etc. and how attitudes can be converted into questions. Solutions to problems were also only superficially dealt with.

Overall, this candidate was awarded 13 marks out of a possible 18 marks for knowledge and understanding and 7 marks out of 12 for evaluation, making 20 marks out of a potential 30.

When we add the marks for Parts (a), (b) and (c), the candidate scores a total of 38 marks out of 60.

Grade A answer

EXAMINATION ADVICE

This candidate demonstrates a good grasp of the concept and illustrates it well by referring to concepts such as status and power. The examples used are excellent. Most importantly, this candidate mentions the concept of 'validity' to show how interview bias might distort research findings. The full 6 marks are awarded for knowledge and understanding of interview bias.

(a) Interview bias occurs when an interviewee is negatively affected by the social status or power of the interviewer. They may feel threatened in some way, e.g. a working-class person may regard a middle-class interviewer as patronising, condescending, etc. because of their accent, body language, tone of voice and so on. They may therefore may be unwilling to open up to them. This will therefore affect the validity of the data collected.

(b) Firstly, most of the Scottish and Welsh sample thought of themselves as Scottish and Welsh first rather than British. For example, the majority of Scots (64%) saw their Scottish identity as more important than their British identity. The Welsh were not so definite but 48% saw Welsh identity as most important to them.

Secondly, only a small minority of Scots and Welsh saw their British identity as more important than their Celtic identity. For example, only 9% of Scots saw their British identity as all-important, although 25% of the sample saw it as equally important. The Welsh were a bit more accepting of British identity – 21% saw it as more important than their Welsh identity and nearly a third of this sample saw Welsh and British identity as equally important.

The candidate clearly focuses on two major similarities and uses the data precisely and in detail to illustrate the points being made. This candidate is awarded the full 8 marks.

This candidate has adopted an interesting strategy. Instead of picking two bullet points and assessing their weaknesses, he or she has focused on weaknesses from the point of view of two methodological concepts – representativeness and validity – and applied these to all or most of the bullet points. This is perfectly acceptable and allows the candidate to be detailed in their response.

In this response, we can see that the emphasis on representativeness enables the candidate to make excellent points about:

– the typicality of the area and its population
– the effect of recent events
– the problem of using quota samples
– the problems of focus group interviews
– problems of generalising to the rest of the population.

This candidate uses sociological concepts in a confident way throughout this part of their response.

(c) In this design the representativeness of the research population can be queried. It is probably not a good idea to select an urban area that has recently had race riots because these residents may not be typical either of the general white population or of socially mixed areas who may not have had riots. There is a danger that such a population is still emotionally involved in particular racial issues about their area and therefore the research will probably show higher levels of prejudice. Such results may therefore be biased by recent events and their effect upon the population. Representativeness may also be undermined by the use of a quota sample. Interviewers may find themselves consciously or unconsciously only stopping people who look as though they are articulate, co-operative, etc. Also, a busy supermarket on a busy Friday afternoon probably won't have a cross-section of the community – it is likely to be biased towards women, the unemployed, etc. Choosing such a busy place and time is not going to result in selecting a sample that can give careful thought to the research. Focus group interviews may also not produce a representative sample. It is likely that people who volunteer to take part are already interested in the issue of racial conflict. They may be people who are either openly racist or anti-racist and they will therefore bring biases to the research. They will not be typical members of the population. For all these reasons, then, it will be difficult to generalise to the rest of the population from the sample generated by these methods.

Secondly, the research design can be criticised because the data likely to be generated will probably lack validity, i.e. it will not reflect reality or be a true interpretation of those who take part in the research. For example, the busy afternoon and location selected for carrying out five-minute interviews is likely to result in rushed and ill-considered responses. The format of the actual interview, i.e. responding to racist statements, is most unsatisfactory. Racism is a loaded emotional issue and people are likely to hide their real feelings so as not to be judged as a racist. It has also been found that people who take part in research prefer to please the researcher (yea-saying). In addition, they may be suspicious of the motives of the researcher and how what they say might be used against them (i.e. demand characteristics). All of these influences may well lead to false and invalid responses. Finally, a potential problem with focus groups is that unless they are managed well, strong personalities can dominate the debate and actually lead other members into agreeing with them. Racism may not be the most appropriate subject to discuss in a focus group because it is a sensitive subject and consequently people may not admit to their real feelings it in front of others.

The second part of the response focuses on weaknesses relating to validity. The concept is clearly explained at the beginning of the paragraph. Various factors which may undermine validity are confidently discussed, e.g. racism as a loaded issue, people's preference for agreeing with the interviewer, the influence of demand characteristics and the problems of managing strong personalities in focus groups.

The candidate clearly focuses on two weaknesses in a detailed way and is awarded the full 8 marks for knowledge and understanding. The examples and illustrations used throughout are focused on the context of the research situation. The candidate is therefore awarded the full 8 marks for interpretation and analysis. 16 marks are awarded altogether.

(d) The research focuses on the social attitudes of council house tenants so I would therefore use unstructured interviews. These types of interview are like informal conversations. The researcher has a group of topic areas in order to guide the interview but the interviewee is generally allowed total freedom to speak at length and in some depth on the chosen topic.

Unstructured interviews would be particularly good for collecting information about attitudes towards asylum seekers. This is a particularly emotive topic, i.e. it is very similar in attitude to racism, and people may be aware that if they express negative opinion that they might be interpreted as being racist. Unstructured interviews are usually organised in such a way that hopefully my respondents will see that I am not making judgements about them or imposing my version of reality on them. Unstructured interviews will also hopefully allow my interviewees to respond freely and this will allow trust and rapport to develop. Realistically, I may need to conduct two or three interviews with the same person. People will be able to see that I value their views on asylum seekers and hopefully this will generate more valid qualitative data.

Such interviews also allow me to probe for deeper meanings, i.e. what do people understand by asylum seekers? Why do people think they are here? Where do people's prejudices come from? Structured interviews and questionnaires would not be appropriate because the closed question format would only result in superficial responses to questions about motives for prejudice. Even open questions on such questionnaires are unlikely to provide the depth required for such a topic. In addition, questionnaires would not allow me to follow up ambiguous responses. With an unstructured interview I can explore any vague or ambiguous answers as I go along.

I now need to think about how I will access council house tenants. A sampling frame will be available in the form of a list of tenants kept by local councils. I intend to access three groups of such tenants. Both Glasgow and Sheffield will be targeted as they have received substantial numbers of asylum seekers in recent years. In order to provide a comparative analysis, a third sample will be made up of council tenants drawn from an area that has received no asylum seekers.

Unstructured interviews are not really suited to large numbers of people. They take time and patience. Therefore I will focus on about a dozen or so people from each area. I will use a systematic sampling technique to access about 100 people from each sampling frame who have lived in the area for over ten years. Each of these people will get a letter outlining the aims of the research and assuring them of anonymity and confidentiality. It is likely that I will get a high non-response rate because of the sensitivity of the issue but hopefully I will get 20–30 people responding, of which 12 will be selected per area.

There may, of course, be problems with my research design. I am only using a small sample because unstructured interviews are time-consuming. Therefore it will be difficult to generalise to the whole population. However, my case-study type approach will still be able to offer useful insights into similar populations if my sample is reasonably typical or representative of white people who have lived on council estates for long periods of time. Some positivist sociologists might claim that my method is also unreliable because my relationship with the council tenants is likely to be unique and therefore not replicable. It will therefore be difficult to verify my data. Unstructured interviews also generate a great deal of qualitative data and I will have to be selective in what I finally decide to include in my report. I will have to make sure that I don't find myself only using that material that supports my hypothesis.

Finally, interview bias may be a problem. Respondents might be put off telling me the truth by the nature of the topic, my status, my social characteristics, etc. People may feel that I will use their prejudices about asylum seekers against them in some way and therefore withhold information, lie, exaggerate, and so on. They may feel that they may lose their council houses if they admit prejudice. Therefore my data may not result in a valid picture of reality.

Margin annotations (left)

An appropriate method is chosen, i.e. unstructured interviews, and is clearly defined.

The method is linked intelligently to the research context. The candidate is sensitive to the nature of the research topic, i.e. attitudes towards asylum seekers. The candidate clearly understands the research process, as seen in the reference to the need for more than one interview. The candidate has a good grasp of sociological concepts.

The candidate is thinking about how they might access council tenants across a range of cities. This is obviously a student who keeps up with contemporary events. The sampling frame idea is fine. The idea of conducting a comparative analysis is a very good one.

This is a relevant point but unfortunately it is dealt with in a very rushed fashion and so loses some of its power. The references to 'social characteristics' need following up. The concept of validity is used appropriately but it would be worth following it up in a little more detail. This section is therefore too superficial.

Margin annotations (right)

The candidate demonstrates the need to operationalise particular elements of the research question. There is a focused attempt to justify the choice of unstructured interviews by referring to the inadequacy of other methods, i.e. structured interviews and questionnaires.

The candidate recognises a potential problem and adapts their plans accordingly. This is a very practical paragraph and suggests that the candidate is comfortable with the technicalities and stages necessary to conduct successful research. Problems like low non-response are successfully anticipated.

This is a strongly evaluative paragraph that uses concepts such as generalisability well and also connects well to the theoretical framework, i.e. how positivists might see his or her research. It is a shame, however, that the candidate has not made a similar connection to the interpretivist theory of methodology. However, implicitly many of the points made about the nature of their research device are interpretivist.

This candidate is fairly comfortable with the idea of conducting research and confident in their knowledge about how to do so. He or she demonstrates strong knowledge and understanding of their chosen research method, and sees the need to locate that method firmly within the research context of council tenants and asylum seekers. However, the answer doesn't achieve full marks for knowledge and understanding because it doesn't use sociological concepts like reliability and validity consistently enough. It is therefore awarded 16 marks out of a possible 18 marks for knowledge and understanding.

The evaluation is mostly consistent in structure, but is let down by neglecting interview bias – a major factor if considering any form of interview – and so the candidate is awarded 10 marks out of a possible 12 for this skill.

Overall, then, for Part (d), this candidate is awarded 26 marks out of a possible 30 marks.

> If we add the marks for Parts (a), (b) and (c), the candidate scores **56 marks out of a possible 60 – an excellent mark that achieves an A grade with plenty to spare.**

Coursework: the research report

Unit 2535 is the alternative to the Sociological Research Skills examination (Unit 2534). It is worth 30% of your AS marks and 15% of the full A level.

You have to choose a piece of original sociological research (with the guidance of your teacher) and write a critical report on it. It is always a good idea to choose a piece of research that fits into your study of either The Individual and Society or Culture and Socialisation so that you can kill two birds with one stone, i.e. the material you use will probably also be useful to use as supporting evidence in examination questions.

You are expected to write 1000 words for the research report. You will find that if you significantly overshoot this length it is impossible to get top marks. In other words, the examiners expect you to be concise. The good news is that OCR provide you with an official Answer Book, which is divided into sections that clearly recommend how many words you should use.

*Keep to the word limits in this Unit.

The four sections of the Research report

Each of the four sections begins with a prompt which tells you what ought to be in that section and how many words you ought to be writing.

- **Section A** is a short section that requires details of the research you are reporting on, i.e. its title, its author and the date of publication. You must give this information in full, e.g. the complete title including subtitle should be included. Don't rely on your teacher to fill this section in. It is your responsibility.

- **Section B** should be between 210 and 300 words. It focuses on the aims of the research and the research methods used by the sociologist. You should examine the process of research, especially the sample and sampling frame/technique used, the hypothesis/research question, ethics, etc. It is important that you use sociological concepts such as reliability, validity, representativeness and generalisability in your response.

- **Section C** should be between 250 and 300 words. It focuses on the reasons why the researcher chose the method(s) that they did. In other words, you have to think about the justification for the chosen method, i.e. did it aim to gather quantitative or qualitative data, or both? Was the emphasis on scientific method or was the researcher more interested in getting a first-hand account of the group being studied?

- **Section D** should be between 350 and 400 words. It focuses on summarising some of the key findings of the research. It is a good idea to illustrate these with extracts that you can put into the appendix – these will not be included in the word count. This section also requires you to give an opinion about whether the research worked well or not in terms of the data collected. It is a good idea, when answering this question, to make use of the key concepts of reliability, validity, representativeness, generalisability and ethics.

The skills

The research report is worth 90 marks, divided up as follows:

- Knowledge and understanding: 48 marks
- Interpretation and analysis: 24 marks
- Evaluation: 18 marks.

Marks for these skills are awarded for the whole report rather than any specific section. Once you hand in the report, your teacher will mark it and send off a sample of their marking to OCR for moderation. You and your teacher will need to sign a front-cover sheet attached to the Answer book confirming that the work is all your own.

When writing the research report, you should:

- respond in detail to the prompts in each section
- apply the four key concepts, i.e. reliability, validity, representativeness and generalisability throughout
- make sure every methodological point made is clearly related to the research context
- keep to the word count.

Example of an A-grade research report

This section aims, through the use of an A-grade response, to give you some ideas about how to do well in this form of assessment.

The report is accompanied by commentary written by an experienced senior examiner.

The words in bold are the exam board's instructions, which are in the Answer Book.

Section (a)

Please give details of the research on which you are reporting

Title: Racism in Children's Lives: A Study of Mainly White Primary Schools

Authors: Barry Troyna and Richard Hatcher

Date of publication/completion: 1992

Publisher or source: Routledge, London.

Note that the candidate has given the sub-title as well as the main title for this piece of research. All details have been completed accurately.

Section (b)

Outline of the research design (210–300 words)

You should state the objective of your chosen piece of research, and use this section to outline how the researcher(s) carried out their research. You should describe the aims of the research and the research methods that were used. (You may wish to consider methods, sample size, access to sample, ethics, etc).

The primary aim of this ethnographic study was to uncover how 'race' was perceived and interpreted by children in primary schools by exploring the role it played in their everyday lives, and especially their relationships with other children. The researchers aimed to show that race and in particular racism played a significant role even in the lives of very young children. The researchers took an interpretivist approach – they were mainly interested in how children made sense of their world in every day life.

The candidate has a clear understanding of the aims of the research and how ethnography as a methodological approach links into interpretivist perspectives.

The researchers spent a term each in three primary schools interacting with about 30 pupils aged 10 and 11 who were in their final years of primary school education. Interestingly, from an ethical point of view, they did not tell the children about their interest in issues of 'race'. Instead they told them that they were in the school collecting material for a book about children in general. Their rationale for this was that they did not want to put preconceived ideas into the children's heads but wanted spontaneous thinking about racial issues in order to increase validity.

The candidate sees the opportunity to make a point about the ethics of the research. Sociological guidelines to research often state that researchers should be open with those being researched. This was obviously not the case for this piece of research but the candidate clearly explains why and uses the concept of validity to reinforce their point.

This section clearly describes how the unstructured interviews were organised and managed.

They used a variety of methods to explore how the children felt about racial issues. Most of the research took the form of discussion with children – in the form of unstructured interviews with individuals and in small self-selected groups. All interviews took part outside the classroom. The researchers were keen not to impose a format on these interviews but there were obviously themes that they were keen to explore. These interviews were carried out on several occasions. Most lasted about half an hour. Materials such as photographs, stories, poems and case-studies were used to stimulate the children's interest. In addition, the researchers spent break and lunch-times with the children. Some of the children were asked to keep diaries.

Section (c)

Reasons for selection of research design (250–300 words)

Use this section to outline the reasons why the researcher(s) chose the methodology outlined above. You should explain why the methodology was thought to be suitable for achieving the kind of data required by the researcher(s).

These researchers are aiming to examine the children's behaviour and attitudes in their natural environment. This is an interpretivist approach. Interpretivists are generally concerned with achieving 'verstehen' or empathetic understanding, i.e. they want to see the world through the eyes of the people they are studying rather than impose their view of reality on their research subjects. The unstructured interview is a typical interpretivist research device because it allows the research subject the freedom to allow discussions to take a natural course, i.e. the children could talk about what mattered to them. In this sense, it is regarded as having high validity.

The candidate demonstrates a good knowledge of how theoretical considerations affect the choice of research device. The use of the unstructured interview is justified in terms of its validity.

The unstructured interview is also preferred because it should result in rich, valid qualitative data about how the children see the world, especially if the researchers can establish a relationship of trust and rapport with the children. The researchers attempted to build this relationship by conducting several interviews with the children. The researchers also stressed to the children that they were not teachers and believed that, as a result of this, the children welcomed the opportunity to talk freely and without fear of being in trouble. In addition, the researchers promised the children that everything they said would be treated in complete confidence. The researchers also made the point of listening seriously and sympathetically to everything the children had to say and made a point of not making judgements about the children's statements or behaviour. All of these things combined to produce data which looked at the 'why' and 'how' rather than just giving priority to the 'what'.

This paragraph is very focused on the advantages of unstructured interviews in terms of the relationship that can be established between researcher and subject. The candidate clearly shows how a relationship likely to generate qualitative and valid data is established.

You should use this section to outline briefly the main findings of the study, making reference to a limited sample of the research data to illustrate particular points. (The sample may be attached to the report as an appendix and may take the form of a graph, table, text quotations etc. It will not be included in the word count.) You should also identify the parts of the research that appear to have worked well and those that have not. You will need to show that you are aware of ways in which the methods selected have affected the quality of the data collected and produced, using the concepts of reliability, validity, representativeness and/or generalisability.

Section (d)

Evaluation of research findings (350-400 words)

Troyna and Hatcher found that white children often engaged in racist name-calling. They often felt sorry afterwards because they realised it hurt the feelings of the Asian children. It was also out of keeping with their own beliefs that all children were equal (see appendix, point 1). However, some children did see racist name-calling as a legitimate tactic in arguments with black children. (see appendix, point 2). Many children were unaware of the impact of racist name-calling – many said when they told Asian children 'to go back to their own country', this was the equivalent of calling someone 'titch' or 'four eyes'. Differences in the degree of racist name-calling was mainly the consequence of the effectiveness of the stance the school took towards racist incidents. Troyna and Hatcher conclude that most children are ignorant of the processes of racial discrimination in society but listening to parents, watching television, etc. gives them a stock of commonsense knowledge about race which they actively select from, interpret and sometimes act upon in terms of racist name-calling.

Positivists would not be happy with the reliability of the research method because unstructured interviews involve establishing unique relationships. Positivists regard this method as unscientific. It would be very difficult for another group of sociologists to establish the same type of relationships in order to verify the data collected from the children. There is also the danger of interviewer bias undermining the validity of the data. At the end of the day, Troyna and Hatcher were adults and the children may have been so eager to please people of a higher status that they worked out that Troyna and Hatcher were looking for certain types of response and gave them what they wanted. There is also the danger that the materials used to stimulate the children in thinking about racism may have 'led' the children in a particular direction.

Troyna and Hatcher's 'evidence' involves using a good deal of conversational analysis. There are two problems here which might undermine validity. The researcher's own interpretations of what the children meant cannot be taken for granted. These may be an adult interpretation of children's motives that may not equate with how children see things. Qualitative research of this nature also means selecting quotations from hundreds of hours of material – such selection may consciously or unconsciously be based on the researcher's ideological beliefs about racism.

Finally, it is not clear how representative these samples of white children are. Troyna and Hatcher do not mention a desire to generalise so we can safely assume that this is meant to be a case study of children's attitudes in three primary schools.

Appendix

1   Angelina said ' Today I had an argument with Gurjit Bains in netball. She fell out with me and she kept pulling faces at me. So I called her a Paki. I felt bad about it but it just came out. So I said 'sorry, let's make friends and we played races together'.

2   K said 'I've called racist things. I didn't call it because I'm nasty, because at the old school we didn't have any different coloured children. I didn't know anything about racist. I didn't know what it meant and I know what it means now, and I called Jagdeep 'Bobble 07' because they wear bobbles on their heads for their religion. I'd heard people calling him that name and I know he gets upset about it, so if I know he gets upset about it, I call him that name.

The candidate identifies key findings and illustrates these in the appendix. There could have been some examples given of children's quotations in regard to parents and television, but the main conclusions of Troyna and Hatcher are well summarised

A good theoretical link focusing on the concepts of reliability and validity. The points made about verification and interview bias are relevant and focused on the context of the research. The point made about the materials is perceptive.

The candidate is aware of how interpretivist research itself can be problematic – much of it relies on the interpretation of the sociologist and despite best intentions, there may be a gap between the researcher's interpretations and the subject's motives. The point made about ideological beliefs questions the objectivity of this sort of research.

It was difficult for the candidate to make a point about representativeness and generalisability because the research does not focus on either of these two concepts. However, the point made by the candidate is valid.

Overall, this candidate demonstrates a knowledge and understanding of methodological issues of a very high standard throughout the report. The key concepts are applied confidently and the candidate has an excellent grasp of both theoretical and practical influences on the research process and how these impact on the quality of the data collected. The findings are clearly summarised. The candidate evaluates intelligently, and overall there is a reasonable balance between strengths and weaknesses throughout the report. Finally, the candidate pays due consideration to the prompts and the word count. Overall, this is an excellent report that would pick up full marks across all three skills – 90 out of 90 marks.

Answers to self-assessment questions

Section 1
The individual and society
(pp. 40–1)

1. a ii; b i; c iii
2. Any three of: canalisation; appellation; manipulation; differentiated activity.
3. A Marxist term used to describe people who must sell their labour for a living, i.e. the working class.
4. a ii; b i
5. a
6. a A young man who rejects the 'New Man' image of masculinity and who follows the norms of traditional male stereotyped behaviour.
   b A young woman who rejects traditional female stereotyped behaviour and behaves more like a traditional young male.
   c Roles in the family that are to do with caring and nurturing; traditionally associated with female behaviour.
   d A man who is willing to display his sensitive 'feminine' side, perhaps taking on more childcare and domestic labour.
7. a i; b ii
8. Domination by males over females.
9. Mead studied small-scale social interaction – a micro approach. Marx and Durkheim studied society as a whole – a structural or macro approach.
10. a ii; b i
11. Any three of: Pakistanis, Indians, Bangladeshis, African Asians, African Caribbeans, Africans, Chinese, Caribbean Asians.
12. • A person may have a mixed ethnic identity.
    • Ethnic identity is often a matter of self-perception rather than anything objective or easily visible.
13. A peer group is the people with whom one is more or less equal in age and status.
14. a The process of learning new norms and values, or adjusting existing norms and values, as we experience new situations and relationships throughout our lives.
    b The many and varied ways in which people relate to each other in everyday life.
    c The first stage of socialisation, which is part of early childhood and early school life. It is how we acquire our first norms and values.
15. a ii; b iii; c i
16. a iii; b ii; c i
17. Any two of: Religion, clothing, language, custom, festivals, media, body adornment, food, sport, mass media.
18. The dispersal of a group of people from a single place or country to destinations around the world.
19. a Objective class
    b Subjective class
20. • There has been a decline in the industries involving manual labour (e.g. coalmining, manufacturing, dockwork, agriculture).
    • There has been an increase in professional and white-collar office work, particularly in the public sector (welfare state).
    • More people have achieved higher educational standards.
21. a ii; b i; c iii
22. a ii; b i
23. a i; b ii
24. a i; b ii
25. a

Section 2
Families and households
(pp. 84–5)

1. Any three of:
   • nuclear family
   • extended family
   • lone-parent family
   • reconstituted family.
2. a iii; b i; c ii
3. Any two of:
   • looking after grandchildren through babysitting and childminding
   • supporting their own elderly parents
   • through continuing in employment, possibly part-time
   • making financial contributions to children and grandchildren
   • through support with domestic chores and labour.
4. a iii; b i; c ii
5. b
6. Household: the person or people who live in a house, such as a family (perhaps with servants), students in a shared home, or people in a community group such as a commune.
7. a in terms of blood or marriage relationships
   b in terms of kinship – that is, a sense of responsibility for family members
8. The term 'extended family' is used to describe those relations who may live close to or with the parents and children. In some cultural groups, brothers and sisters will share a household. This is a 'horizontal extended family'. In other cultural groups, the elderly are very much part of family life, and so there are a number of generations living in the household. This is a 'vertical extended family'. The difference lies in the number of generations who are part of the family group.

continued.../

9 c

10 a false – it is rising
    b false – the peak year was 1993
    c true

11 c

12 Any three of:
    • an ageing population
    • longer life-spans
    • increased female working
    • the tendency to marry later in life
    • the falling birth rate
    • the rising divorce rate

13 a iii; b i; c iv; d ii

14 • Free communes in which people express their
      individuality and face issues or make rules as they
      develop their lifestyle. These communes tend to be
      characterised by transient living and a short
      organisational life-span.
    • Structured communes share a basic set of rules and
      an underlying philosophy. There may be a pooled
      economic structure and an organised leadership
      system. This is typical of religious groupings.

15 c

16 a

17 patriarchy

18 a symmetrical family
    b conjugal roles
    c New Men

19 Over 70% of divorces are initiated by women.

20 divorce, death, separation or choice

21 b

22 a false – it is 10 years
    b true
    c false – it is 25–29 years
    d false – it is the poorer social groups who are
       vulnerable to divorce

23 No, nearly three-quarters of never-married, childless
    people aged under 35 who were cohabiting expected to
    marry each other. Thus, for most people, cohabitation is
    part of the process of getting married and is not a
    substitute for marriage.

24 • Changes in divorce law – divorce law reform has
      generally made divorce more accessible to larger
      numbers of people.
    • Secularisation of marriage – fewer people feel bound
      by traditional Christian teaching with regard to
      divorce.
    • Changes in the economic status of women – women
      no longer require marriage as a means of economic
      support; other sources of income are available to
      them through work or the welfare benefits system.
    • Changes in women's expectations of marriage –
      abusive relationships may have been tolerated in the
      past because people had fewer options; today,
      people know that they do not have to stay in
      situations that they find unbearable.

Section 3
Mass Media
(pp. 118–19)

1	c	15	d
2	b	16	d
3	b	17	a
4	d	18	c
5	b	19	a
6	d	20	d
7	a	21	a Philo
8	b		b Klapper
9	c		c Lull
10	d		d Morley
11	d	22	b
12	c	23	b
13	b	24	b
14	b	25	b

Section 4
Research methods
(pp. 140–1)

1 b

2 c

3 a

4 b

5 d

6 c

7 a i; b ii

8 d

9 d

10 a secondary
    b primary
    c secondary
    d secondary
    e primary

11 b

12 a iv; b ii; c v; d i; e iii

13 a and c

14 a

15 a ii; b i; c iii

16 d

17 d

18 a iii; b iv; c i; d ii

19 b

20 a backed up by good
       evidence.
    b reliable
    c valid
    d representativeness

21 c

22 b

23 • choice of topic
    • resources (time,
      money)
    • theoretical
      perspective
    • interests and
      values
    • current debates in
      sociology
    • access to the
      subject of the
      research

24 It is the ethical
    principle that research
    participants should be
    fully informed about
    the research and
    should have agreed to
    take part.

25 • survey by postal
      questionnaire
    • survey by
      structured
      interview
    • survey by
      unstructured
      interview
    • participant
      observation
    • case study

Glossary

Agency: The ability of people, individually or collectively, to take decisions and to act.

Agencies of socialisation: Institutions such as the family, education system, religion, mass media, etc. from which we learn the culture of our society.

Anthropology: The study of the culture of small pre-industrial societies.

Ascribed status: Social standing or status allocated at birth.

Asymmetrical: Unequal.

Beanpole families: Families that are very small, perhaps consisting of one or two adults and a single child, with the pattern repeated through the generations.

Birth rate: The number of live births per thousand of the population in one year.

Case study: The study of a single example of a phenomenon.

Catchment area: The area around a school. Children living in a school's catchment area are normally given priority when places are allocated.

Co-educational: A school attended by both boys and girls.

Cohort: A group of people who share a significant experience at a point in time, for example, being born in the same year, or taking A levels in the same year.

Commune: A number of families and single adults sharing accommodation and living expenses, usually for ideological and social reasons.

Conjugal roles: The roles played by adult males and females within a family; may be 'joint' or 'segregated'.

Consensus: Broad agreement on basic values.

Consumption: The process of buying and using goods and services.

Contested: Debated and discussed, with disagreement.

Convergence: The coming together of different types of media, either in one company or one technology.

Co-parenting: Where separated or divorced parents take equal roles in caring for children, who spend some time in one household and the rest of their time in the other.

Correlate: To show the relationship between two variables; may be positive or negative.

Correspondence theory: The view that what happens in schools mirrors (corresponds to) what will happen at work, with different classes having different experiences.

Couple: Two adults who share a sexual relationship and a home.

Crisis of masculinity: A term describing how the traditional ways of being a man (such as being a breadwinner) are increasingly questioned.

Cultural capital: The values, knowledge or ideas that parents pass on to their children, which can then influence their success at school and later in life.

Cultural resistance: Ways in which ethnic and other minorities resist pressure from dominant cultures and work to maintain their own cultural traditions.

Culture: The accumulated knowledge, norms and values of a particular group; their way of life.

Custody: Rules that govern the rights of a parent or other carer with regard to a child.

Death rate: The number of deaths per year per thousand of the population.

Decriminalised: When behaviour is no longer punishable by law.

Deferred gratification: Putting off immediate satisfaction in order to get a greater reward later.

Demography: The study of population.

Deregulation: The removal of legal restrictions and rules on broadcasters.

Desensitisation: Becoming immune to having feelings or to showing emotions as a result of over-exposure to, for example, violent images.

Determinism: The view that all events are fully determined (caused) by previous events. In the context of human social behaviour, it is contrasted with 'voluntarism'.

Deviance: The breaking of norms, mores, values or rules.

Digital channels: TV channels only available via digital, satellite or cable.

Digital underclass: People who do not have the material means to access new media technology.

Domestic labour: The work of the household, usually known as housework.

Dual shift: The work that women do in the home after they have completed paid work outside the home.

Empirical: Based on observation or experiment rather than on theory.

Estates: The system of stratification in the medieval period, with division between clergy, nobility and commoners.

Ethnicity: Shared culture based on common language, religion or nationality.

Ethnocentrism: Looking at an issue from one particular cultural point of view

Ethnography: The use of direct observation, sometimes combined with other methods, to help the researcher to understand the world view of those being studied.

Extended family: Nuclear family plus grandparents, uncles, cousins, etc.; may share a home or keep in close contact.

Familial ideology: The view that the traditional family is 'better' than any alternatives.

Family: A group of people to whom we may be biologically related and to whom we feel a sense of kinship.

Feminism: A theoretical perspective adopted mostly by women, which sees females as being oppressed by a patriarchal society.

Fertility rate: The number of live births per thousand women of childbearing age (defined as 15–44 years).

Fit thesis: A functionalist theory suggesting that families evolve to suit the needs of industrial society.

Fragmentation: The breaking up of class structures and loyalties.

Free market: An economic system based on free competition between those willing to invest and/or take risks with capital.

Function: A term used by functionalists to describe the way in which a social institution contributes to the survival and well-being of a society.

Functionalism: Theories that explain social institutions in terms of the functions they perform for the society.

Functionalists: Sociologists who explain social institutions in terms of the functions they perform for the society.

Gatekeepers: Media personnel who decide what counts as news.

Gay families/couples: These are same-sex individuals who choose to live in a partnership.

Gendered division of labour: Work is allocated on the basis of gender, so women do domestic work and men work outside the home.

Ghettoise: To imply that a group or issue should not be a mainstream concern.

Global economy: Describes the global market in which goods and services are traded across the world, particularly by multinational corporations.

Globalisation: The processes by which societies and cultures around the world become increasingly interdependent economically, culturally and politically.

Grandparenting: As life expectancy increases and more women go out to work, the role of grandparent is becoming more significant. For example, in many families, grandparents provide childcare for their grandchildren.

Hegemonic masculinity: Dominant and traditional ideas about the role of men that stress individualism, competition and ambition.

Hegemony: Cultural domination, usually by an economically powerful group.

Hidden curriculum: The ways in which pupils learn values and attitudes other than through the formal curriculum of timetabled lessons.

Homogeneous: Sharing the same social characteristics.

Household: An individual or a group of people who share a home and some meals, e.g. a family (perhaps with servants), students in a shared home or people in a community group such as a commune.

Icon: Figure to be worshipped or admired.

Ideology: A set of ideas and claims that explains how society is or ought to be. In Marxist usage an ideology is always false (the ideology exists to serve the interests of a class rather than to explain reality).

Impartiality: Neutrality.

Individualism: An emphasis on individual people – e.g. in terms of happiness and success – rather than on groups, communities or societies.

Industrialisation: The set of changes by which a society moves from being predominantly rural and agricultural to being predominantly urban and industrial.

Institutional racism: This occurs when the way in which an organisation or institution operates has racist outcomes, regardless of the intentions of individuals within it.

Integrity: Trustworthiness.

Interactionism: A perspective within sociology that focuses on small-scale social interaction rather than on structures and institutions.

Interactive relationship: A relationship in which the parties respond to each other.

Interpretivist: An approach in sociology that focuses on the meaning that social phenomena have for the people involved.

Interview schedule: The list of questions used by the researcher.

Kibbutz: A form of community living that developed among Jewish families in what is now known as Israel before World War II. It involved groups of families sharing childcare and domestic duties, and was often based on farming.

Kinship: The sense of duty we feel towards family members.

Labelling: The process in which individuals or groups are thought of by teachers, or other agents of social control, in terms of types or stereotypes.

Macro: Large scale.

Marginalised groups: Groups of people who are excluded from economic and political power, e.g. the poor.

Media conglomerates: Large-scale media companies that often have global economic interests.

Meritocracy: A system in which the rewards go to those who have talent and ability and who work for the rewards.

Meta-narratives: A postmodern term to describe 'grand' theories such as Marxism.

Micro: Small scale.

Misogynist: Hating, demeaning and devaluing women.

Modernity: The period of history from the late eighteenth to late twentieth centuries, marked by a belief in progress through science and rationality.

Moral panic: Exaggerated social reaction to a group or issue, amplified by the media, with consequent demands for action.

Multicultural education: Education that teaches all children about the cultures of some of the minority groups.

Multicultural: The inter-mingling of a number of cultures.

Multi-ethnic society: A society in which a number of different ethnic groups live together.

Nation: This can mean 'a country' but is used in sociology to define a group of people with a shared common culture and history.

National identity: This is a sense of belonging to a particular nation state or cultural group.

Nationalism: This is a social and political concept that describes how people feel loyalty to a geographical region or culture.

Nationality: This is a legal concept. A person's nationality refers to the country of which they are a legal citizen with rights of residence and voting.

New masculinities: This is the change in traditional male roles whereby men are enabled to get in touch with their caring and domestic side.

New man: A man who challenges traditional male gender roles and is willing to take on domestic and other traditionally female roles.

New Right: A political philosophy that emphasises traditional moral and social values, particularly with regard to the family.

New vocationalism: A view of education that sees the meeting of the needs of the economy as being very important; it also refers to the policies connected to this view.

News values: What journalists think is newsworthy.

Norm: A rule of behaviour in everyday life.

Nuclear family: Parents and children in a single household.

Objective: (a) Existing independently of the observer; (b) being free of bias.

Objectivity: Without bias.

Operationalise: To define something so that it can be measured or counted.

Participant: Anyone who takes part in research. Some researchers use the term 'subject' but 'participant' is preferable because it suggests that the person is an equal in the process rather than an inferior.

Patriarchy: A system where men have social, cultural and economic dominance over women.

Phenomena: Anything that can be seen or perceived.

Pirate radio stations: Radio stations that transmit illegally because they don't have government broadcasting licences.

Population: All the people, or other unit, relevant to the research.

Postmodernism: The theory that suggests industrial society has been superseded by a media-saturated society in which the old indicators of identity – e.g. social class – have been replaced by new forms of identity based on consumption of style, fashion, etc.

Postmodernity: The period of history after the modern period.

Power élite: The minority who control economic and political power.

Primary data: Data collected by the researcher.

Primary definers: Powerful groups (e.g. the government) that have easier and more effective access to the media.

Primary socialisation: The process of learning knowledge, skills and values in early childhood, within the home and usually from parents.

Private capital: Financial resources in the hands of private investors.

Privatisation: A government policy designed to reduce the public sector by allowing a greater role for private companies.

Procreation: The process of having children; the process of creating new members of society.

Proletarianisation: A process whereby middle-class people become more working class.

Qualitative: Research where the sociologist aims to understand the meaning of social action.

Quantitative: Research that concentrates on collecting statistical data.

Race: A concept that views human beings as belonging to separate biological groupings.

Reification: When the results of human interactions seem to take on an independent reality of their own.

Reliability: A reliable method gives the same result when the research is repeated.

Representative: A sample is representative when what is true of the sample is true of the population from which it is drawn.

Republican ideas: Set of ideas opposed to hereditary power, e.g. arguing that the Queen should be replaced by an elected Head of State.

Response rates: The percentage of the sample who return completed questionnaires.

Rite of passage: A ceremony to mark the transition from one stage of life to another; for example, marriage ceremonies.

Role: The set of norms and expectations that go with a status.

Sampling frame: The list of people, or other unit, from whom a sample is drawn.

Secondary data: Data collected by others and used by the researcher.

Secularisation: The gradual loss of formal religious belief from society.

Self-fulfilling prophecy: A predicted outcome that helps to bring about that outcome.

Sexism: Discrimination against people because of their sex; most sexism has been against women.

Socially constructed: An agreed social definition of how to think or behave.

Social control: Social forces and pressures that encourage conformity and punish deviance, either formally or informally.

Social mobility: Movement up and down between social classes – for example, from working class to middle class.

Socialisation: The process of learning how to behave in a way that is appropriate to your culture or society.

Status: A position in society.

Subculture: A group sharing values and ways of behaving that are different from the rest of society.

Symmetrical family: A family in which men and women have some degree of equality.

Terrestrial television: Broadcasting using land-based transmitters.

Underclass: A group at the bottom of the social ladder, said to be characterised by violent crime, illegitimacy, unemployment and dependency on welfare benefits.

Urbanisation: The proportion of a country's population living in towns and cities.

Valid: Valid evidence is evidence of what it claims to be evidence of.

Values: The set of beliefs and morals that people consider to be of importance.

Voluntarism: The assumption that individuals are agents, with some choice and control over their actions. Usually contrasted with determinism.

Weberians: Sociologists who draw on the ideas of Max Weber (1864–1920).

References

Abraham, J. (1995) *Divide and school: Gender and class dynamics in a comprehensive school*, Falmer Press, London.

Adams, E. (1985) *Television and 'the North'*, Centre for Contemporary Cultural Studies, University of Birmingham.

Adonis, A. and Pollard, S. (1998) *A class act: The myth of Britain's classless society*, Penguin, London.

Akinti, P. (2003) 'This is a message to TV broadcasters: There is a black audience that is sick of the mediocre fare you are feeding it', *The Guardian*, 21 February.

Allen, I. and Bourke Dowling, S. with Rolfe, H. (1998) *Teenage mothers: Decisions and outcomes*, Policy Studies Institute, London.

Althusser, L. (1971) *Lenin and Philosophy and other essays*, New Left Books, London.

Anderson, A. (1993) 'Source-media relations: the production of the environmental agenda' in A. Hansen (ed.) *The mass media and environmental issues*, Leicester University Press, Leicester.

Aries, P. (1962) *Centuries of childhood*, Jonathan Cape, London.

Ballard, C. (1979) 'Conflict, continuity and change' in V. S. Kahn (ed.) *Minority families in Britain*, Macmillan, London.

Ballaster, R., *et al.* (1991) *Women's worlds: Ideology, feminism and the women's magazine*, Macmillan, Basingstoke.

Barker, C. (1997) 'Television and the reflexive project of the self: Soaps, teenage talk and hybrid identities', *British Journal of Sociology*, Dec, vol. 48 (4), p. 611.

Barker, E. (1984) *The making of a Moonie: Brainwashing or choice?*, Basil Blackwell, Oxford.

Barlow, A., Duncan, S., James, G. and Park, A. (2001) 'Just a piece of paper? Marriage and cohabitation' in A. Park *et al.* (eds) (2001).

Baudrillard, J. (1985) 'The ecstasy of communication' in H. Foster (ed.) *Postmodern culture*, Pluto, London.

Beishon, S., Modood, T. and Virdee, S. (1998) *Ethnic minority families*, Policy Studies Institute, University of Westminster, London.

Bell, C. and Newby, H. (1977) *Doing sociological research*, George Allen & Unwin, London.

Bell, C. and Roberts, H. (1984) *Social researching*, Routledge & Kegan Paul, London.

Belson, W. (1978) *Television violence and the adolescent boy*, Gower Press, Aldershot.

Ben-Yehuda, B. and Goode, E. (1994) *Moral panics: The social construction of deviance*, Blackwell, Oxford.

Berger, P. and Luckmann, T. (1967) *The social construction of reality*, Penguin, Harmondsworth.

Bernardes, J. (1997) 'Understanding family diversity' in *Sociology Review*, Sept. 2001, Phillip Allan Publishers, Oxfordshire.

Bernstein, B. (1990) *The structure of pedagogic discourse, Vol. 4: Class, codes and control*, Routledge, London.

Berrington, A. (1996) 'Marriage patterns and inter-ethnic unions' in D. Coleman and J. Salt (eds), *Ethnicity in the 1991 Census, Volume one, Demographic characteristics of the ethnic minority populations*, HMSO, London, pp. 178–212.

Bettelheim, B. (1969) *The children of the dream*, Thames and Hudson, London.

Bhatti, G. (1999) *Asian children at home and at school*, Routledge, London.

Bottomore, T. and Rubel, M. (1963) *Karl Marx – Selected writings in sociology and social philosophy*, Penguin, Harmondsworth.

Boudon, R. (1974), *Education, opportunity and social inequality*, John Wiley and Sons, New York.

Bourdieu, P. (1973) 'Cultural reproduction and social reproduction' in R. Brown (ed.) (1973) *Knowledge, education and cultural change*, Tavistock, London.

Bourdieu, P. (1984) *Distinction*, Routledge, London.

Bourdieu, P. and Passeron, J. (1977) *Reproduction in education, society and culture*, Sage, London.

Bowles, S. and Gintis, H. (1976) *Schooling in capitalist America*, Routledge, London.

Braverman, H. (1974) *Labor and monopoly capital*, Monthly Review Press, New York.

Brozier, C. (1999) 'Gender canyon', *New Internationalist*, No 315, August.

Brittan, A. (1989) *Masculinity and power*, Blackwell, Oxford.

Britton, L., Chatrik, B., Coles, B., Craig, G., Hylton, C. and Mumtaz, S. with Bivand, P., Burrows, R. and Convery, P., (2002) *Missing ConneXions: The career dynamics and welfare needs of black and minority ethnic young people at the margins*, JRF/The Policy Press, York.

Broad, B., Hayes, R. and Rushforth, C. (2001) *Kith and kin: Kinship care for vulnerable young people*, Joseph Rowntree Foundation and National Children's Bureau, London.

Buckingham, A. (1999) 'Is there an underclass in Britain?', *British Journal of Sociology*, March, vol. 50 (1), p. 49.

Buckingham, D. (1996) *Moving images*, Manchester University Press, Manchester.

Buss, D. M. (1998) 'The psychology of human mate selection: Exploring the complexity of the strategic repertoire', in C. Crawford and D. L. Krebs (1998).

Butler, J. (1999) *Gender trouble: Tenth anniversary issue (Thinking gender)*, Routledge, London.

Campbell, B. (1993) *Goliath: Britain's dangerous places*, Methuen, London.

Carvel, J. (1997) 'Graduates paid more', *The Guardian*, 22 May, 1997.

Chan, M.Y. and Chan, C. (1997) 'The Chinese in Britain', *New Community*, vol. 23(1).

Channel 4 television (1988) *Baka People of the Rainforest*, produced and photographed by Phil Agland.

Chapman, S., (2001) 'Toffs and snobs? Upper-class identity in Britain', *Sociology Review*, vol. 11 (1).

Charlesworth. S, (2000) *A phenomenology of working-class experience*, Cambridge University Press, Cambridge.

Cohen, S. (1972) *Folk devils and moral panics*, MacGibbon and Kee, London.

Collier, R. (1992) 'The New Man: Fact or fad', *Achilles' Heel*, 14.

Commission for Racial Equality (1992) *Set to fail? Setting and banding in secondary schools*, Commission for Racial Equality, London.

Connell, R. (2002) *Gender*, Polity Press, Cambridge.

Connell, R. W. (1995) *Masculinities: Knowledge, power, and social change*, University of California Press, Berkeley and Los Angeles.

Connolly, P. (1998) *Racism, gender identities and young children: Social relations in a multi-ethnic, inner-city primary school*, Routledge, London.

Connor, H. and Dewson, S. (2001) *Social class and higher education: Issues affecting decisions on participation by lower social class groups*, DfES, London.

Cooper, D. (1970) *The death of the family*, Random House, New York.

Coote, A., Harman, H. and Hewitt, P. (1990) 'The family way: a new approach to policy making', *Social Policy Paper No.1*, Institute for Public Policy, London.

Crawford, C, and Krebs, D. L. (eds) (1998) *Handbook of evolutionary psychology: Ideas, issues and applications*, Lawrence Erlbaum Associates, London.

Cumberbatch, G. (1990) *Television advertising and sex role stereotyping*, Broadcasting, Standards Council Research.

Curran, J. and Seaton, J. (1991) *Power without responsibility (4th edn)*, Routledge, London.

Curtice, J. and Heath, A. (2000) 'Is the British lion about to roar?', in the *British Social Attitudes 17th report*, 2000–01 edition, 'Focussing on Diversity', NCSR/Sage.

Dahrendorf, R. (1992) *Understanding the Underclass*, Policy Studies Institute, London.

Dallos, R. and Sapsford, M. R. 'Patterns of diversity and lived realities' in J. Muncie, M. Wetherell, M. Langan, R. Dallos and A. Cochrane (1997) *Understanding the family* (2nd edn), Sage, London.

Davidson, A. (1997) *From subject to citizen, Australian citizenship in the twentieth century*, Cambridge University Press, Cambridge.

Davie et al. (1972) *From birth to seven*, Penguin, Harmondsworth.

Davis, K. and Moore, W. E. (1945) 'Some principles of stratification' in R. Bendix and S. M. Lipset *Class, status and power*, Routledge and Kegan Paul, London.

de Beauvoir, S. (1953) *The second sex*, (H. M. Parshley, trs & ed.), Alfred A Knopf, New York.

Delamont, S. (2000) 'The anomalous beasts: Hooligans and the sociology of education', *Sociology*, vol. 34 (1), Feb.

Delamont, S. (2001) *Changing women, unchanging men: Sociological perspectives on gender in a post-industrial society*, Open University Press, Buckingham.

Delanty, G. (1995) *Inventing Europe: Idea, identity, reality*, Macmillan, London.

Delphy, C. and Leonard, D. (1992) *Familiar exploitation*, Polity Press, Cambridge.

Denscombe, M. (1999) *Sociology update*, Olympus, Leicester.

Denscombe, M. (2000) *Sociology update*, Olympus, Leicester.

Denscombe, M. (2001) *Sociology update*, Olympus Press, Leicester.

Denscombe, M. (2002) *Sociology update*, Olympus Books, Leicester.

Department for Education and Science (1985) *Education for all* (The Swann Report), HMSO, London.

Dore, R. P. (1976) *The diploma disease*, Allen & Unwin, London.

Dunn, J. and Deater-Deckard, K. (2001) *Children's views of their changing families*, Joseph Rowntree Foundation, York.

Dunscombe, J. and Marsden, D. (1993) 'Love and intimacy: the gender division of emotion and "emotion work"' in *Sociology*, vol. 27 (2), pp. 221–41.

Durkheim, Emile, (1964) *The division of labor in society* (trs. George Simpson), Free Press paperbacks, New York; London: Collier-Macmillan (Originally published by Macmillan (1933), Translation of: *De la division du travail social*).

Easthope, A. (1986) *What's a man gotta do: The masculine myth in popular culture*, Paladin, London.

Edgell, S. (1980) *Middle-class couples*, Allen & Unwin, London.

Edwards, T. (1997) *Men in the mirror*, Cassell, London.

Elkins, M. and Olangundoye, J. (2000) *The Prison population in 2000: A statistical review*, HMSO (http://www.homeoffice.gov.uk/rds/pdfs/r154.pdf)

Elwood, J. (1999) 'Gender achievement and the gold standard: Differential performance in the GCE A level examination', *Curriculum Journal*, vol. 10 (2).

Eversley, D. (1984) *Changes in the composition of households and the cycle of family life*, Council of Europe, Strasbourg.

Eyre, R. (1999) 'The 1999 McTaggart Lecture to the Guardian International Television Festival', *The Guardian*, 28 August, 1999.

Ferguson, M. (1983) *Forever feminine: Women's magazines and the cult of femininity*, Heinemann, London.

Festinger, L. *et al*. (1956) *When prophecy fails*, Harper and Row, New York.

Freire, P. (1972) *Pedagogy of the oppressed*, Penguin, Harmondsworth.

Frosh, S., Phoenix, A. and Partman, K. (2002) *Young masculinities*, Palgrave, London.

Furedi, (1995) 'A plague of moral panics', *Living Marxism*, January.

Galtung, J. and Ruge, M. (1970) 'Structuring and selecting news' in S. Cohen and J. Young, *The manufacture of news, social problems, deviance and the mass media*, Constable, London.

Garfinkel, H. (1967) *Studies in ethnomethodology*, Polity Press, Cambridge.

Gauntlett, D. (1995) *Moving experiences: Understanding television influences and effects*, John Libbey, Eastleigh, Southampton.

Gauntlett, D. (2000) (www.theory.org.uk)

Gerwitz, S., Ball, S. J., Bowe, R. (1995) *Markets, choice and equity in education*, Open University Press, Buckingham.

Giddens, A. (1979) *Central problems in social theory*, Macmillan, London.

Gillies, V., Ribbens McCarthy, J. and Holland, J. (2001) *Pulling together, pulling apart: The family lives of young people*, Family Policy Studies Centre, London.

Gilroy, P. (2000) *Between camps: Race, identity and nationalism at the end of the colour line*, Allen Lane, London.

Glass, D. V. (ed.) (1954) *Social mobility in Britain*, Routledge and Kegan Paul, London.

Goffman, E. (1969) *The presentation of the self in everyday life*, Penguin, Harmondsworth, (first published 1959, Doubleday, New York).

Goldthorpe, J. (1987) *Social mobility and class structure in modern Britain*, Clarendon Press, Oxford.

Goldthorpe. J.H., Lockwood, D. *et al*. (1969) *The affluent worker in the class structure*, Cambridge University Press, Cambridge.

Goode & Ben-Yehuda (1994) see Ben-Yehuda and Goode.

Gordon, D. (2000) 'Inequalities in income, wealth and standard of living in Britain' in C. Pantazis and D. Gordon (eds) (2000).

Gordon, D., Adelman, L., Ashworth, K., Bradshaw, J., Levitas, R., Middleton, S., Pantazis, C., Patsios D., Payne, S., Townsend, P. and Williams, J. (2000) *Poverty and social exclusion in Britain*, Joseph Rowntree Foundation, York.

Gramsci, A. (1971) *Selections from the prison notebooks*, Lawrence and Wishart, London.

Greer, G. (1971) *The female eunuch*, Paladin, St Albans.

GUMG (1993) *Getting the message: News, truth and power*, Routledge, London.

GUMG (2000) 'Media coverage of the developing world: Audience understanding and interest' (www.gla.uk/departments/sociology/debate.html)

Hall, S. (1978) 'Cultural identity and Diaspora' in J. Rutherford (ed.) *Identity, community, culture and difference*, Lawrence and Wishart, London.

Hall, S. and Young, J. (eds) (1981) *The manufacture of news*, Owen and Young, London.

Halsey, A. H., Heath, A. and Ridge, J. M. (1980) *Origins and destinations*, Clarendon Press, Oxford.

Halstead, M. (1994) 'Between two cultures? Muslim children in a western liberal society', *Children and Society*, vol. 8 (4), pp. 312–326.

Hammond, P. (1964) *Sociologists at work*, Basic Books, New York.

Hargreaves, D. H. (1967) *Social relations in a secondary school*, Routledge, London.

Harvey, D. (1990) *The condition of postmodernity*, Blackwell, London.

Hattersley R. (2001) 'New Labour's creeping poverty gap' in *The Guardian*, Monday 16 July.

Hechter, M. (1975) *Internal colonialism: The Celtic fringe in British National development*, Transaction Publishers, New Brunswick, NJ.

Hester, M. and Radford, L. 'Contradictions and compromises', in Marianne Hester, Liz Kelly and Jill Radford (eds) (1996) *Women, violence and male power*, Open University Press, Buckingham.

Hey V. (1997) *The company she keeps: an ethnography of girls' friendships*, Open University Press, Milton Keynes.

HMSO (published annually) *Social Trends*, HMSO, London (www.statistics.gov.uk)

HMSO (published annually) *Population Trends*, HMSO, London (www.statistics.gov.uk)

Hockey, J. and James, A. (1993) *Growing up and growing old: Ageing and dependency in the life course*, Sage, London.

Holdaway, S. (1983) *Inside the British Police*, Basil Blackwell, Oxford.

Illich, I. (1973) *Deschooling society*, Penguin, Harmondsworth.

Jackson, P. W. (1968) *Life in classrooms*, Holt, Rinehart and Winston; (1991) Teachers College Press.

Jagger, E. (2001) 'Marketing Molly and Melville: dating in a postmodern, consumer society', *Sociology*, vol. 35 (1) February.

Jones, K. (1998) 'Death of a princess: public mourning, private grief', *Sociology Review*, Sept.

Jones, M. (2000) 'The moral panic revisited', *Sociology Review*, Feb.

Jones, N. (1993) *Living in rural Wales*, Gomer Press, Llandysul.

Kellner, D. (1995) *Media culture*, Routledge, London.

Kidd, W. (1999) 'Family diversity in an uncertain future', *Sociology Review*, vol. 9 (1).

King, A. (2000) 'Football fandom and post-national identity in the New Europe', *British Journal of Sociology*, vol. 51 (3), Sept. p. 419.

Klapper, J. T. (1960) *The effects of mass communication*, The Free Press, New York.

Koerner, Ernst F. K. (1972) *Bibliographia Saussureana, 1870–1970. An annotated, classified bibliography on the background, development and actual relevance of Ferdinand de Saussure's general theory of language*, Scarecrow Press: Metuchen, NJ.

Laing, R. D. (1960) *The divided self: a study of sanity and madness*, (in the series 'Studies in existential analysis and phenomenology'), Quadrangle Books, Chicago, IL.

Langford, W., Lewis, C., Solomon, Y. and Warin, J. (2001) *Family understandings: Closeness, authority and independence in families with teenagers*, Joseph Rowntree Foundation and Family Policy Studies Institute, London.

Lash, S. and Urry, J. (1994) *Economies of signs and space*, Sage, London.

Liebow, E. (1967) *Tally's Corner*, Routledge and Kegan Paul, London.

Lockhurst, I. (1999) 'Men: The silent victims', *S – the A-level Sociology Magazine*, Issue 4, May.

Low Pay Commission (2000) http://www.lowpay.gov.uk/ Low Pay Unit, Manchester.

Lull, J. (1990) *Inside family viewing: ethnographic research on television audiences*, Routledge, London.

Lyotard, J. (1984) *The postmodern condition: a report on knowledge*, Manchester University Press, Manchester.

Mac an Ghaill, M. (1988) *Young, gifted and black: Student–teacher relations in the schooling of black youth*, Open University Press, Milton Keynes.

MacBeath, J. and Mortimore, P. (eds) (2001) *Improving school effectiveness*, Open University Press, Buckingham.

MacIntosh, M. and Mooney, G. (2000) 'Identity, inequality and social class', in K. Woodward (ed.) *Questioning identity: Gender, class, nation*, Open University Press, Milton Keynes.

Macionis, J. J. and Plummer, K. (1997) *Sociology: A global introduction*, Prentice Hall Europe, New Jersey.

Mack, J. and Lansley, S. (1985) *Poor Britain*, George Allen & Unwin, London.

Maclean, C. (1979) *The wolf children: Fact or fantasy?*, Penguin Books, Harmondsworth.

Manning, P. (1999) 'Who makes the news?', *Sociology Review*, September.

Marshall, G., Newby, H., Rose, D. and Vogler, C. (1988) *Social class in modern Britain*, Hutchinson, London.

Marsland, D. (1989) 'Universal welfare provision creates a dependent population', *Social studies review*, Nov.

McAllister, F. with Clarke, L. (1998) *Choosing childlessness*, Family Policy Studies Centre, London.

McNeill, P. (1990) *Research methods*, Routledge, London.

McQuail, D. (1994) *Mass communication theory: An Introduction* (3rd edn), Sage, London.

McRobbie, A. (1982) 'Jackie: An ideology of adolescent femininity' in B. Waites (ed.) *Popular culture: Past and present*, Open University Press, Buckingham.

McRobbie, A. (1995) 'Re-thinking 'Moral panic' for multi-mediated social worlds', *British Journal of Sociology*, 46.

Mead, G. H. (1934) *Mind, self and society*, Chicago University Press, Chicago, IL.

Mirza, H. (1992) *Young, female and black*, Routledge, London.

Mitsos, E. and Browne, K. (1998) 'Gender differences in education', *Sociology Review*, vol. 8 (1), Sept.

Modood, T. (ed.) (1997) 'Church, state and religious minorities', *PSI Report No. 845*, Policy Studies Institute.

Modood, T., Berthoud, R., Lakey, J., Nazroo, J., Smith, P., Virdee S. and Beishon, S. (1997) *Ethnic minorities in Britain*, Policy Studies Institute, London.

Morley, D. (1980) *The 'Nationwide' audience*, BFI, London.

Morris, D. (1975) *The naked ape*, Corgi, London, (first published 1967, Cape, London).

Morrison, D. (1992) *Television and the Gulf War*, John Libbey, Eastleigh, Southampton.

Morrison, D. (1999) *Defining violence: The search for understanding*, Broadcasting Standards Council/Institute of Communication Studies, University of Leeds, Leeds.

Mort, F. (1988) quoted in Chapman, R. and Rutherford, J. (1988) (eds) *Male order: Unwrapping masculinity*, Lawrence and Wishart, London.

Mulvey, L. (1975) 'Visual pleasure and narrative cinema', *Screen*, vol. 16 (3).

Murdoch, G. and McCron, R. (1979) 'The television and delinquency debate', *Screen Education*, vol. 30 (Spring).

Murdock, G. P. (1949) *Social structure*, Macmillan, New York.

Murphy, P. and Elwood, J. (1998) 'Gendered experiences, choices and achievements – exploring the links', *Journal of Inclusive Education*, vol. 2 (2), pp. 95–118.

Murray, C. (1984) *Losing ground: American social policy, 1950–1980*, Basic Books, New York.

Murray, C. (1993) 'The time has come to put a stigma back on illegitimacy', *Wall Street Journal*, 14 November.

Nairn, T. (1988) *The enchanted glass: Britain and its monarchy*, Radius, London.

Newson, E. (1994) 'Ordeal by media: A Personal Account, *The Psychologist*, April.

Newson, E. and Newson, J. (1968) *Four years old in an urban community*, Allen & Unwin, London.

Nixon, S. (1996) *Hard looks – Masculinities, spectatorship and contemporary consumption*, UCL Press, London.

Oakley, A. (1981) *Subject women*, Robertson, Oxford.

OFSTED (1999) *Raising the attainment of minority ethnic pupils*, HMSO, London.

OPCS (1994) *OPCS Monitor: National population projections (1992 based)*, HMSO, London.

Opie, I. and Opie, P. (1969) *Children's games in street and playground*, Clarendon, Great Britain.

Osler, A., Street, C., Lall, M. and Vincent, K. (2002) *Not a problem? Girls and school exclusion*, National Children's Bureau.

Pahl, R. E. and Wallace, C. (1988) 'Neither angels in marble nor rebels in red' in D. Rose (ed.) *Social stratification and economic change*, Hutchinson, London.

Pantazis, C. and Gordon, D. (eds) (2000) *Tackling inequalities*, The Policies Press, Bristol.

Park, A. et al. (eds) (2001) *British social attitudes, the 18th RSA report: Public policy, social ties*, Sage, London.

Park, R. E. (1927) *Introduction to the science of sociology*, University of Chicago Press, Chicago, IL.

Parsons, T. and Bales, R. F. with James Olds (and others) (1955) *Family, socialisation and interaction process*, Free Press, Glencoe, Ill.

Philo, G. (1997) *Children and film/video/TV violence*, Glasgow University Media Group, Glasgow.

Philo, G. (2001) 'Media effects and the active audience', *Sociology Review*, February.

Pilcher, J. (1995) 'Growing up and growing older', *Sociology Review*, September.

Pilcher, J. (1998) *Women of their time*, Ashgate Publishing, Aldershot.

Reay, D. and Mirza, H. (2000) 'Spaces and places of black educational desire: Rethinking black supplementary schools as a new social movement', *Sociology*, vol. 34 (3).

Redhead, S. (1992) *Rave off and the end of the century party*, Routledge, London.

Rex, J. (1996) 'National identity in the democratic multi-cultural state', *Sociological Research Online*, vol. 1 (2) (www.socresonline.org.uk)

Robinson, M. (1991) *Family transformation through divorce and remarriage: A systemic approach*, Routledge, London.

Rose, S. (1998) *Lifelines: Biology, freedom, determinism*, Penguin, Harmondsworth.

Rosenthal, R. and Jacobson, L. (1968) *Pygmalion in the classroom*, Holt, Reinhart and Winston, New York.

Sarlvik, B. and Crewe, I. (1983) *Decade of dealignment: The Conservative victory of 1979 and electoral trends in the 1970s*, Cambridge University Press, Cambridge.

Saunders, D. G. (1995) 'A typology of men who batter: three types derived from cluster analyses', *American Journal of Orthopsychiatry*, 62, pp. 264–275

Saunders, P. (1995) *Capitalism: A social audit*, Open University Press, Buckingham.

Savage, M., Barlow, J., Dickens, P. and Fielding, T. (1992) *Property, bureaucracy and culture: Middle-class formation in contemporary Britain*, Routledge, London.

Schlesinger, P. (1990) 'Rethinking the sociology of journalism' in M. Ferguson (ed.) *Public communication: The new imperatives*, Sage, London.

Schudson, M. (1994) 'Culture and the integration of national societies', *International Social Science Journal*, vol. 46.

Scott, J. (1982) *The upper classes*, Macmillan, London.

Scott, J. (1986) 'Does Britain still have a ruling class?', *Social Studies Review*, vol. 2 (1).

Selbourne, D. (1993) *The spirit of the age*, Sinclair-Stevenson, London.

Sewell, T. (1997) *Black masculinities and schooling – How black boys survive modern schooling*, Trentham Books, Stoke on Trent.

Shropshire, J. and Middleton, S. (1999) *Small expectations: Learning to be poor?*, York Publishing Services, York.

Slater, D. (1997) *Consumer culture and modernity*, Polity Press, Cambridge.

Smart, C., Wade, A. and Neale, B. (2000) 'New childhoods: Children and co-parenting after divorce and objects of concern?', *Children and Divorce*, Centre for Research on Family, Kinship and Childhood, University of Leeds.

Smith, P. (1991) *Ethnic minorities in Scotland*, Central Research Unit Papers, The Scottish Office, The Stationery Office, Edinburgh.

Southerton, D. (2002) Boundaries of 'us' and 'them': Class, mobility and identification in a new town, *British Sociology Association*, vol. 36 (1), 171–193, Sage Publications, London.

Spender, D. (1983) *Invisible women: Schooling scandal*, Women's Press, London.

Stacey, J. (1990) *Brave new families: Stories of domestic upheaval in late twentieth century America*, Basic Books, New York.

Sullivan, A. (2001) 'Cultural capital and educational attainment', *Sociology*, vol. 35 (4).

Thornton, S. (1995) *Club cultures: Music, media and subcultural capital*, Polity Press, Cambridge.

Tunstall (1983) *The media in Britain*, Constable, London.

Turak, I. (2000) Inequalities in Employment in C. Pantazis and D. Gordon (eds) (2000)

Van Dijks, T. (1991) *Racism and the Press*, Routledge, London.

Warnock Report, *The (1984) Report of the Committee of Inquiry into Human Fertilisation and Embryology*, Chairman of Commission: Dame Mary Warnock, HMSO, London.

Weber, M. (1978) *Economy and society*, vols. 1 & 2, (eds) G. Roth and C. Wittich, University of California Press, Berkeley.

Wedderburn, D. and Crompton, R. (1972) *Workers' attitudes and technology*, Cambridge University Press, Cambridge.

Westwood, S. (1999) 'Girls just want to have fun: Re-presenting gender', *Sociology Review*, September.

Whannell, G. (2002) 'David Beckham: Identity and masculinity', *Sociology Review*, February.

Whyte, W. F. (1955) *Street corner society: The social structure of an Italian slum*, University of Chicago Press, Chicago, IL.

Willis, P. (1977) *Learning to Labour: How working-class kids get working-class jobs*, Saxon House, Farnborough.

Winship, J. (1986) *Inside women's magazines*, Pandora, London

Winston, R. (2002), *Human instinct*, Bantam Press, London.

Wolf, N. (1990) *The beauty myth*, Vintage, London.

Woodward, W. and Ward, L. (2000) 'End bias, élite universities told', *Guardian Weekly*, 8 to 14 June.

Yip, A. (1999) 'Same sex couples', in *Sociology Review*, vol. 8 (3).

Young, J. (1971) *The Drugtakers*, Paladin, London

Young, M. and Willmott, P. (1973) *The symmetrical family*, Penguin, London.

Index